Gods and Myths of the
ANCIENT WORLD

Gods and Myths of the
ANCIENT WORLD

The Archaeology and Mythology of Ancient Egypt, Ancient Greece and The Romans

Mary Barnett

Photography by Michael Dixon

Grange BOOKS

Published in 1997 by
Grange Books
An imprint of Grange Books PLC
The Grange
Grange Yard
London
SE1 3AG

**Copyright © 1997 Regency House
Publishing Limited**

ISBN 1 84013 081 4

Printed in China

All photographs supplied by the CM Dixon Picture
Library

CONTENTS

EGYPT

GREECE

THE ROMANS

Egypt

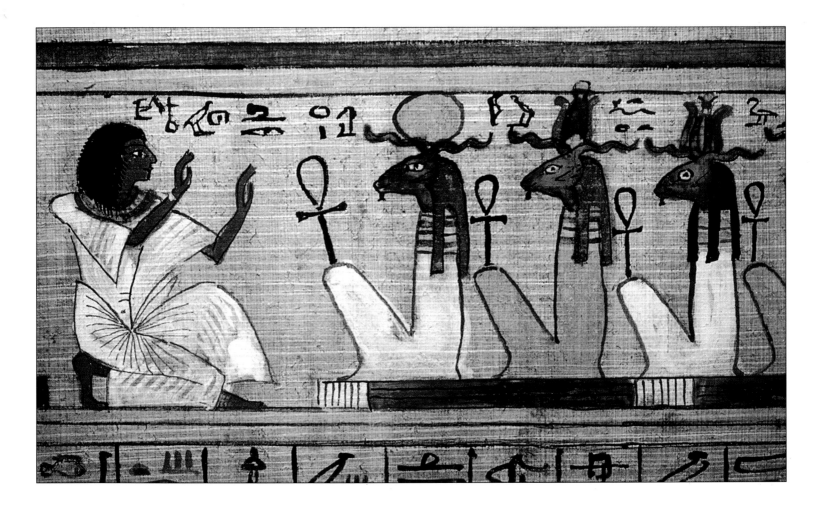

INTRODUCTION

Most people coming into contact with the remains of the ancient Egyptian civilization – through books, films, visits to museums or to Egypt itself – find a colourful and fascinating array of evidence which at first is confusing and largely unintelligible. It is possible to wander among the monuments, the mummies and the hieroglyphs in a museum admiring one thing, wondering at another, but finding it difficult to understand what we see, except in the most simple way.

The experience of everyday modern life hardly equips us to find a common ground with such an alien past, even though much of that past has been so well preserved. The dry climate of Egypt, which slows the processes of decay, and the culture of ancient Egypt, which produced so much in durable material like stone, and preserved so much by elaborate burial practices, have combined to conserve an impressive array of evidence, which is now available for study but remains difficult to comprehend.

To understand the myths and religion of a foreign culture is not easy either, particularly when the culture is as distant in time as that of the ancient Egyptian civilization. The Egyptians used symbols to express abstract ideas, often producing conflicting and contradictory images to express different aspects of the same thing. This book aims to describe some of the elements that formed their myths and helped to give expression to their religious ideas, and to illustrate some of the ways in which those ideas were symbolically represented, particularly in visual terms.

The myths and religion of a country or culture are normally concerned, in their early development at least, with ideas about creation and existence itself, about the relationship of humans with the cosmos and about social order: the ideas that bind and stabilize society, that explain annual and daily events like the recurrence of the seasons and the rising and setting of the sun, and that deal with good and evil, and with dangers and fears, real and imagined.

For the Egyptians the state religion, once established, was concerned with the maintenance of divine order through the king's intercession with the gods; if the gods were propitiated and the king's duties to them were properly performed the state would prosper. This divine order was known as *maat*, meaning truth, order, and harmony. Ritual and magical means as well as practical methods were used to establish and maintain the harmony of *maat* in the state.

For the individual, who was excluded from much of the ritual of the state religion, the concept of *maat* was also important. Ritual, magical and practical means were also used to bring success, to maintain order and to avert misfortune. Household and family gods were probably more important at a personal and everyday level than were the great exclusive state cults. At a personal level too, ethical concepts were evolved which could help an individual to achieve a righteous and worthy life in the present and to attain a pleasant and everlasting afterlife in the future.

One of the difficulties experienced in studying

ancient Egyptian mythology and religion is that images are used symbolically to illustrate a number of different aspects of the same thing. This results in an array of apparently conflicting images. For instance, the sun-god can be illustrated as the sun itself, or as a falcon, or as a human being. What is being worshipped is not the sun, the falcon, or the human image, but the abstract power and qualities that these symbols represent. In this sense the images are not contradictory but are compatible. This book aims to show how some of these symbolic ideas are represented visually, in order to help the reader to understand the concepts they express.

Yet understanding can take us only so far. It is important to remember that Amun, the great god of ancient Egypt, is known as 'the hidden one' and the real name of Ra, the all-powerful sun-god of Egypt, is secret. If Ra's real name were known, his power would be diminished. Amun must always remain the hidden one, otherwise something of his divine mystery and power would also be lost.

A relief from the Temple of Rameses III on the West Bank, Luxor (ancient Thebes) showing prisoners of the campaigns of Rameses against the Sea Peoples.

9

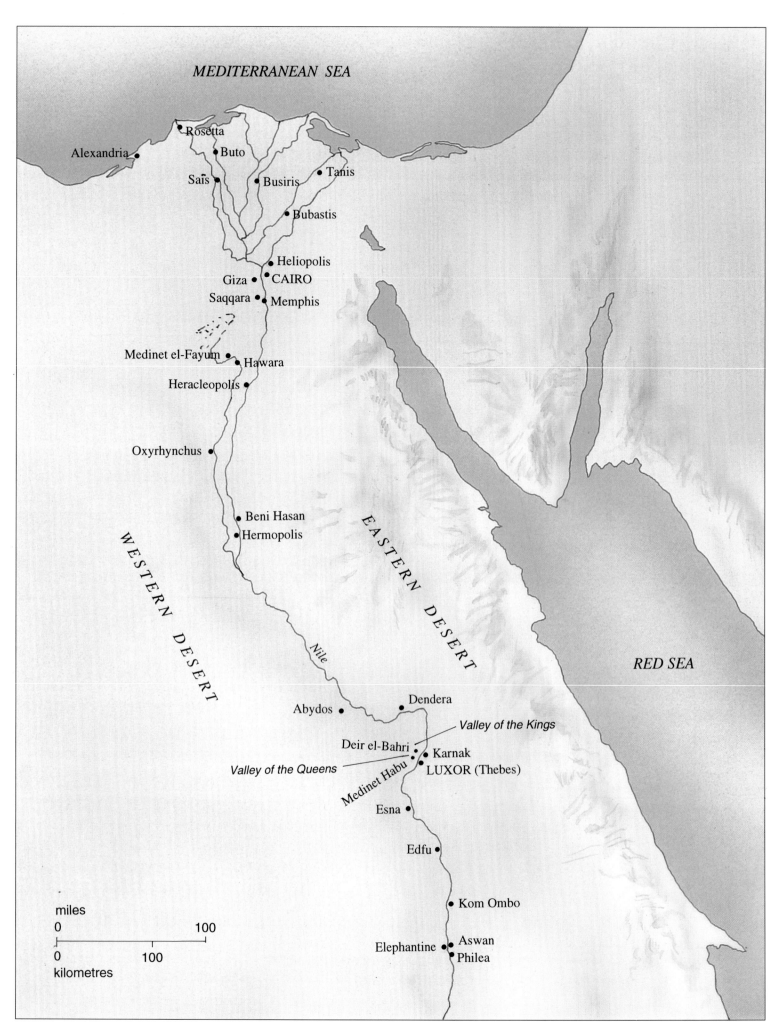

MEDITERRANEAN SEA

Rosetta

Alexandria

Buto

Saïs

Busiris

Tanis

Bubastis

Heliopolis

Giza

CAIRO

Saqqara

Memphis

Medinet el-Fayum

Hawara

Heracleopolis

Oxyrhynchus

WESTERN DESERT

Beni Hasan

Hermopolis

EASTERN DESERT

Nile

RED SEA

Dendera

Abydos

Valley of the Kings

Deir el-Bahri

Karnak

Valley of the Queens

Medinet Habu

LUXOR (Thebes)

Esna

Edfu

Kom Ombo

miles

0

100

0

100

kilometres

Elephantine

Aswan

Philea

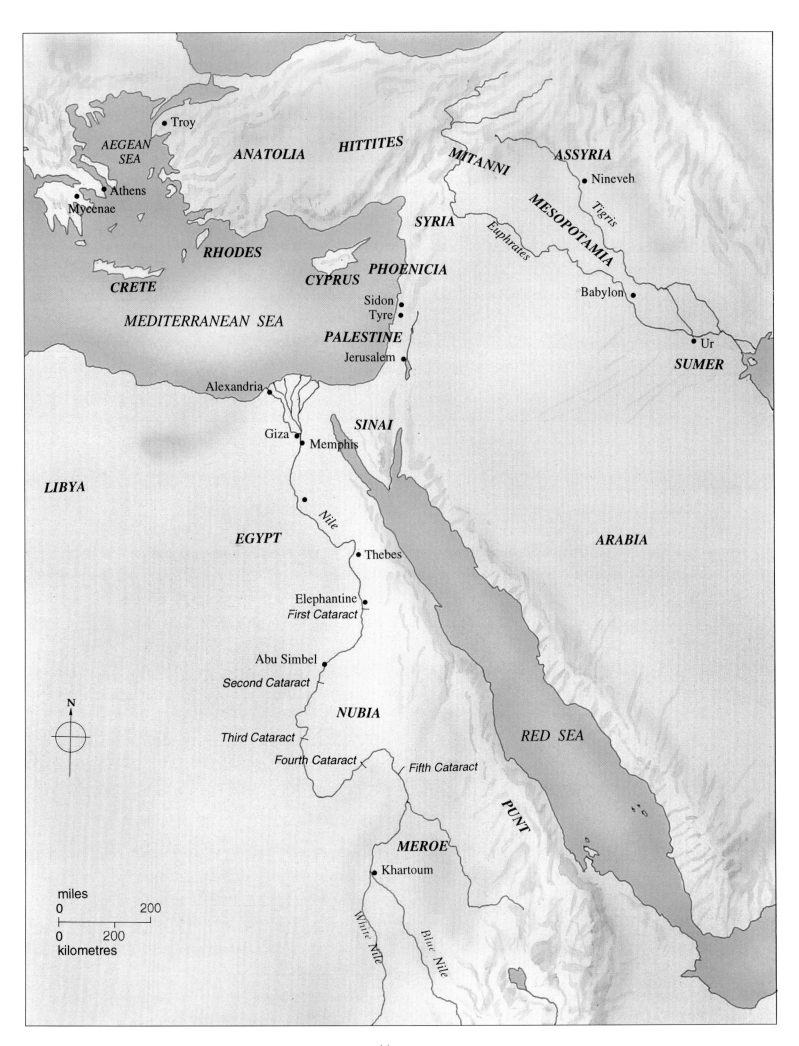

Troy

AEGEAN
SEA

ANATOLIA   HITTITES   MITANNI   ASSYRIA

Athens   Nineveh

Mycenae   SYRIA   MESOPOTAMIA   Tigris

RHODES   PHOENICIA   Euphrates

CRETE   CYPRUS   Sidon   Babylon

MEDITERRANEAN SEA   Tyre

PALESTINE

Jerusalem   Ur

Alexandria   SUMER

SINAI

Giza   Memphis

LIBYA

Nile   EGYPT   ARABIA

Thebes

Elephantine
First Cataract

N   Abu Simbel

Second Cataract

NUBIA   RED SEA

Third Cataract

Fourth Cataract   Fifth Cataract

PUNT

MEROE

Khartoum

miles
0   200

0   200
kilometres

White Nile   Blue Nile

11

CHAPTER ONE
ANCIENT EGYPT:
LAND, PEOPLE & HISTORY

A stone hand-axe of the Palaeolithic period.

The nature of the gods and myths of any culture is to some extent conditioned by the nature of the land in which the first tellers of their stories lived. The characteristics of the gods and the myths that support their cults and explain their influence change over time as physical, historical and even political events modify the culture that has engendered them. The gods and myths of Egypt have certain features in common with those of many other cultures, but there were also special factors about the geography of Egypt and the development of a strong kingship and priesthood there that have fashioned the myths in a particular way. It seems wise therefore to begin with a general survey of the geographical features of the land of Egypt, and the framework of historical events that influenced the development of its culture.

Egypt lies between the Mediterranean Sea in the north and Sudan in the south and consists mainly of a limestone plateau about 200 to 300m (600 to 1,000 ft) high, which is cut in a south to north direction by the valley of the Nile. On the west the Western, or Libyan, Desert is part of the Sahara Desert, and the mainly limestone rocks are barren and sand-covered. To the east the Eastern, or Arabian, Desert consists of limestone and volcanic rocks forming ranges of low mountains between the Nile Valley and the Red Sea.

The prevailing winds over Egypt are from the north, so that the coastal area receives a moderate rainfall from the Mediterranean and has a Mediterranean climate: but further inland, to the south, the climate becomes that of a subtropical desert. Alexandria on the north coast has about 30 days of rainfall each year, totalling about 180mm (7 in) of rain per annum, while Cairo, about 160km (100 miles) to the south, usually has only about six days rain per year, amounting to about 25mm (1 inch) in total and Luxor hardly sees rain at all, with a rainfall of only about two-thirds that of Cairo.

Without the Nile, most of Egypt would be a barren desert, unable to support any but a tiny nomadic population, and certainly unable to provide a home for a flourishing civilization. But the Nile is one of the world's great rivers, and at about 6,700km (over 4,000 miles) it is one of the longest. Its two main sources are the White Nile, rising from Lake Victoria on the Equator and the Blue Nile, rising in the Ethiopian highlands. The two rivers join at Khartoum, and their waters are later joined by the Atbara from the east.

The White Nile provides a fairly constant supply of water throughout the year, but the Blue Nile and the Atbara are both swollen to a flood by the summer rains in the mountains of Ethiopia. These rains last from late May to early September and in the past, before the building of the Aswan High Dam, they caused the waters of the Nile to rise quickly during June and July and continue rising, more slowly, to reach their maximum level in early September. The waters then subsided quickly during October, and continued to subside more slowly until they reached their lowest point in May when the annual cycle began again.

Over many millennia the Nile carved a channel through the rocks of the Egyptian plateau, making a valley that was only a few miles wide in Upper Egypt but that divided into several channels just north of modern Cairo, and then fanned out into a broad delta before reaching the Mediterranean Sea.

The flood brought large quantities of silt from the Ethiopian mountains, depositing it in the Nile valley where it provided a supply of fertile soil that was renewed annually and that is now over ten metres thick in much of the valley, and up to forty metres thick in parts of the Nile Delta. This régime of annual flooding, which has continued from prehistoric times and throughout the historical period up to the 20th century, has been considerably modified by the building and completion in 1971 of the High Dam at Aswan. This forms Lake Nasser, which stretches southwards as far as the Sudan. As well as

Flint arrowheads from the Sahara, 6th millenium BC.

(British Museum) Detail of the Hunters' Palette from an Egyptian burial of the predynastic period (about 3000 BC) showing hunters with stone axes and clubs, flint knives, spears, bows and hunting dogs.

regulating the floods to provide a more even flow of water in the Nile throughout the year, the dam has meant that much of the silt is held back at the lake, consequently the annual renewal of fertile soil does not now take place.

In palaeolithic times, large areas of Egypt were covered with forests and grassland and the Nile carried huge amounts of water, and silt, from the highlands of Ethiopia, where the rainfall was much greater than it is today. Groups of men hunted game across the whole of North Africa, following a nomadic or semi-nomadic way of life, and settling in the areas that were most favourable to them. Archaeologists have studied evidence of settlements along the plateau overlooking the Nile valley, and have found many flint implements that were used in their hunting and fishing. These settlements and the artefacts were very similar to other Stone-Age settlements in the rest of North Africa and Mediterranean Europe.

There appear to have been movements of people to Egypt from both the east, from Libya, and from the west, from Asia. During the late Palaeolithic period the climate became drier, forest diminished and grasslands gave way to desert. Water and vege-tation became restricted to a few oases – and to the valley of the Nile. While the surrounding land became more of a desert, the Nile valley became more attractive to the human population.

When the Nile began to rise in late June, the people would move to the higher parts of the valley and during September, when the flood was at its highest, they could hunt gazelle and other animals on the desert plateau. Then in October the water receded, leaving a rich deposit of new mud, and pools and streams full of fish. Wildfowl were also abundant as the Nile provided a natural route for migratory birds. Many plants, including primitive wheat and papyrus, flourished in the rich soil and there was plenty of food. The water level of the river reached its lowest point in the spring so vegetation grew less, but wooded areas in the valley still gave cover for animals that could be hunted for food. When the waters rose again in the following July, the annual cycle was repeated.

Gradually, the population grew and became more settled and became farmers as well as hunters. Those living in the southern part, later known as Upper Egypt, tended more to pastoral activities, while those to the north in the Delta (Lower Egypt)

took advantage of the rich soil and the more temperate climate to become agriculturalists. Simple communities developed along the Nile that were independent of one another for the most part. Archaeology shows that they buried their dead near their dwellings, or in cemeteries on the edge of the desert. They already appeared to believe in an afterlife, for the dead were buried with weapons, tools, jewellery, pottery and food as if it was felt that these things would be needed in the future. The corpse was usually buried in a crouched position, with knees drawn up to the chest, and wrapped in skins or matting. The dry climate often dessicated the body, thus preserving it in a form of mummification that was entirely natural.

Settlements grew in size and labour was organized in the communities to attend to the seasonal work of irrigation, drainage, clearing of channels and building of banks to control and exploit the annual Nile flood for the benefit of agriculture.

A pattern was thus being established that was to develop into the sophisticated structure of the Egyptian civilization. Already there was a natural division of Egypt into two lands, Upper Egypt to the south, and the Delta, or Lower Egypt, to the north.

These areas were to develop into two kingdoms and then they were later to be united to form the one kingdom of Egypt. The capital of Lower Egypt (the Delta region) was Buto; its king wore the red crown; it adopted the bee as its symbol, and the cobra, associated with the goddess Neith, was its chief deity. Similarly, Upper Egypt had its capital at Nekhen, south of Luxor; its king wore the white crown; the sedge was its emblem and its chief deity was the vulture.

The ancient Egyptian period of civilization is traditionally considered to have begun about 3100 BC when Menes, who was possibly the same person as Narmer, united his own kingdom of Upper Egypt with that of Lower Egypt in the Delta. Although the two kingdoms were united by Menes, they kept their separate identities: the king was not 'King of Egypt' but 'King of Upper and Lower Egypt', and the kings of the First Dynasty had two tombs, one near Memphis in Lower Egypt and one near Abydos in Upper Egypt.

Manetho, an Egyptian priest living around 305–285 BC, wrote a history of Egypt and his list of dynasties has been the basis of the modern structuring of Egypt's history. However, the actual order, the

A strain of primitive wheat, similar to that which would have grown in ancient Egypt, growing on an experimental farm at Butser, England.

The Pharoah between two goddesses. The goddess on the left wears the Red Crown of Lower Egypt, the goddess on the right wears the White Crown of Upper Egypt and the Pharoah has the Double Crown of Upper and Lower Egypt. Relief from the outer wall of the Temple of Horus at Edfu, Ptolemaic period.

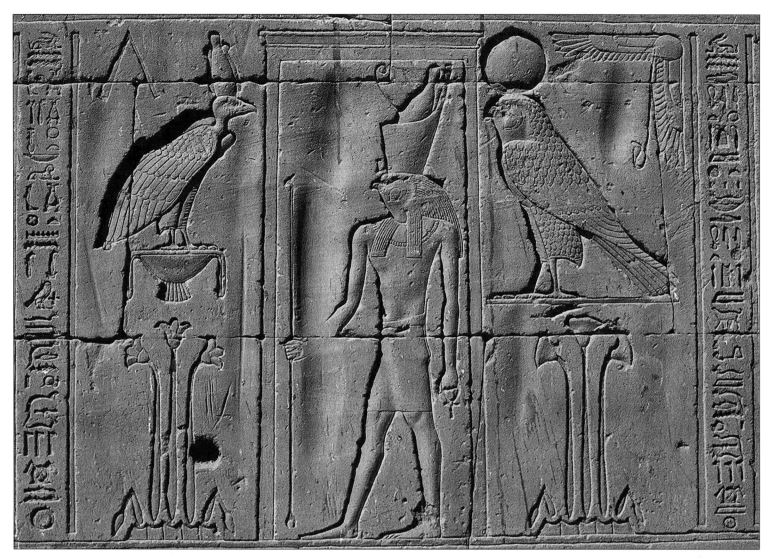

correct names and the exact dates of some of the earlier kings are not precisely known even today. Altogether, there were over 30 dynasties before the conquest of Egypt by Alexander the Great in the 4th century BC, after which Egypt was governed by Macedonian, Greek (the Ptolemies), Roman, Byzantine and Persian rulers before Arab invaders took control in the 7th century AD. The dynasties themselves may be grouped to form several main periods which are summarized here:

EARLY DYNASTIC PERIOD: 1st and 2nd Dynasties: 3100-2686 BC

A new capital was founded at Memphis, south of present-day Cairo, and royal tombs were built at nearby Saqqara and at Abydos much further south. The kings of the 1st Dynasty were buried in *mastaba* tombs, which were formed by digging out a pit in the rock and building a superstructure of mud-brick above it. They were buried with rich tomb furniture, most of which was stolen or destroyed by tomb-robbers, and other burials accompany the main burial, apparently of servants sacrificed at the time of the king's death, to serve him in the afterlife. After the

2nd Dynasty this practice ceased and instead models of servants were buried with the king or other important persons, in the belief that magical spells could bring them back to life to serve their master.

OLD KINGDOM: 3rd to 6th Dynasties: 2686-2181 BC

In this period important buildings began to be built in stone rather than mud-brick, and the first pyramids were built as royal tombs. The most famous 3rd-Dynasty ruler was Djoser (Zozer) for whom the Step Pyramid was built at Saqqara. His chief minister and architect of the Step Pyramid was Imhotep, who was later deified and identified with Asklepios, the Greek god of medicine, becoming a popular domestic deity among the ordinary citizens of Egypt.

Pyramid-building was further developed in the 4th Dynasty, particularly by Sneferu, who built at least three pyramids, including the 'Bent' Pyramid at Dahshur, south of Saqqara, and by his son Khufu who built the Great Pyramid at Giza. Records survive from the 5th and 6th Dynasties of trading expeditions to Nubia, Libya and the nearer parts of Asia. Power became more decentralized, with local courts

Falcon-headed Horus, the mythical king of ancient Egypt, holds the ankh, *the symbol of life, in his left hand and the* was *sceptre in his right and wears the Double Crown of Upper and Lower Egypt. On the left is the vulture of Upper Egypt wearing the White Crown, standing above lotus plants. On the right is the hawk of Lower Egypt, perched above papyrus reeds. Relief from the outer wall of the Temple of Horus at Edfu, Ptolemaic period.*

and administration in the regions, later called *nomes* by the Greeks. The size of royal tombs decreased, which suggests that royal power and wealth declined then. Worship of the sun-god Ra of Heliopolis increased in importance, and with this the prestige of the priests of Heliopolis increased.

FIRST INTERMEDIATE PERIOD: 7th to 10th Dynasties: c.2181-2055 BC

This was a period of instability, possibly exacerbated by a series of poor harvests, low Nile inundations, and a general decline in central power. Other centres of local power developed as well as the old capital, Memphis. The 9th and 10th Dynasties were centred on Heliopolis, and Thebes became another important centre. Finally a Theban ruler, Mentuhotep II gained control of the whole country, founding the 11th Dynasty and bringing in the next period.

MIDDLE KINGDOM: 11th to 13th Dynasty: c.2055-c.1700 BC

Central power was increased and there was expansion into Nubia. The 12th Dynasty kings ruled from Memphis, and introduced co-regency, whereby the king appointed a successor, usually one of his sons, who ruled with him during the last years of his reign to facilitate a stable transfer of kingship on his death. During the 13th Dynasty, central power declined and the borders of Egypt were subject to invasions by foreigners.

SECOND INTERMEDIATE PERIOD: 14th to 17th Dynasties: c.1700-c.1550 BC

Settlers from Asia established themselves in the eastern Delta and this region, even as far as Memphis, came under the rule of the Hyksos kings, who came from Palestine. The 15th and 16th Dynasties consisted of two contemporary dynasties: Hyksos dynasties ruled in the Delta, while at the same time the 17th-Dynasty Egyptian kings ruled from Thebes. The Hyksos introduced the use of horses and chariots in warfare, and also new forms of weapons, which the Egyptians were later to adopt themselves for their own benefit.

NEW KINGDOM: 18th to 20th Dynasties: c.155-1069 BC

The Theban kings eventually took power from the Hyksos rulers and under Ahmose I, who founded the 18th Dynasty, they gained control of the Delta and of the whole of Egypt. Later, they expanded the Egyptian empire as far as the Euphrates in the east and into the land of Kush in the south. In addition,

useful alliances and political marriages were made with other rulers in Western Asia.

Great buildings, especially temples, were built during the period, and the 18th Dynasty included many rulers who are well recorded in the archaeological record and famous still today, for example: Queen Hatshepsut, Amenhotep III, Akhenaten, Tutankhamun, Horemheb. The 19th Dynasty continued with Rameses I and II and Seti I and II among others, and the 20th Dynasty had a succession of Rameses as rulers.

The New Kingdom period, which had started as a period of expansion and of great architectural, artistic and literary achievement, declined by the end of the 20th Dynasty. There were increasing attacks from abroad, notably by the Sea Peoples, and power shifted away from the kings towards the priesthood of Amun.

THIRD INTERMEDIATE PERIOD: 21st to 24th Dynasties: 1069-747 BC

Power was now decentralized. Smendes, the founder of the 21st Dynasty, ruled Northern Egypt from Tanis in the Delta: at the same time the priest-kings of Amun at Thebes (such as Pinudjem I) controlled Southern Egypt. A Libyan, Sheshonq I, gained power in the Delta, founding the 22nd Dynasty, and for a short time he established his son at Thebes. Then Egypt was again divided, with the 22nd, 23rd and 24th Dynasties ruling simultaneously in different parts of the country. The 25th Dynasty, Kushite, expanded northwards from Kush and gained control of Thebes, but could not displace the 24th Dynasty that was still ruling the Delta from Saïs.

LATE DYNASTIC PERIOD: 25th to 30th Dynasties: 747-332 BC

The 25th Dynasty Kushite ruler, Shabaqo, moved his capital northwards from Thebes to Memphis, but a number of Assyrian invasions aided by rulers from the Delta culminated in the overthrow of the Kushite Dynasty and the rule of Egypt by the Assyrians. When the Assyrians withdrew from Egypt because of troubles nearer home, Psamtek I established the Saïte Dynasty, the 26th, as the major power in Egypt. At this time Greek mercenaries were brought into the Egyptian army and Greek traders settled along the Mediterranean coast.

The Greeks and Egyptians had a common enemy – the Persians – and in 525 BC the Persians invaded Egypt and established the 27th Dynasty. In 404 BC the Egyptians shook off Persian rule and during the 28th, 29th and 30th Dynasties Egyptians ruled their own land again until

The Step Pyramid of Djoser stands on the edge of the Western Desert overlooking the Nile flood-plain. The palm trees mark the western edge of the Nile Valley at Saqqara, near Memphis, which was the capital of Egypt at the time of Djoser.

The Pyramids of Khufu, Khafre and Menkaure (from right to left) at Giza. These were the largest pyramids built by the Pharoahs.

the Persians returned under Artaxerxes III and held Egypt from 343 to 332 BC.

MACEDONIAN AND PTOLEMAIC PERIODS: 332–30 BC

In 332 BC, Alexander the Great, having beaten Darius III of Persia at the Battle of Issus in Asia, made a brief diversion from his conquest of the Persian Empire in Western Asia to free Egypt from the Persians. On Alexander's death, Egypt passed briefly to his immediate successors, then to Ptolemy I Soter, who had been the Macedonian administrator of Egypt. The Ptolemies ruled from 305 to 30 BC, establishing a new capital at Alexandria, increasing the influence of the Hellenistic world upon Egypt but also retaining the existing Egyptian religious and

(British Museum) Horse and chariot and attendant. Wallpainting from the tomb of Nebamun at Thebes, c.1400 BC.

political system. They repaired, enlarged and founded new temples and introduced the cult of Serapis which assimilated both Egyptian and Greek religious ideas.

ROMAN PERIOD: 30 BC–AD 337

Egypt played its part in the power struggle between Pompey, Julius Caesar, Mark Antony and Octavian (Augustus) for control of Rome, and Cleopatra VII, her brother and her son Caesarion were to be the last of the Ptolemies. The Roman Emperors succeeded as Pharoahs, but Egypt was seen by the Romans chiefly as a source of food, of exotic goods and of taxes. Some Emperors, notably Hadrian, travelled in Egypt and showed an interest in Egyptian culture and religion.

Cleopatra and her son by Julius Caesar, called Caesarion, making offerings to the gods. Relief on the outer wall of the Temple of Hathor at Dendera. Cleopatra wears the cow's horns holding the sun-disc of Hathor, who was regarded as the divine mother of the reigning Pharoah. She holds a libation vessel and a sistrum. Caesarion wears the double crown and the ram's horns of Amun, and holds out a censer to present incense to the gods. Above him a hawk , symbol of Ra the sun-god or of Horus, stretches out its wings protectively.

In the 4th century AD the Emperor Theodosius ordered that all Egyptians should become Christians and that all pagan temples should be closed. Some areas survived this measure for a while, but in AD 553 the Emperor Justinian finally closed the temples at Philae and Siwah, effectively making an end of the ancient Egyptian religion. A special form of Christianity, Coptic Christianity, had developed in Egypt and its early forms show some assimilation of Egyptian religious elements, and of Greek mythological ideas also.

Egypt became part of the Byzantine Empire, and its borders were raided by North Africans from the west, by Nubians from the south and by Sassanian Persians from the East, until in the 7th century AD a successful invasion established the Arabs and Islamic religion in Egypt.

With the destruction of the Egyptian religion and the scattering of its priesthood, the meaning of hieroglyphic writing was lost until its decipherment in the 19th. century. Consequently there developed a mystery about the Egyptians and their religion which remains to this day.

24

CHAPTER TWO
UNCOVERING ANCIENT EGYPT

Any real understanding of Ancient Egyptian civilization was dependent upon the decipherment of Egyptian hieroglyphics, which did not come about until the 19th century. Yet Europeans retained an interest in the civilization and, over the intervening centuries, gleaned what they could from visiting the country and observing and collecting its antiquities. Even though the secret of hieroglyphics was lost, other early sources of information about ancient Egypt were available to Europeans.

The most important of these was the description of Egypt by the Greek writer Herodotus in his *Histories,* written about 425 BC. He had visited Egypt in about 450 BC and writes mainly about the Delta, although it seems possible that he travelled as far south as Aswan. He obtained much of his information from Egyptian priests. Nevertheless, he was a close observer at first-hand and describes the country's religious customs, including festivals, the use of magic, animal cults, burial customs and mummification. Although some of his information has proved unreliable, later research has shown that a great deal of it was true.

Another Greek writer, Diodorus of Sicily, visited Egypt in about 60 BC and his World History contains a description of Egypt based partly on material from earlier sources including Herodotus. Interestingly, he added material on mummification not recorded by Herodotus. He also gave a brief account of the Osiris myth, which the writer Plutarch, a Greek citizen of Rome, later described in more detail.

Many travellers visited Egypt during the Roman period. They usually arrived at the port of Alexandria and followed the Nile to Memphis, Giza and Thebes, sometimes travelling as far as Elephantine. Strabo, one of the great, learned travellers of the Roman world, went to Egypt in 25 BC, spent a few years in Alexandria and travelled as far as the First Cataract. The last book of his *Geographia* contains an account of Egypt, particularly of Lower Egypt, that became an important reference work for later travellers. Pliny, Plutarch and Josephus were other writers from the Roman world who added to the early accumulation of knowledge about ancient Egypt.

Later, some of the evidence for the ancient civilization was destroyed during the Christian period in Egypt, in the first millenium AD. Many of the temple reliefs and inscriptions were defaced because Christians regarded them as idolatrous. Parts of some temples were actually converted into Christian churches, while others had houses built within them or were used as convenient quarries to provide stone for local builders.

In fact, few travellers visited Egypt from then until the 16th century, when it became a Turkish province. At that time trade with Europe increased, encouraging more European visitors to Egypt. In the 18th century travel became fashionable among wealthy Europeans, many of whom visited Egypt. An interest in collecting Egyptian antiquities developed among these visitors and created a considerable

Strabo described the Colossi of Memnon (Amenhotep III) at the site of his mortuary temple. The temple stood in the inundation zone of the Nile, and the flooding and robbing of the stone by later kings to build their own temples completely effaced the building, leaving only these two colossal figures of Amenhotep III which stood at the entrance to the temple. The former flood-plain of the Nile can be clearly seen, and beyond this is the steep western edge of the Nile valley. The Valley of the Kings, where many of the New Kingdom kings were buried, lies in these hills behind the colossi. Strabo mentioned that one of the figures emitted a singing sound when the first rays of the morning sun struck it. At first Strabo thought the sound was caused by locals, but became convinced of its supernatural origin. It may have been caused by a flaw in the stone and expansion caused by the sun's heat. The sound ceased when Septimius Severus later repaired the monument.

ABOVE
The defaced head of Amenhotep III in his chariot at the Temple of Amun at Karnak.

RIGHT
The Rosetta Stone showing hieroglyphic, demotic and Greek scripts.

industry among both the local people and the collectors. Antiquarians from France, England, Germany and Italy acquired collections of Egyptian antiquities that can now be seen in the museums of Paris, London, Berlin and Turin as well as in other cities throughout Europe. Interest in the country was also indicated by the many detailed topographical studies that were published.

When Napoleon Bonaparte invaded Egypt in 1798 he instigated a programme of research into all aspects of Egyptian civilization – scientific, cultural and historical. It was carried out during the period of French occupation and resulted in a 19-volume work: *Description de l'Égypte*, published from 1809–1828.

One of the most significant findings of the French came by chance, however. In 1799, while the French army was working near Rosetta to improve coastal defences against the British, they found a stone that bore three long inscriptions written in three language forms: hieroglyphic, demotic and Greek. This stone passed into British hands after their victory over the French. It now lies in the

British Museum and is known as the Rosetta Stone. There was no difficulty in translating the Greek text inscribed on it, which proved to be a decree issued by Ptolemy V in 196 BC. Then it was realized that the demotic and hieroglyphic texts were direct translations of the Greek text, and thus the possibility of deciphering hieroglyphs was at last glimpsed.

After a few false starts by various scholars, one Thomas Young realised that hieroglyphs could be used either phonetically, where each hieroglyph stands for a sound, or ideogrammatically, where each hieroglyph stands for an idea related to is pictorial value. By referring to the Coptic language and script, Young was able to decipher the demotic part of the inscription and go a little way towards deciphering the hieroglyphs. A Frenchman, Jean-François Champollion, continued the work and, in 1822, published a description of Egyptian hieroglyphs that at last made the ancient texts, papyri and inscriptions accessible after about 1500 years of obscurity.

Briefly, hieroglyphic script was the original form of writing developed by the Egyptians; it used signs written in lines without punctuation marks or spaces to indicate breaks between words or sentences. The letters 'face' towards the beginning of the line they are in: thus, if the human or animal heads face to the left, the line should be read from left to right, and vice versa. Columns are always read from top to bottom. There are no signs for vowels, only for consonants. This means that the exact pronunciation of ancient Egyptian cannot be known, although some clues have been obtained from the Coptic language, which is a later form of Egyptian written with Greek letters together with a few signs derived from hieroglyphs.

The signs could be used in three ways. First, they could be used as phonograms, with each sign representing a single consonant such as p, or with each sign representing two or three consonants such as pr or nfr. Second, they could be used as logograms, in which a picture sign of an object would actually mean that object. Third, they could be used as determinatives placed at the end of a word made up of phonograms to modify the meaning of the word; for example the letters making up the word

(British Museum) Hieroglyphs on the stela of Inyotef from Abydos. 12th Dynasty, c.1930 BC.

for wife may be followed by a sign, the determinative, illustrating a seated woman.

Hieratic script developed about 2700 BC and has simpler forms than the hieroglyphic signs. It allowed faster writing on papyrus, and hieratic script was used chiefly for literary and administrative texts. Demotic script evolved from hieratic script about the 7th century BC and was used in commercial and administrative documents, and later in literary, technical and even religious documents. Its use died out in the second century AD as Roman administrators used Greek for official and legal documents, while the Copts used the Egyptian language written in a Greek script with a few additional signs.

The ability to understand what was written in texts and papyri and on inscriptions on stone obviously encouraged new, more informed, work on the antiquities of Egypt and enabled a far more scholarly approach to be instigated. In 1858 the Egyptians appointed their own Director of Antiquities, and began to control the export of antiquities from the country and to form a national collection, which they eventually housed in its own purpose-built museum, The Egyptian Museum in Cairo. Many other countries have nevertheless continued to excavate, to conserve and to research, so that our understanding of the gods and myths and the civilization of ancient Egypt continues to grow year by year.

CHAPTER THREE
EGYPTIAN RELIGION

A first introduction to Egypt's past, through books, museums, or a visit to Egypt itself, leaves a fascinating, colourful, and confused impression. The impression is also a biased one, particularly in the case of myths and religion. One reason it is biased is that most of what has been preserved has come from tombs and burials. Much of our knowledge of everyday life in ancient Egypt is derived from tomb furniture, objects buried in tombs, models placed in tombs, scenes painted in tombs.

They give an impression of a society obsessed with death, or at least with the afterlife. They show evidence of great wealth and luxury when we know that the majority of the population would have been poor, or at least not very rich, and would have left very little behind them for us to see. We, of course, are not able to visit them in their ordinary houses, nor to observe them going about their daily activities.

When we examine their religion we find literally hundreds of gods, many of them animals, or humans with animal heads, some of them monsters unlike any animal we have ever seem. It is not possible to know what the innermost religious thoughts of these ancient Egyptians were. It would have been true then, as it is true today, that at any one time there would be a hundred different people with a hundred different shades of religious feeling, and as times changed, those religious ideas would have changed too.

Myths would also have changed and become

(Egyptian Museum, Cairo) The Pharoah stands between Sekhmet (the lion-headed goddess) and Ptah. On the left is the vulture of Upper Egypt wearing the White Crown, balanced on the right by the cobra of Lower Egypt. The king wears the Blue Crown and carries the flail and crook, symbols of royal authority. Pectoral from the tomb of Tutankhamun, 14th century BC.

adapted, been created and been forgotten. The Egyptian civilization lasted over three thousand years, a time-scale that would take us back from our present day to a time before the beginnings of Rome and before the flowering of ancient Greece. Words spring to mind to describe the religion we see in ancient Egypt: totemism, fetishism, polytheism, magic – all true in sense. Yet it has been argued that despite all this there is a strong monotheistic tradition in ancient Egyptian religious thought. A reading of the so-called Wisdom Literature and other ethical writings confirm this view and will be discussed later in this book.

Furthermore, our own society is so different from theirs, and our own religious cultural background, whatever our own specific religious beliefs, is again so different that it is impossible to know precisely what was the religious experience of the ancient Egyptians. However, we can study the rituals, the outward forms, the symbolism, the development and evolution of their religion and thereby gain some understanding of its mysteries.

The Nile itself was an important element in ancient Egyptian thought. The black alluvial soil of the Nile valley contrasted with the red rocks of the desert on either side: the Egyptians called them the Black Land and the Red Land. The narrow valley of Upper Egypt contrasted with the Delta region of Lower Egypt. The annual cycle of inundation suggested the concepts of creation, and of death and rebirth. The sun, rising daily above the hills of the east and setting in the deserts to the west suggested another regular cycle of renewal. These natural events tended to provoke similar mythologies among many primitive peoples, but the marked contrast between valley and desert, and the special conditions of the annual Nile flood made a unique impression upon the early inhabitants of Egypt.

The Nile was the main thoroughfare of ancient Egypt, and the boat was the best means of travelling any distance. Consequently, when the ancient Egyptians thought of the sun-god travelling across the sky by day, they imagined that there was a river in the sky along which the sun-god sailed in his solar

The Temple sacred to Amun, Mut and Khons at Luxor. Sphinxes line the processional way which led from the Temple of Amun at Karnak to Luxor, ending at the great pylons of the temple.

boat. Similarly, they believed that at night the sun sank below the western horizon and travelled through the underworld, sailing over water in his boat, to emerge next morning at the eastern horizon. At these latitudes the power of the sun could be both beneficial and life-threatening, and the absence of the sun during the dark and cold desert nights was a contrasting feature of the environment. This could be the basis of the thread of dualism which runs through Egyptian thought: day and night, east and west, desert and river, flood and drought, sowing and harvest, death and rebirth, good and evil. These are universal themes of myth, but they were perhaps more intensely felt in the Nile valley than they were elsewhere.

In predynastic times the dead were buried with objects that may have had some kind of religious significance. There were female figures of baked clay and of ivory, small animal figures that might have been worshipped, and slate palettes in the form of animals such as the hippopotamus. Useful everyday objects were also buried with the dead, and these might have been buried with the intention of providing them for use in an afterlife.

Early predynastic Egyptian pottery, particularly from the Delta region, sometimes bears painted designs which resemble the standards displayed on boats or carried by men. The Narmer palette (c.3100 BC) shows a procession of four standard-bearers, each standard surmounted by a bird, mammal or other object. These may be totems, and may be the forerunners of the animal cults that continued throughout the period of Egyptian civilization. The word 'totem' actually comes from North America but is commonly used to express a concept found in Ancient Egypt. It is derived from an Algonquin word meaning the emblem of a tribe or group. The totem usually took the form of an animal (less commonly a plant or other natural object) that identified the tribe or group. The animal itself was often perceived as an ancestor of the group, and seen as a guardian spirit who might be appealed to or worshipped.

The early inhabitants of the Nile valley formed independent groups with their own territories within the Nile valley and, when Egypt was united, the country was divided into regions based on these territories. In Ptolemaic times these regions were called by the Greek word *nomes*. There were about 40 nomes in the whole of Egypt, and each had an insignia, or standard, and could be described as the 'jackal nome' or 'ibis nome' after the animal or other device on its standard. A group probably chose a particular animal because it had certain qualities they respected or feared. A snake, hawk, jackal, scorpion or crocodile are all obvious choices from the local animal population.

Some of the objects on the standards were not animals but other objects, which might have been fetishistic in character. A fetish (the word comes from West Africa) is an object worshipped for its magical powers, acting as a charm or amulet, and revered in its own right rather than as an image or symbol of something else. There are many examples of fetishism, magic, and the use of amulets and spells throughout the history of ancient Egypt, for example the shield and crossed arrows that were a symbol of the warrior-goddess Neith have been found on emblems dating from as far back as predynastic times.

Different regions had their own local gods, and cult centres developed with their own gods and their own mythologies. The chief ones are set out on the chart opposite.

The god of a particular district would be worshipped locally, but would rise to prominence nationally if the rulers of that district became national rulers. Thus Horus, the god of the rulers from Hieraconpolis who unified Egypt at the start of the dynastic period, gained status from their political success. Similarly Amun, who had been an obscure local god, rose to national importance as the god of the Theban kings who drove out the Hyksos from Egypt. Neith, a warrior-goddess from Saïs, became important in the 26th Dynasty when Egypt was ruled by kings from Saïs. Throughout the history of ancient Egypt political events shaped the development of religion while myths were invented or modified to suit political ends, as we shall show.

A profusion of gods existed, and the priests of

MAIN CULT CENTRES IN ANCIENT EGYPT.

Locality:	Local Deity:
Buto	Edjo (cobra goddess), later Horus
Saïs	Neith
Tanis	Seth
Busiris	Osiris
Heliopolis	Atum or Ra
Memphis	Ptah & Sekhmet
Hermopolis	Thoth
Thinis	Onuris
Abydos	A Jackal, later Osiris
Dendera	Hathor
Koptos	Min
Ombos	Seth
Thebes	Amun
Edfu	Horus
Elephantine	Khnum

Seti I offering incense to the god Horus. Wall painting from the sanctury of Horus in the Temple of Abydos.

the cult centres would modify existing traditions to develop complicated mythologies in order to establish the superiority of their own local cult and gods above those of their neighbours and rivals. The practice of the cults became exclusive to the king and the priesthood. Temples were not built for public worship, but for the private practice of the cult by the king and the priests.

The king was seen as the son of Ra, the sun god, and as the living king he was Horus, the mythical king of Egypt and successor of Osiris. When he died, the king was carried to the sky to live with Ra and to take his place among the stars. But with the rise to prominence of the Osiris cult, the dead king was thought of as Osiris, the mythical dead former king, who ruled in the underworld.

The most important duty of the king was to maintain the *maat* of Egypt, *maat* being the state of divine order and justice, and this involved a daily ritual in each temple, before the shrine of the god. The king was meant to perform the ritual in person, but as he obviously could not do this at every temple throughout the land, his place was taken by a priest as his representative. The daily ceremony started as a procession to the temple followed by the ritual purification and dressing of the king in the House of Morning. A censer was charged with charcoal and incense for the king and he proceeded to the shrine of the cult statue of the god. The doors of the shrine were unsealed and opened and the king offered incense to the god and presented the figure of Maat to the god to represent order in his kingdom. The figure of the god was then stripped of its garments, purified and re-clothed in fresh garments.

A ritual feast was prepared on an offering-table in front of the shrine. The courses of food were consecrated and offered to the god, more incense was offered and the doors of the shrine were closed and re-sealed. Then the room which contained the shrine was purified and all footprints were swept away as the king retreated from the room. The public did not attend this ceremony; it was a ritual that involved only the king and senior priests, and like many aspects of the state religion it was remote from the experience of ordinary people.

Only at the great annual festivals, when the gods would be brought out of the temples did the general population participate in the great state cults. In the second month of the inundation, Amun would travel from his temple at Karnak to visit the shrine of his consort, Mut, at Luxor. At another time, Hathor would make the long journey by boat on the Nile from Dendera to celebrate her divine marriage to

Horus in his temple at Edfu. There were pilgrimages and festivals at the shrine of Osiris at Abydos, a festival of the Coming Forth of Min at harvest time, a festival of Sokar near the end of the inundation season. Such festivals were times of holiday for the ordinary people.

The *sed* festival was concerned with the role of kingship rather than with one particular god and was first documented in the reign of king Den in the 1st Dynasty. This festival celebrated the royal jubilee after the king had reigned for 30 years, although in some cases it was celebrated well before the full 30 years had elapsed. There was a double coronation to confirm the king as King of Upper Egypt and of Lower Egypt. As part of this ceremony, the king ran a course between markers, probably to symbolize the boundaries of his kingdom, although the running of the course may have been to demonstrate his physical fitness for the kingship. Then the king fired four arrows, one to each of the four cardinal points, symbolically directed at the enemies of his realm.

The temple was a dwelling-place for the gods

The first courtyard of the great Temple of Amun at Karnak, with statues of Osiris.

A singer of Amun, Meresimen, adores Osiris and the Four Sons of Horus (these four are also the guardians of the canopic jars which hold the organs taken from the body during mummification).

where the king could commune with them and act as an intermediary between them and the people. The inner rooms of the temples were covered with paintings showing the king worshipping and making offerings to the gods. It was believed that these images could take the place of the king in his absence and perform the essential rituals that were required by the gods. The status of the king was reinforced by images on the temple walls that showed him being blessed by the gods, and in the birth-houses attached to the temple the king would be shown symbolically as a child of divine origin.

The king was the First Prophet or High Priest of every temple, but a chief priest was appointed to deputize for him. This person would often be the nomarch, or ruler of the local province of which there were some 40 in Egypt, or some other high local official. Another senior priest would manage the economy of the temple and other priests would attend to specialized duties within the temple, including the study of astronomy, the teaching of writing and the copying of religious texts, singing

42

and making music for the temple ceremonies.

The ordinary priests were organized in four groups: each group would serve at the temple for one month and then return to its secular life for the next three months. During its month of office the group was paid from the temple revenues, and the position could be a lucrative one. It was believed that only the essence of the food offerings brought to the gods every day was consumed by them so the priests were free to consume the actual offerings. The priests were thus concerned with the temple and its organi-zation. It seems very unlikely that they performed any kind of pastoral role.

Many temples and priesthoods were granted freedom from taxes and state service and were able to become rich and powerful, at times even rivalling the authority of the king. The consequent rivalry between temple and king is well illustrated by the events of the reign of Akhenaten who reduced the power of the priests of Amun at Thebes and favoured the hitherto less important cult of Aten, retaining exclusive control of that cult to himself. On the death

of Akhenaten, the priests of Amun were able to regain their lost power and influence and to efface much of the work of Akhenaten. Temples developed into great administrative centres, and the priests became substantial landowners, employing large non-priestly staffs to run the temple estates.

The records show that Rameses III endowed about one tenth of all cultivable land in Egypt to temples, while the temples also received income from private donations and from tithes. When the temples acquired land they also acquired control of the people who lived on that land so that, although the state religion itself was often remote from the people, the religious institutions actually had a direct influence on the lives of many of them.

The ancient Egyptians held the fundamental belief that life could continue after death in some form or other, but for life to continue in a form similar to that of their present life, the body and the spirit of the individual had to be preserved and the needs of both body and spirit had to be attended to. In addition, to gain an eternal afterlife the person had to show piety to the gods and lead a good and just life in the present world.

The preservation of the physical self was achieved by mummification of the body, and by the encasing of the mummy in a suitable coffin within a tomb that would protect it from decay and destruction. In many simple burials of predynastic times the body was preserved by natural dessication arising from the dry climate and contact with the sterile sand of the burial place. Later, when the dead were buried in more elaborate tombs this natural process of

preservation did not take place and putrefaction of the body occurred. In order to preserve the body under these conditions, a process of mummification was evolved, which gradually achieved the desired result.

By the time of the New Kingdom this process was quite advanced. The brain and viscera were removed from the body, as these speeded the process of decay, and they and the body itself were dehydrated by the application of natron, which is a naturally-occurring form of sodium carbonate and sodium bicarbonate found in a number of locations in Egypt, particularly at Wadi Natrun in Lower Egypt. The heart, regarded as the seat of intellect, was usu-

ally left in the body. The body was treated with oils, resins and spices and then packed out to restore its original contours as the dehydration process caused the flesh to shrink and the body to become mainly skin and bone. Amulets were placed on the body as a form of protection, and it was wrapped in linen bandages. This became a very skilled process, which reached its highest standard in the 21st Dynasty but tended to deteriorate thereafter.

The internal organs, which had been taken out earlier, were also carefully preserved because no part of the body should be missing if it was to be perfect in the afterlife. They were stored in four canopic jars, and placed near the mummy at burial. The word

canopic, used to describe these jars, arises because their swollen shape and animal-headed stoppers reminded early scholars of the story of Canopus, the pilot of Menelaus, who was buried at Canopus in Egypt, and was worshipped there as a jar with a human head and a swollen body.

The contents of the canopic jars were protected by the four sons of Horus, each assigned to a particular organ. Duamutef, identified by his jackal's head, protected the stomach: Hapi, with the head of an ape, protected the lungs: Imsety, with a human head, guarded the liver and Qebehsenuef, with the head of a falcon, looked after the intestines. The goddesses Isis, Neith, Nephthys and Selket provided

extra protection to the canopic gods and to the coffin. In Ptolemaic and Roman times mummies were less well preserved; the organs were often left in the body and dummy canopic jars were used.

Strangely, also in the Ptolemaic and Roman periods, animal mummification became very popular and large cemeteries devoted to the appropriate animal were found close to certain cult centres. For example, ibises were buried at Hermopolis, the cult centre of Thoth, who was associated with the ibis.

Cats were mummified and buried at Bubastis where the cat-goddess Bastet was sacred. Exactly what was intended by this animal mummification is not clear, as research on the cat mummies shows that rather than dying a natural death, most had had their necks broken, and they consisted mainly of two groups – either young kittens or two year-old cats. Perhaps they were sent to serve the goddess Bastet in their after-lives.

The Egyptians believed that an individual was made up of five different elements: the physical body, the *ka*, the *ba*, the name and the shadow. At death the *ka* lived on and so required food and drink just as the body had done in life. This was supplied by the family of the deceased bringing food and drink to an offering-table at the tomb, or by making an endowment to a temple so that the priests could perform this function for them. In case this actual physical supply of offerings should cease, or in place of it altogether, the necessary offerings could be sup-

plied by magical means, by illustrating the offering process on the tomb walls, on the coffin, or on papyri placed in the tomb with the body. It was then believed that a kind of sympathetic magic would cause the event illustrated to happen.

The *ba* was the manifestation of the non-physical attributes of a person, and has sometimes been thought of as his soul, although this is not a strictly accurate equivalent. It is usually illustrated in the Book of the Dead and in other contexts as a bird with a human head and often with human arms, called a *ba*-bird or soul-bird. The *ba* was free to travel from the tomb by day, but it had to return to the mummy every night so that the physical body could survive in the afterlife. The *ba* travelled to the underworld to unite with the *ka* of the person to form the *akh*, which was the afterlife equivalent of the physical body of the deceased. Tombs had a false door that allowed the *ka* and *ba* to pass from the tomb to the world of the living and back again, and coffins had eyes painted on them so that the dead person could see out. These illustrate the strange mixture of abstract and concrete and of physical and mystical elements in the thinking of the ancient Egyptians.

One early notion of life after death was that the deceased rose to the sky and became one of the stars. A later idea, particularly bound up with the Osiris myth, was that the dead person carried on a life in the part of the underworld called the Field of Reeds in a manner similar to present life on earth. In the myth,

Osiris was killed and brought back to life again, eventually becoming ruler of the underworld. The texts and spells buried with the body were designed to help the resurrection into the afterlife, and to protect and guide the deceased person during the perilous journey through the underworld.

Before being placed in the tomb the mummy was placed in front of the tomb and the ceremony of Opening the Mouth was carried out in order symbolically to bring the mummy or dead person to life by means of rituals that would restore to it the power of speech, sight and the other senses. This ceremony was performed by the son or heir of the dead person, in the case of a king, by his successor. The deceased was also judged in the ceremony of the Weighing of the Heart in which the heart of the dead person was weighed against the Feather of Truth, which symbolized the *maat*, or sense of order and justice of the universe. The heart was chosen because the ancient Egyptians believed that the heart was the organ of the intellect, transmitting its commands to all parts of the body via the bloodstream. These subjects are dealt with in more detail in the chapter on the Book of the Dead.

There are also a number of ancient Egyptian texts which are today known as 'Wisdom Literature'. Some of these are didactic in purpose, giving precepts for the conduct of everyday life, such as a father would give to his son, or a king to his heir. Others are more reflective in nature and are often called 'pessimistic' literature because they deal with the condition of order and particularly the disorder of the times they describe.

The earliest surviving didactic texts come from the 4th and 5th Dynasties and one, the *Instructions of Ptahhotep*, consists of the advice given by a senior state official to his son whom he wishes to succeed him when he retires from service. They include such maxims as:

'Consult the ignorant man as well as the wise one.'

24712

(British Museum) Wooden shabti-*box of Anhai showing Anhai and her soul-bird (*ba*) receiving refreshment from the goddess of the sycamore tree. The goddess is often portrayed as Hathor, but in this case she is shown as Nut.*

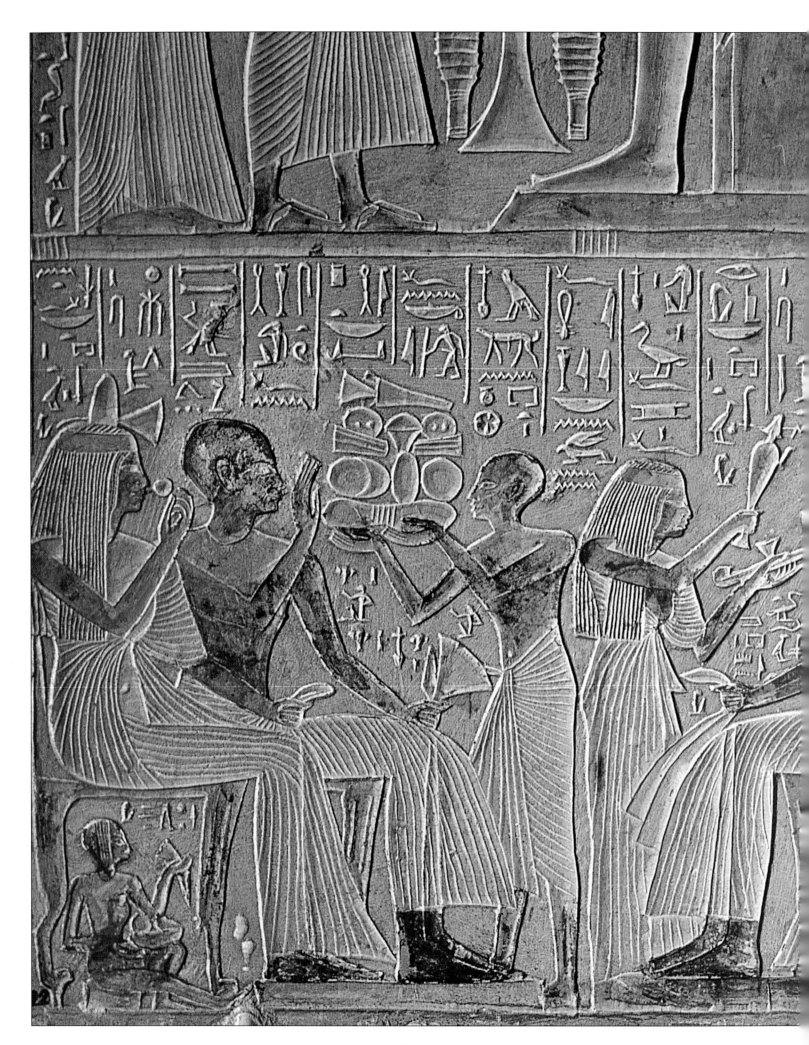

'If you abase yourself in the service of a perfect man, your conduct will be fair before God.'

'If you have been of no account, you have become great and if having been poor you have become rich and if you have become governor of a city, do not be hard-hearted because of your advancement, because you have become merely the guardian of the things which god has provided.'

'What is loved of god is obedience; God hates disobedience.'

A later text is the *Teaching of Amenemipat*, which is reminiscent of the Biblical Book of Proverbs. If there is any connection between this text and the Book of Proverbs, it is not certain which came first or which was the model for the other.

Examples of the reflective texts occur from the Middle Kingdom onwards, and these show a variety of philosophies which range from the deeply pessimistic to the hedonistic. The *Song of the Harper* shows this latter view:

'*Follow your desires as long as you live. Put myrrh on your head, clothe yourself in fine linen ...*'

A later text says much the same thing:

'*... cease not to drink, to eat, to get drunk and to make love. Make holiday, pursue your desire day and night.*'

These texts give an insight into personal, religious and ethical views quite different in character from those of the state religion, and demonstrate that many aspects of ancient Egyptian religion are not obvious on first inspection.

(National Archaeological Museum, Florence) Relatives bring food and offer incense to the dead. Painted limestone tomb relief.

51

CHAPTER FOUR
THE CREATION MYTHS

Creation myths are concerned with the moment at which the cosmos came into being and they attempt to elucidate for mankind, if only by creating a series of comprehensible images, the problem of how a force could exist within a state of non-being and how it could initiate the creation of a cosmos and its separation from the void. The images used in the detail of such explanations are naturally dependent upon the topography and circumstances of different areas of the world. It is not surprising that the dominant images in the Egyptian creation myths are water, a hill that rises from the water, and the sun that vanishes at night but rises each day to cross the sky once again.

There is no way of knowing how old such myths are, or in what form they were originally handed down orally from generation to generation. The first indications of such myths in Egypt are found in the Pyramid Texts from the late years of the Old Kingdom and the Coffin Texts from the Middle Kingdom. They had probably been in existence long before that, however, in a number of different forms, and ideas on the subject of creation probably affected pictorial language and ritual during the earliest period of the Pharaohs in ways we are unable to detect.

Our knowledge of the creation stories is derived from texts that have been influenced by the structuring of the myths by the priests at three chief centres, each of which was a cult centre for a particular deity. It is possible that political considerations played some part in the formulation of the myths as each centre in turn achieved importance and its priests attempted to locate significant events in the myths in their own area and relate them particularly to their favoured god. It should be remembered that alternative explanations or images that changed and developed over time were acceptable to the Egyptians, even when they were contradictory, and this is something to which the modern mind has to adjust. Nevertheless, in spite of the different ways found in the cosmogonies to express what are, after all, the very remarkable facts of creation, it will be seen that certain images are consistent.

The Cosmogony of Heliopolis

Heliopolis, the City of the Sun, was the name used by the Greek historian Herodotus for the Egyptian city containing the sanctuary of Yunu, which was a very important and very early temple of the sun-god. One of the most significant Egyptian cosmogonies, or creation myths, the one that later seemed to achieve perhaps the greatest degree of acceptance, was formulated there possibly about 3000 BC.

This tells us that in the beginning there was nothing but water. It was not merely an ocean or a lake with boundaries, but a limitless expanse of motionless water. It was called Nun. Even after the world was created Nun continued to exist at its margins and would one day return to destroy it and begin the cycle again.

By some unexplained means, a self-created god called Atum, 'The All', rose from the waters, even although they had no surface, and created the primeval mound of earth on which he could stand.

This primeval mound was important to all the cosmogonies and it has been suggested that it was an image that came naturally to people who were used to seeing such fertile mounds or islands reappearing after the obliterating flood-waters of the Nile had withdrawn, and that such a mound was possibly the inspiration for the building of the first pyramids.

In a sense, the priests of Heliopolis claimed the first land as their own in that they cherished a sacred stone called the Benben stone, alleged to be a relic of the event, that symbolized the primeval mound, where the rays of the first light of dawn may have struck and where a temple to the sun-god was built.

Because the creator, Atum, the All, as his name suggests, represented and contained within himself everything, he was able to create other deities from himself. Two explanations are given for the method by which he was able to induce life. The first says that he produced two children from his own semen by using his hand, which some versions of the story suggest may have represented the female principle also contained within him. The other explanation is

that he sneezed out the god Shu and spat out the goddess Tefnut. It is possible that there is a punning connection between the word Shu and the Egyptian word for sneeze.

Shu was a god of air, whose name comes from a root meaning 'empty.' His sister Tefnut, whose name may mean 'moist air', seems appropriately connected with spitting. In typically dualistic fashion, Shu was the air through which the sun shone, that is the kind of dry air that preserves things; Tefnut, on the other hand, was the kind of moist air that rots and corrodes.

The two deities were brought up by Nun, the waste of water, and watched over by the eye of Atum, which he could separate from his body. The eye, or *udjat*, plays a part in a story told about the childhood of Shu and Tefnut. Atum sent his eye to look for the children when they were lost from him in the wastes of Nun. Meanwhile he replaced it with a brighter eye, which was resented by the first eye when it returned with the children. Atum therefore placed the first eye on his forehead where it could

(British Museum) Nun, god of the primeval waters, holding the emblem of long life. His body is usually shown as blue or green, symbolizing water and fertility. Detail of the Papyrus of Ani.

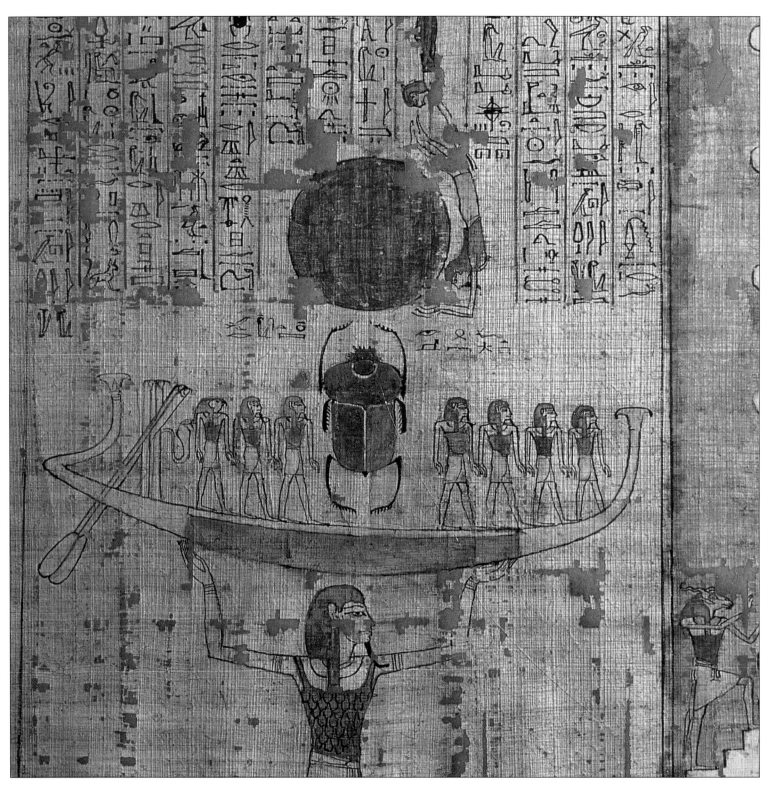

A detail from the Papyrus of Anhai which suggests both Creation and the daily rising of the sun. A god holds the boat of the sun containing the beetle-god Khepri (symbolic both of Creation and of the rising sun at dawn) and the red disc of the sun is received by the sky-goddess, Nut.

keep watch on the world once he had created it. Later, it became associated with the snake-goddess that was worn as the *uraeus* by the pharaohs on their foreheads. Another story says that he was so glad to see his children again that he wept for joy, and mankind was created from his tears.

The union of Shu and Tefnut produced two further deities – Nut, the sky goddess, and Geb, the earth god. It is interesting that Egyptian mythology is unlike Greek and other Indo-European mythologies in making the sky female and the earth male. Once again the brother and sister united to produce chil-

dren – the gods Osiris and Seth and their consorts, the goddesses Isis and Nephthys. From Nun had therefore sprung a family of nine gods, the so-called Ennead of Heliopolis, although Osiris and Isis also produced the god Horus in the next generation.

It seems possible that the priests of Heliopolis had at some stage grafted the generation of gods headed by Osiris on to the family of Atum in a deliberate move to connect the great god Atum's creativity with the gods of kings and men, and by doing this both to relate the kings of Egypt to the solar god and to reinforce the idea of the continual cycle of life and death in the universe that was so important in Egyptian thought. The myths concerning Osiris, which emphasize these notions, will be dealt with later.

Once Nut and Geb had produced their children, Shu separated them for ever. Illustrations show Nut, the sky, arching over Geb, the earth, who lies beneath her while Shu, the air, forces them apart, making space for himself. In doing this, he continued the creative principle of distinguishing and dividing the elements from one another.

By maintaining her posture, with her limbs at each cardinal point of the world, Nut creates a barrier to the waters of Nun. She is usually shown as a woman, decorated with stars, but is sometimes portrayed as a cow. It was said that every evening she swallowed the sun-god, Ra, who then travelled through her body at night to be born from her each morning, when the red sky suggested the blood caused by his birth. In an alternative account of the sun's journey, Ra travelled in a boat beneath her body by day and through the underworld at night.

At Heliopolis, the sun-god Ra was the cult deity, and aspects of Atum, 'the All', had been fused with him in several manifestations by the time of the Pyramid Texts. For example, the emerging sun was seen as Khepri, the scarab beetle, rolling the sun's disc before him just as the beetle propelled a ball of dung; the full, shining sun's disk was known as Ra, and the distant sun, was called Harakhti, the hawk. These names could be combined with the name of Atum, or Ra, the sun god as in Ra-Harakhti, for example.

Atum's birth as a sun god was also described in this set of myths by the image of a lotus flower that rose from the flood of Nun at the same time as the primeval mound. From the flower emerged a child who was the self-created sun god. In yet another image, the sacred bird of Heliopolis, the Benu-bird also acted as a manifestation of Atum as sun-god. The Benu-bird was associated with the benben stone, and their names may both be derived from the Egyptian verb *weben*, 'to shine' or 'to rise', which may also have suggested the otherwise mistaken

(British Museum) The dead Ani, portrayed as a swallow standing on a mound. This may refer to the primeval mound which rose out of the waters at the time of Creation, and to the benu bird which alighted on that mound. Detail from the Papyrus of Ani.

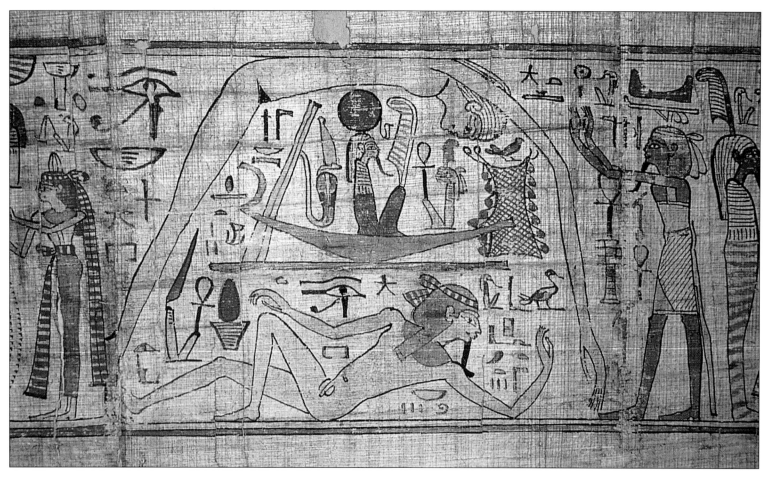

relationship Herodotus noted between the Egyptian
bird and the Greek Phoenix. The bird is shown as a
yellow wagtail in the Pyramid Texts and as a grey
heron in the later Book of the Dead, but its association with the sun remains constant.

The Cosmogony of Hermopolis

Hermopolis is the Greek name given to the city in
Upper Egypt that is known today as Ashmunein. It
was earlier called Khmun, 'the Eight', for reasons
that will become clear, and it was the cult centre of
the god Thoth, the god of wisdom who is said to
have given hieroglyphs to the Egyptians. The Greeks
equated Thoth with their god Hermes, hence their
name Hermopolis for the city.

The cosmogony developed at Hermopolis actually deals with events before that of Heliopolis
because it concerns the nature of the featureless
water before the act of creation, dealing with its negative characteristics, with what was not there before
something was. It says that the waters either were, or
produced out of themselves, four beings or deities
and their female counterparts. These were Nun and
Nunet, the primal waters; Heh and Hehet, whose
name has been thought to mean infinity although it
has also been suggested that it actually means the
flood force inherent in water; Kek and Keket, darkness, and Amun and Amunet, whose name suggests
a number of qualities: hiddenness, unseen energy, air

56

or wind. These eight deities were known as the Ogdoad, or Eight, of Hermopolis. The four gods were shown with frogs' heads and the goddesses with serpents' heads; thus they were perceived in the form of creatures who seemed to appear spontaneously each year from the mud and slime of the Nile's inundation.

It can be seen that Nun who, in the Heliopolitan myth, was himself the containing watery substance, is in the Hermopolitan myth only one element – the watery one – contained within the whole pre-cosmic substance. Of the other deities one, Amun, had the hidden potential energy to cause the disturbance that might have initiated creation from within the dark, inert waters.

By some means, a cosmic egg was formed within the dark waters, and when it broke light came from it. In some versions of the story, the cosmic egg was laid by a goose, the Great Primal Spirit in the form of the 'Great Cackler', whose cry was the first sound in the primal silence. It was probably a particularly local version of the story that claimed that the god Thoth in his form as an ibis flew to the primal mound with the egg. Again, there are two versions of what came from the egg: one says that Ra, in the form of a bird of light, hatched from it, another that it contained air which, once released, separated the sky from the earth and provided the breath of life for future creation.

In Hermopolis, this first burst of energy was also said to have thrust up a primeval mound, which was here described as the 'Isle of Flame' because the birth of the sun god there brought with it the first, flaming sunrise. Only later was the mound equated with Hermopolis itself.

Three pairs of the Ogdoad remained undeveloped and stayed where they were, being responsible for the flow of the Nile and the rising of the sun. Amun, the hidden, unknowable force was a different matter, however. His role as a creator grew more important, particularly in Thebes when it became a major religious centre later on. By a complex intellectual process of the priests, he was developed from being merely one of the elements present at the creation to being a transcendental force who created himself and actually energized the eight deities, of whom he was one, into the act of creation.

In Thebes he developed as the sun god, and can often be seen inscribed as Amun-Ra.

The Cosmogony of Memphis

The city of Memphis was built near the Nile Delta in about 3000 BC and deliberately developed as a political and religious centre, which doubtless felt the

need to compete with other centres like the ones already discussed. Its cult-god was Ptah, who had been worshipped in very early times as a supreme artificer, a great craftsman; later he was fused with Tatenen, which was the name given to the primeval mound, so that he was actually conceived, as Atun was in some of the versions of the Heliopolitan myth, as not only concerned in the creation of the mound, but as himself being it. His importance had, nevertheless, waned over the years. Evidence for the cosmogony formulated at Memphis comes from the so-called Shabaka Stone, on which was copied the contents of a much earlier text that has not survived.

It is in some ways the most interesting of the cosmogonies to a modern reader because it stresses intellect as a primary principle of creation. It claims

(Egyptian Museum, Cairo) The head of Tutankhamun as a child, emerging from the lotus flower is a symbol of the creation of the sun. From the tomb of Tutankhamun. 18th Dynasty.

(British Museum) Thoth, the ibis-headed god, leads Pensenhor to the underworld. Detail from the mummy-case of Pensenhor, from Thebes, c.900 BC.

that the god Ptah was the creator of the world, that he was also Nun, and that he created the Ennead, the nine gods of Heliopolis, with his heart and his tongue. To the Egyptians the heart is the seat of thought, the place where ideas are conceived, and the tongue controls speech and therefore the commands that determine action. Names were important to the Egyptians and, in a sense, the act of naming the gods would have given them life.

Ptah therefore created the other gods, including Atum, the first god of the Heliopolitan system, whose own acts of creation were simply the result of following Ptah's instructions. Ptah was thus responsible for the whole of creation, and present in it all. Having made the gods, he allotted them to places where they would be worshipped. He not only made the physical world, but also devised moral order, and he created political order in Egypt by devising the system of nomes or departments. He remained the great artificer and was, for that reason, equated by

others over the centuries. Behind them probably lie earlier stories and less developed great gods. They all suggest the overwhelming importance of the annual rise of the earth from the Nile's flood, and the daily falcon-like rise and fall of the sun that sometimes seemed to come too close to the earth. Behind them all is the sense that the flood waters are only just restrained, the whole process could start all over again, and the first act of creation was a wonderful moment that is constantly repeated in a less glorious fashion.

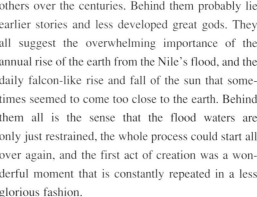

LEFT
Amun-Ra shown as the ram of Amun with the sun-disc of Ra. Relief from the Temple of Amun at Karnak.

LEFT
(Musée Borely, Marseilles)
Bronze figure of the god Ptah.

the Greeks with their god Hephaestus. But he was also 'Lord of Truth'. In Ptah, the priests of Memphis combined the intellectual force of creation by means of the word with the primeval mound itself, thus uniting mind and matter.

Khnum and the Creation of Mankind

The main cosmogonies are concerned primarily with the physical universe and with the chief gods, but the god Khnum concerned himself with making human beings. He was a potter, and thus a craftsman, like Ptah. Khnum was, however, depicted as ram-headed, having the horizontal horns of an early breed, and was thus associated with creativity among the animal world. His home was Elephantine at Aswan, in the cataract region of the Nile, where also lived Hapy, the god who controlled the annual inundation. Nile clay in that area provided material for potters, and the fertile soil brought Khnum a reputation for the provision of prosperity. At Esna, further north in Upper Egypt, Khnum was worshipped as the creator of all human creatures. Inscriptions there show in anatomical detail how he fashioned the human body, with its skeletal structure, its skin and internal organs. In him are combined the sources of animal energy, creativity and fertility, upon which life depends.

These have been merely summaries of some of the most outstanding Egyptian creation myths, and it is important to realize that they evolved and developed over time, that there are different, local versions of the myths and that some gods merged with

59

CHAPTER FIVE
THE MYTH OF OSIRIS

The myth of Osiris is one that developed and changed over the centuries as the god increased in importance and popularity. Stories about him were gathered into a complex myth that eventually wove together a number of important strands of Egyptian thought to form a pattern in which concepts of death and rebirth, order and disorder, vegetative growth and aridity, kingship and rightful inheritance were all balanced against one another and given a place.

His story has been pieced together by scholars from evidence found in many scattered sources from different periods, including the Pyramid Texts of the Middle Kingdom, inscriptions in temples and on stele, a variety of papyri, and the account of the Greek writer Plutarch. Consequently there are a number of versions of some incidents in the myth and the emphasis placed on certain events varies according to the period and the circumstances of their recording.

Although the first archaeological evidence for Osiris dates only from the middle of the 3rd century BC there is some reason to suppose that he existed earlier than that as a god of vegetation, having power over the germination and growth of grain crops in particular. The association between the god who lived on after death to rule in the underworld and the annual sowing of seed in the earth and the subsequent harvest is, in any case, a natural one. The continuity of his reputation as a god concerned with vegetation is confirmed by the 'Osiris beds' found in some tombs, in which a model of the god was filled with earth and sown with seeds that actually germinated inside the tomb. Naturally, new growth from the apparently dead seed was primarily meant in these circumstances to suggest his very strong association with the possibility of the rebirth of the dead in the underworld.

As the cult of Osiris increased in importance, he assimilated the natures of gods he replaced. At Busiris in the Delta, for example, he probably replaced the god Andjety, a royal god. It may be from him that he derived the royal insignia he is usually shown with: the crook and the flail and the high crown flanked by plumes, known as the *atef* crown. It will be seen that he became strongly linked with the notion of kingship.

He is said to have been born at Rosetau near Memphis, which was thought to have been the entrance into the underworld. At Abydos in Upper Egypt he assimilated the characteristics of the funerary deity, Khentiamentiu, and thus became known as 'Lord of the Westerners'. The name 'westerners' was given by the Egyptians to the dead because as the sun sets in the west each day it was thought to be the direction in which people also went at the end of their lives. From that time, Osiris was worshipped as a ruler of those buried in the cemeteries in the desert near Abydos, who would have hoped to enter the underworld successfully.

Thus Osiris had associations with vegetative fertility, with kingship and with rule over the underworld. We have already seen how the cosmogony of Heliopolis brought the god into connection with the

61

sun god in his manifestation as Atum by making Osiris his grandson, the eldest child of Nut, the sky goddess, and Geb, the earth god. By doing this, it also linked the older gods to mankind through the role of Osiris as king.

Some of these complexities are expressed in visual representations of the god. He is shown as a man with kingly attributes, but is wrapped in the bandages of a mummy; because of this his body is often white, but sometimes it is black like the mud of the Nile or green like reborn vegetation.

As we have seen, Osiris had two sisters, Isis and Nephthys, and a brother, Seth. One source says that Osiris and Isis fell in love in the womb. All agree that they married, thereby providing a pattern of royal marriage between brother and sister.

Following the rule of the god Shu, succeeded by his son Geb, Osiris became king and he and Isis presided wisely over the kind of golden age commonly found in mythological descriptions of a remote period. Crops grew well, the climate was tempered by breezes, there was order on earth and people behaved justly to one another.

This peaceful episode was brought to an end by the rulers' younger brother Seth, who slew Osiris in order to seize power for himself. It was said that Seth had always represented violence and disorder, to the extent that he had begun life by tearing himself from his mother's womb. Even his pictorial representations suggest his disorder; he is shown as a probably mythical animal, with the long, downward-curving nose of an anteater, and unique upward-pointing, squared-off ears.

The earliest sources of the story of the death of Osiris suggest a reluctance by contemporary Egyptians to dwell on the murder of a reigning king; they merely say that the 'Great One' fell on his side on the bank of the Nedyet river; sources from the Middle Kingdom, however, say directly that Seth attacked and killed him on the river bank.

Osiris's sister and wife, the goddess Isis, sought sorrowfully for her husband and, having found him, she 'gathered up his flesh', possibly preserving his body magically from corruption. From that point, Osiris became ruler of the underworld, or *Duat*.

A much fuller version of the murder of Osiris was recorded well over a thousand years later by Plutarch. It is thought that, although he imposed a Hellenistic influence on the myth, for example by calling the Egyptian gods by their corresponding Greek names, he recorded its current outline accurately enough from the sources he consulted in Egypt, and that the earlier story would inevitably have changed by that date. Plutarch tells the following version of the story.

He begins with an account of the conception and birth of Osiris, saying that at the moment of his birth a voice was heard to say that the lord of creation was born. He describes his period as king of Egypt, emphasizing his devotion to the civilizing and teaching of his people. After his success in Egypt he went on a journey to teach other nations of the world. On his return, the envious god Seth (whom Plutarch calls Typhon, after a monster of Greek mythology) gathered together 72 like-minded comrades and a Nubian Queen, who plotted together to kill Osiris.

They managed secretly to measure his body exactly. Seth invited Osiris to a banquet with other guests. During the feast, some of the conspirators brought a beautifully wrought chest into the hall, suggesting that it might be a gift for the man who best fitted inside it. Osiris took his turn at lying in the chest, which of course fitted him exactly. Seth's followers instantly closed the chest, sealing it with molten lead. They then took it to one of the mouths of the Nile and threw it into the river so that it might be carried away into the sea.

The chest came ashore near Byblos on the coast of Lebanon by the roots of a young tamarisk tree which swiftly grew, enclosing the chest within its trunk. The flourishing tree came to the attention of the king of the country, who ordered it to be cut down to be used as a pillar in his house. While the tree had been growing, Isis had been searching desperately for her husband. When she heard about the wonderful tree, she went to Byblos herself.

She gained entry to the palace by becoming

(Louvre) Osiris, Horus and Isis. Gold and lapis-lazuli. 22nd Dynasty.

LEFT
(British Museum) Osiris-Khentiamentiu. Wallpainting from a Theban tomb c.1200 BC. Osiris as the god associated with the necropolis of the west, and as ruler of dead souls.

OPPOSITE
Statue of Horus at his cult temple at Edfu. He is shown as a falcon wearing the crown of Upper and Lower Egypt, symbol of his mythical kingship of the land after the death of his father, Osiris.

nurse to the king's newly born son, whom she suckled with her finger. In a desire to make him immortal, she put him into the fire each night so that his mortal parts might be burnt away. One night, while this was happening, she had changed herself into a swallow in order to sing out her lamentations. The queen came to listen and, appalled by what she saw,

pulled her son from the flames.

Isis told the queen her story and begged successfully to be given the pillar. She retrieved the chest from inside it, and her cries of grief killed the child she had been nursing.

She took the chest to Egypt where she opened it and hid it in the marshes of the Delta. One night,

Osiris thus served as the first example of the body preserved skilfully enough to ensure the preservation of life after death. He entered the underworld, where he lived on to supervise the judgment of those hoping to enter into eternal life after death. He was often thought of as the underworld counterpart to the sun-god, bringing some share of light to that dark place. Although Osiris and Ra were sometimes perceived as 'Twin Souls', there was occasional rivalry between them and Osiris was sometimes perceived as malevolent. There was no doubt of his power, however.

To return to earth, Isis was now pregnant with the son she had wanted to conceive as the inheritor of the kingdom formerly ruled by Osiris, although there are versions of the story that say she had given birth to a son while Osiris was still alive. The more common versions of the story, however, that describe Isis conceiving her son from the revived corpse of her husband, emphasize the maternal care and guile of Isis as she prepared to give birth to the future heir and to watch over his infancy so that he might grow up to challenge Seth and retrieve his father's kingship from him.

Some sources say that Seth imprisoned Isis, jealous of the honours she had done to the body of Osiris, and that the god Thoth, who acted as the vizier of Osiris, helped her to escape. Most agree that she made her way secretly to the papyrus swamps of the delta to prepare for the birth of her child.

The son she bore to Osiris was the god Horus, the hawk. The myths concerning his growing up to adulthood and his eventual recovery of the kingship, as we shall see, help to explain his complex character as a god. He contains the notion of vulnerability because of his representation at times as a child; his eyes, vital to the falcon, are important in his story, and are sometimes thought of as the sun and the moon; perhaps most importantly, his successful striving for just and rightful kingship lay behind the fact that all Egyptian kings were perceived as the manifestation of the god Horus, and for a long period kings used 'Horus' as the first of their titles.

Once Horus had been born, Isis watched over him, but had to leave him from time to time to find food. On one of those occasions, Seth discovered the child and turned himself into a poisonous snake in order to approach him through the swamp. When Isis returned she found her son near death, suffering from the snake's poisoned bite. She appealed to the surrounding people for help but, although they gave her their sympathy, no one knew a spell strong enough to defeat the poison. She realized Seth was behind the

when she had left the chest unattended, Seth discovered it. He took out the body of Osiris and cut it into 14 pieces, which he scattered throughout Egypt. When Isis heard what had happened she set out with her sister Nephthys, who could not tolerate Seth's action even though he was her husband, and they eventually gathered together the scattered fragments of the body except, says Plutarch, for the phallus, which had been eaten by a fish.

Other Egyptian sources say that the whole body was recovered. Some say that the goddesses buried each part where they found it, thus accounting for the growth in the Osiris cult in certain places. Other sources say that Isis gathered the body together and breathed life into it. She is shown in one illustration hovering over Osiris in the form of a bird, a kite, fluttering her wings to create the breath of life. Because she did this, Osiris revived for long enough to impregnate her. By this means she conceived their son Horus. After this she used her skills to preserve the body of her husband and bind it in linen, and she performed rites that ensured he would have eternal life.

attack, and the episode is presented as the first of a number of attacks by Seth upon Horus, and one in which evil threatens innocence.

Isis called upon the great god for help, and the sun's boat stopped near her so that the god Thoth could descend from it and hear her plea. Thoth spoke on behalf of the sun god and promised that the boat would stop its course, bringing darkness and death to the world, until Horus was cured. The great threat worked as a powerful spell, and Horus was saved. Thoth told the sun-god, Ra, that his son had been saved, for indeed Horus was descended from Ra, or Atum. In this story it can be seen that the people expressed their support and sympathy for the young son of the king, and that the greatest god demonstrated that the world would collapse if any harm came to him. It thus gives cosmic significance to the concept of kingship.

Isis protected Horus herself after this; she is often shown nursing a baby, and there is a reference in the Pyramid Texts to the ruler drinking milk from her breasts. When young, Horus was known as 'Harpa-khered', Horus the Child, from which the Greeks constructed the name Harpocrates by which he is more commonly recognized in the west. He is often pictured at this age sitting on his mother's knee, with his shaven head dressed with the so-called sidelock of youth, although at times he is shown as an innocent force capable of keeping away dangerous creatures, for example when he stands on the back of a crocodiles holding snakes in his hands.

A number of myths developed around the goddess Isis, most of which emphasized her maternal nature, her guile and determination and her skills in magic, all of which were necessary to bring her son to successful maturity on her own.

She was often referred to in spells used to cure children from illnesses resulting from the kind of accidents that naturally occurred to them – snake bites and scorpion stings, falls, burns and so on. She is shown to have a special connection with snakes and scorpions. In one story, she went to visit the Town of the Two Sisters in the Nile Delta, taking with her seven scorpions whom she warned to be discreet so that they did not draw the attention of Seth to the group. A wealthy woman, seeing them approaching her house, barred the door to them, but a poor peasant woman invited them in, offering hospitality as people should.

Six of the scorpions gave their poison to the seventh, who slid into the first house and stung the son of the wealthy woman. Her inhospitable nature was repaid when no one answered her cries for help. Isis,

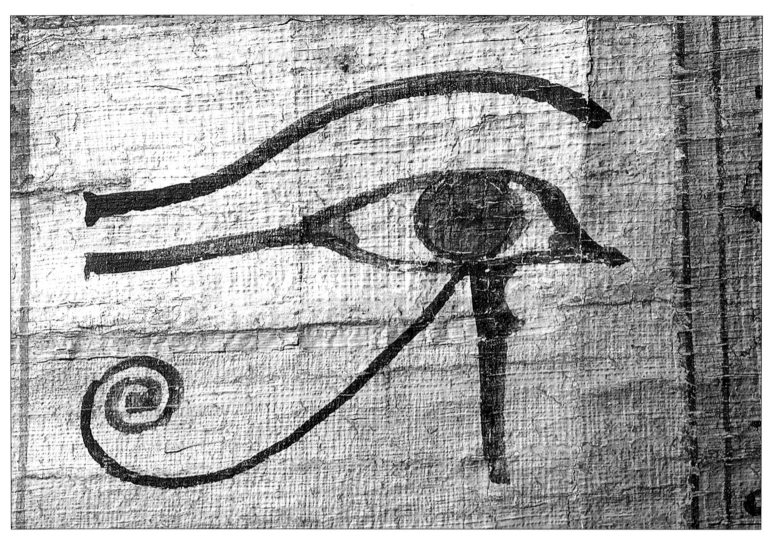

(Rijksmuseum, Leiden) The 'Eye of Osiris' from an ancient Egyptian papyrus.

nevertheless, was unable to refuse help to a suffering child, and cured him with a powerful spell in which she named each scorpion in turn so that she had power over them and their poison, which then became harmless. The woman, in her gratitude, shared her wealth between Isis and the poor woman who had sheltered her.

The greater aspirations of Isis are illustrated by the story of her attempt to take a senior place among the gods when she tired of living on earth as a woman. She determined to discover the secret name of Ra, which she knew would give her power over him so that she could persuade him to help her. She had noticed that saliva sometimes dribbled from the mouth of the ageing Ra. She modelled a poisonous snake from a mixture of some of his saliva and the dust into which it had fallen, then she put the snake where Ra would be sure to walk on it. When the snake bit him, Ra became extremely ill and was unable to help himself because the damage had been done by a creature he had not himself created.

Isis asked if she could help relieve his terrible pain, saying she would overcome it with her spells if he would reveal his name to her. At that, he declared a long list of his many public names, including Khepri in the morning, Ra at midday and Atum in the evening. These did not satisfy Isis, however, for none of them was his hidden name, the one that would give her power over him. When he was persuaded that he would not be cured unless he did as she asked, he withdrew from the other gods and caused his name to pass directly from his heart to hers, forbidding her to reveal it to anyone other than Horus. Then she cured him. The papyrus in which this story is told does not reveal the secret name of Ra, but it does give the spell used by Isis, which could be used by anyone needing a cure for the sting of a scorpion.

In this myth lies an explanation of the way in which the great power of the supreme sun-god passed to the younger family of gods, of which Osiris was the head, and so to future rulers of Egypt, descendants and manifestations of Horus.

Horus eventually arrived safely at adulthood, when he was known as Har-wer, Horus the Elder, or Haroeris in Greek. It was time to make his claim to the kingdom of Egypt and to displace his uncle (in some versions his brother) Seth from power. He went to a tribunal of the gods, presided over by Ra. His great-grandfather Shu, the god of air, supported his claim at once, and Thoth, the god of wisdom, agreed with him. Isis thought all was well and prepared to send the good news, on a wind, to Osiris in the underworld.

At that point Ra intervened to say that he had not yet agreed. When Thoth pointed out the legitimacy of Horus's claim in view of the fact that Osiris was his father, Ra indicated that Seth's great strength perhaps gave him a better claim to rule. It has been suggested that such practical considerations might suggest that the kingship myth is rooted in a real struggle for power early in Egyptian civilization, but there is as yet no evidence for the idea.

It has to be remembered here that Seth was also a complex character, who was chaotic, violent and evil, but who was nevertheless venerated in certain parts of Egypt. Ra supported him as ruler, not only because he was older and stronger than Horus, but also because Seth travelled in the prow of the sun-boat, being the only god who could deal with the serpent Apophis who tried to swallow the sun each evening as it crossed the western horizon.

At the tribunal, Seth characteristically suggested that he and Horus should go outside and settle the matter in a trial of strength, but Thoth restored order and the matter remained unresolved for 80 years. The patience of the tribunal being exhausted, they sent to the great goddess Neith for her advice. She was absolutely decisive in her view that Horus should inherit the throne directly from his father, but sensibly suggested that Ra should console Seth by offering him two of his daughters, Anat and Astarte, as wives. These were goddesses who had entered Egypt from the Middle East during the New Kingdom.

In spite of the tribunal's willingness to accept this advice, Ra refused and soundly abused Horus in a very personal way, emphasizing his youth, weakness and general unsuitability as a potential ruler. A comparatively junior god taunted Ra with his unpopularity and Ra left the tribunal. His good humour was restored when his daughter, the goddess of love, Hathor went to him, showed him her naked body and somehow contrived to make him laugh. He returned to the tribunal and asked Seth and Horus to make their claims to the throne once again.

Seth made his usual claim of strength and of his ability to hold chaos at bay by his attacks on the serpent Apophis. Horus reiterated his legitimate claim through his father Osiris. Isis, losing patience, intervened on behalf of Horus and so infuriated Seth that he threatened to kill the gods in turn, one each day. He said he would take no part in any court into which

Isis was allowed. Ra then removed the tribunal to an island. He ordered the ferryman, Nemty, not to bring across to the island any woman who looked like Isis.

Naturally enough, Isis used her magic skills to disguise herself as an old, poor woman. She placed a gold ring on her finger and carried a bowl of flour with her to the ferry. When Nemty refused to take her across, she pleaded that she needed to go to the island to take food to a young man who had been there for five days tending cattle, and who must be very hungry by now. Finally, the ferryman agreed to take her in return for her gold ring, having refused the cake she first offered him.

When she arrived at the island, Isis chose a moment when the gods were relaxing to make her approach. She changed herself into a beautiful young woman and made sure that Seth could see her. He was instantly attracted and went to talk to her. She threw herself on his mercy, playing her role as a young widow whose son was being threatened by an intruder who intended to take from him the cattle that had belonged to his father and to seize his home. Seth expressed great indignation at this behaviour, putting himself on the side of the son and against the intruder. Isis changed herself once again, this time into a bird, a kite, so that she could keep at a safe distance from Seth. From the branch of a tree she told Seth how he had condemned his own behaviour to Osiris and Horus by his words.

Seth, in tears, reported all this to Ra, who could not find it within himself to be too sympathetic. Showing the unpleasant side of his character, Seth demanded that the ferryman, Nemty, should be brought to the tribunal. It was decided that, because of his disobedience, Nemty should have his toes cut off.

After that incident the court moved once again, this time to the Western Desert, where it decided that the throne of Egypt should go to Horus. The decision was held up once more, however, when Seth demanded that he should challenge Horus to a series of personal contests for the throne. This resulted in a number of bizarre encounters between the two gods.

In the first, Seth suggested that each of them should change himself into a hippopotamus and submerge himself under water for three months. Whoever came to the surface during that time would lose his claim to the throne. After a time, Isis could not contain her concern for what was happening to her son under water so she made a harpoon, which she threw into the water at the point where the beasts had submerged. Unfortunately it first hit Horus and she had to remove it with a spell. When she succeeded in harpooning Seth, he appealed to her as his sister and, unable to resist the argument, she removed it from him, too.

Her action infuriated Horus, who surged from the water and cut off the head of his mother, which he took with him into the mountains of the desert, where it became a headless flint statue. When Ra heard of the action, he vowed that Horus must be found and punished for it. It was Seth who found Horus as he lay asleep by an oasis. He took out the eyes of Horus and buried them, but they grew into lotus blooms. After his savage action, Seth returned to Ra, claiming not to have seen Horus, whom he assumed would by then be dead.

The goddess Hathor found Horus and magically healed his eyes by rubbing them with the milk of a gazelle. In a different story, Seth stole the left eye of Horus, the moon, in revenge for being castrated. In that story too the eye was healed. In both cases the eye of Horus, always referred to in the singular, became stronger, in a sense perfected, by the healing process it had been through. For that reason, representations of it were often used as an amulet, a protective symbol.

At some stage Isis was restored to herself, and she played a part in the next contest between Seth and Horus. Seth invited Horus to a banquet in a gesture of apparent reconciliation. During the evening Seth made a homosexual attack on Horus which Horus ingeniously avoided, catching Seth's semen in his hand. When Horus showed the semen to Isis, she cut off the polluted hand, making him a new one. Then she took semen from Horus, which she spread on lettuces growing in the garden, knowing that Seth would eat them because he was particularly fond of them.

Seth then went to the court of the gods and claimed that he had taken Horus homosexually. The gods expressed their contempt of Horus for allowing himself to be dominated in this way, but Horus demanded that the gods should summon the semen of the two men. When Thoth called on Seth's semen it did not come from Horus but from the waters of the marsh; the semen of Horus emerged as a gold sun disk from the head of Seth.

Even then, Seth devised another contest, in which the two men would build ships of stone in which to race one another. Horus built his of wood, but coated it in plaster to make it look like stone. Seth made his from a whole mountain peak. In the contest before the gods, Seth's boat naturally sank, so he turned himself into a hippopotamus and broke up the boat of Horus. Horus was prevented by the gods from killing Seth in his rage and frustration and went instead to the sanctuary of the goddess Neith to

ask her why he could not gain his inheritance when all the right seemed to be on his side.

The problem was finally resolved when Thoth persuaded Ra to write to Osiris in the underworld, addressing Osiris in flattering terms and giving him a fully royal title. Osiris and Ra disputed their rival powers, Osiris emphasizing his role in feeding the gods with wheat and barley, a claim about which Ra was dismissive. Osiris finally persuaded the other gods of the power of his position by pointing out that everyone came over the western horizon and into his realm in the end.

Then the gods decided as one that Horus should indeed succeed his father as ruler, and he was established on the throne of Egypt. Ra compensated Seth by giving him a place in the sky where he could enjoy himself noisily as a god of storms and thunder. Other versions of the story, however, say that Seth was banished to the desert margins of the country, and so stress his aridity compared with the fertility represented by Osiris.

The Osiris cult was associated with the death of the king and the establishment of a new king when his predecessor passed into an assured life in the underworld. It set the pattern whereby Horus reigned after the rebirth of Osiris into eternal life. As time went on, the cult of Osiris became more popular; it was possibly a myth that people could relate to their own lives, sympathizing with the story of a man who had suffered injustice and attained eternal life through the ministrations and care of a loving wife. In this respect Osiris may have seemed closer to them than most of the other gods; it is interesting, too, that the stories about Isis sometimes concern ordinary people.

Men hoped to achieve eternal life, and they saw Osiris as the means by which they might do it. To this end, at the period when the habit spread further through society, they copied the embalming that had saved him, seeing the process itself as a way of sharing in his suffering. It even became habitual to preface the name of the deceased with the name 'Osiris'.

Although they feared Osiris as a judge of souls, it seems that over time they came to find him more approachable and relevant to their lives than the more remote sun god, whose cult was chiefly the province of monarchs and priests.

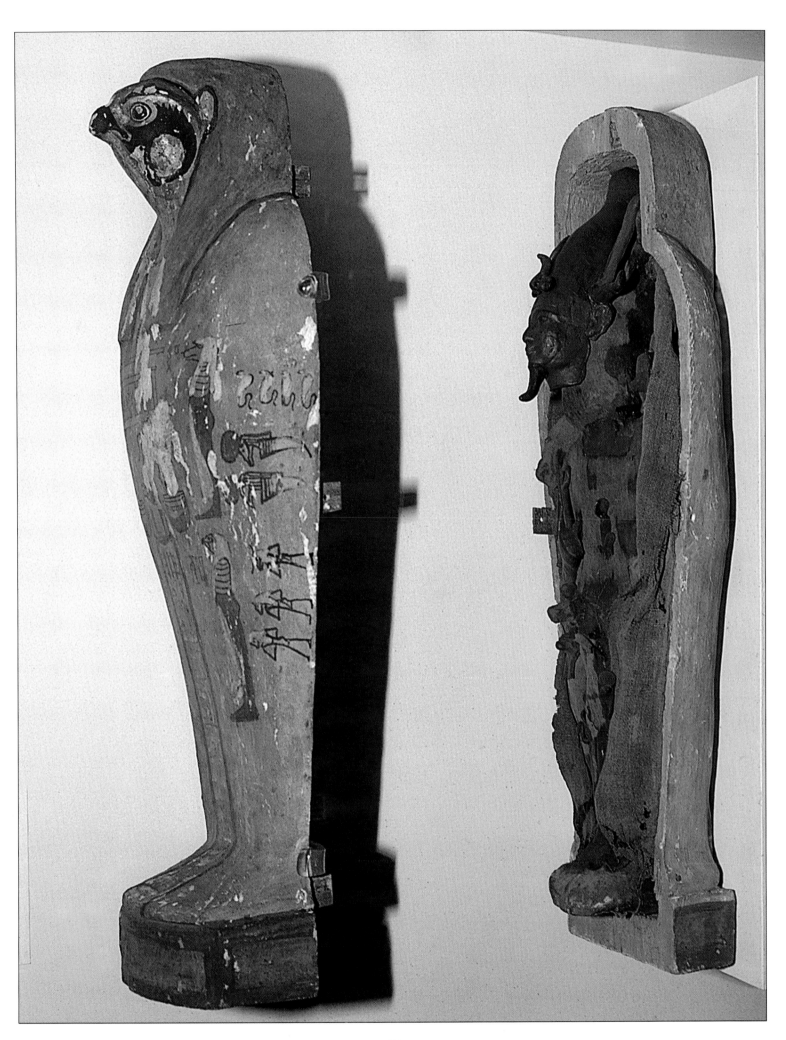

CHAPTER SIX
THE BOOK OF THE DEAD

The scribe, Ani, stands with his hands raised in adoration before an offering table bearing meat, fruit, loaves, cakes and flowers. Behind him stands his wife, Thuthu, a priestess-musician at the Temple of Amun, holding a sistrum and a reed in her left hand.

The name Book of the Dead is applied by Egyptologists to a collection of spells that were placed with a burial to help the deceased person to gain entry to the afterlife, and to pass through the dangers of the underworld to reach a new existence in the Field of Reeds. The ancient Egyptians would have called it something like 'Spells for Coming Forth by Day', which refers partly to the need for the *ba* to be able to leave the tomb and assume different forms outside it. In all, there were over 200 spells but they do not all occur together in any one example. Instead, a selection would be made according to the choice of whoever was ordering the book, and was probably dependent to some extent on the amount of money available to pay for it.

The texts were usually written on papyrus, on a roll up to 41m (135ft) long in the case of the longest one so far discovered and up to 48cm (20in) high. Sometimes the texts would be written on the coffins or on the tomb walls or on linen or vellum, but papyrus was the usual medium. The papyrus would then be placed on or near the mummy, or even be incorporated in the mummy wrappings. Often, the papyrus roll would be placed in a hollow part of a special statuette of the god Ptah-Sokar-Osiris.

Texts of the kind found in the Books of the Dead first occurred as the Pyramid Texts, which decorated the walls of the royal pyramids at Saqqara in the 6th to 8th Dynasties (the first example of the Pyramid Texts is found in the pyramid of King Unas, the last king of the 5th Dynasty). Many of the spells use archaic language and refer to a stellar heaven. The idea that the dead would become stars around the pole star is a much earlier belief than the one held by the occupants of the pyramids, namely that they would journey to the sky and there join the sun-god in a solar kind of afterlife. This suggests that they were originally composed at a date far earlier than that at which they first appear. They also refer to the later Osiris cult, and include the Ceremony of Opening the Mouth, which are prominent in the Book of the Dead texts a few centuries later.

As burial customs became 'democratized' and the practice of elaborate burials spread down from the kings to the nobles and richer subjects, there arose a new form, known nowadays as the Coffin Texts, which were painted on the inside and outside of coffins. These became popular in the Middle Kingdom period, and they continued to describe two kinds of afterlife: the deceased might go to the sky to join the company of Ra, or they might go to the underworld to the kingdom of Osiris. In addition to the necessary spells, a plan of the underworld would often be painted inside the coffin to guide the occupant on his journey.

During the New Kingdom, from about the mid-15th century BC, examples of the Book of the Dead appear. Now the emphasis is on Osiris as the king of the Underworld where the dead will live for eternity. Osiris is also the judge of the dead, and a whole section is devoted to the judgment process, including the Weighing of the Heart. The texts also illustrate the belief that in the afterlife, in the Field of Reeds,

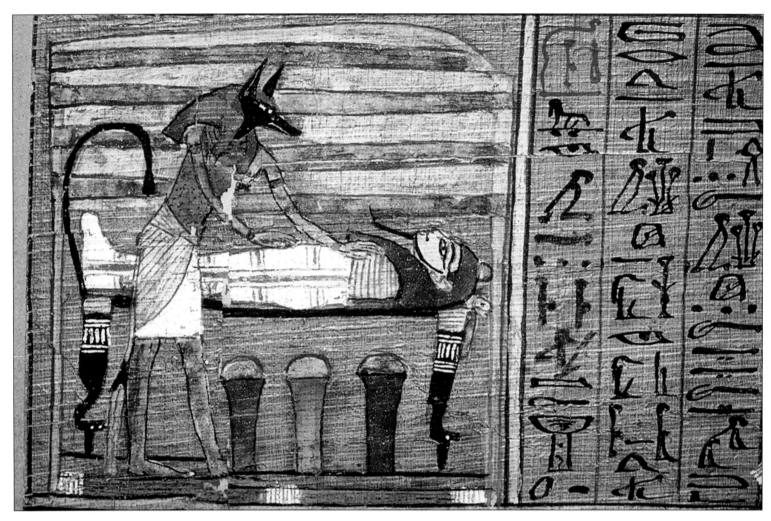

Anubis prepares the mummy of Ani. The mummy lies on a bed, and wears the false beard with upturned end, as worn by the divine mummy of Osiris. The jackal-headed figure attending to the mummy may be regarded as either the god Anubis himself, or as a priest wearing an Anubis mask.

the familiar agricultural tasks would have to be carried out as on earth, hence the need for *shabti* figures to deputize for the dead person and to do his work. Spells were needed to bring these models and figurines to life, and to make them do the work when called upon. These spells would often be written upon the *shabti* figures as well as recorded on the papyrus scroll. There were also spells designed to keep the body whole, such as the spell to prevent him losing his head in the realm of the dead. Many of the spells rely on the magic power of knowing how to name someone; often this would be a minor god or doorkeeper at some gate through which the dead must pass.

The production of the Book of the Dead texts must have become quite thriving industry for the scribes and illustrators. The texts were written in cursive hieroglyphic, hieratic or demotic scripts, and illustrated by vignettes, which could be in full colour or simple black-and-white outlines. Often the vignettes and the scripts were produced by different people, and sometimes different sets of scribes and illustrators would work on different sections of the book, joining them up later to make a continuous roll. Some of the texts were regarded at the time they were copied as being very ancient and mysterious

and difficult to understand, and mistakes were often made in the copies. Sometimes sections would be repeated in error, or illustrations would not be appropriate for the adjacent text. Often the vignettes would be drawn first, and the text filled in later, and sometimes not enough room would be left between the drawings for the text to fit in, so parts would be omitted. There could also be great unevenness of quality: a particular book could have excellent drawing and very poor quality text, and vice versa. The book would usually be made to order, according to whatever spells were considered appropriate or necessary, or what could be afforded. The name of the dead person would be incorporated into the text as the book was produced, but sometimes books were produced beforehand with spaces left for the names to be filled in later when a customer was found.

The details that follow are mostly from the Book of the Dead of the scribe Ani, from Thebes, dated about 1250 BC. He was an accountant and manager of the granaries of the lords of Abydos and a scribe of the lords of Thebes. His wife Thuthu was a noble lady who was also a musician-priestess of Amun-Ra and she is shown in the vignettes carrying a musical instrument, the sistrum. The papyrus is about 24m (79 ft) long, and after the first quarter of its length the

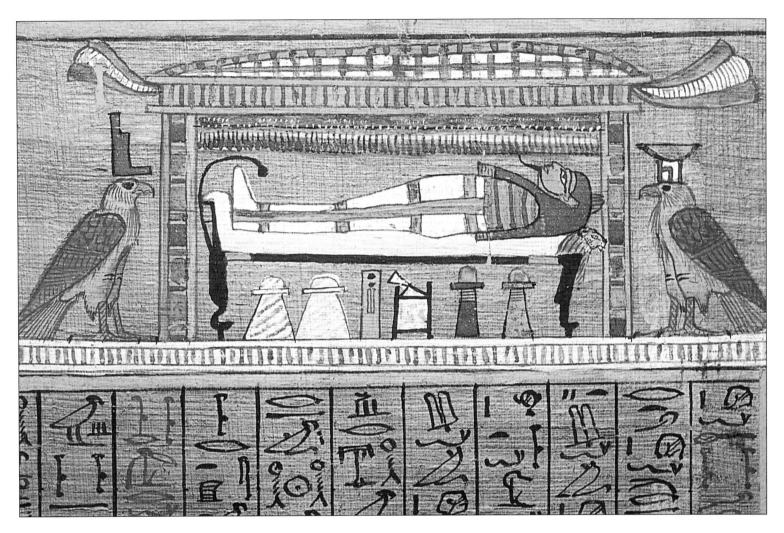

name of Ani has been filled in, which suggests that the papyrus was bought from stock, and only the first part was individually produced for Ani. There are over 200 spells, and a selection of them are listed below.

For coming out into the day.

For going out into the day and living after death.

For not doing work in the land of the dead.

For have a shabti *work for one in the land of the dead.*

An appeal to Thoth to speak for him at the tribunal of the gods.

To open the mouth of the deceased.

For not permitting his heart to be taken from him.

For not letting his heart speak against him in the judgment.

To prevent him losing his head in the land of the dead.

For not putrefying in the land of the dead.

To drive away a crocodile who comes to take away his magic.

For protection against being bitten by a snake in the land of the dead.

For breathing air and having power over

water in the land of the dead.

To allow transformation into any shape desired.

For being transformed into a lotus.

For being transformed into a swallow.

For bringing a ferry-boat in the land of the dead.

For embarking on the boat of Ra.

To worship Osiris.

To escape from the Catcher of Fish.

For not dying again.

To leave yesterday and to come into today.

The spells themselves are repetitive and rely heavily on the magic of naming. A paraphrase of the spell for being changed into a benu bird runs like this: '*I came into existence from unformed matter, I created myself in the image of Khepri and grew in the form of plants. I am made out of the essence of all the gods.....I am crowned, I become a shining one, I am strong and holy among the gods. I am the god Khonsu who drives back all who oppose him.*' Or the spell for being changed into a lotus reads: '*I am the pure lotus who comes forth from the god of light, the guardian of the nostrils of Ra, the guardian of the nose of Hathor. I come forth and hasten after him who is Horus. I am the pure one who comes forth from the field.*'

The mummy of Ani lying on a bed in the form of a lion. Under the bed are a scribe's palette and some containers. Two kites stand as guardians at each end of the bed. The kite at the foot represents Isis, as shown by the throne-shaped headdress. Nephthys stands at the head of the mummy; her headdress is the hieroglyph for gold.

Detail of the Papyrus of Ani. This vignette accompanies a hymn to Osiris. Isis and Nephthys adore the sun-disc which is held aloft by an ankh, symbol of life, which stands on a djed pillar. This takes place beneath the blue vault of the sky, bounded by the mountains of the Eastern and Western horizons. The baboons are shown adoring the sun because they chatter and are active at sunrise; they are regarded as wise animals associated with Thoth.

Another, perhaps more practical, spell is the one for not dying a second time, which meant to die for all eternity, whereas after the first death there was a chance of eternal life if one passed the judgement. Parts of the spell are perfectly understandable as the fears and wishes of a person facing death. *'What kind of land have I come to? There is no water, nor air, it is deep and unfathomable, black as night and men wander helplessly here. In here a man cannot live in peace of mind, nor can the longings of love be satis-*

fied here. But let the state of the shining ones be granted to me for water and air and for satisfying the longings of love, and let peace of mind be given to me as food and drink ... may my heir be strong, may my tomb and my friends who are left upon the earthn flourish and may my enemies be destroyed. I am your son and Ra is my father. For me you have also made life, strength and health. Horus is established upon his throne...' (The deceased person lives again in the form of Horus) *'...he shall wear the atef crown for*

76

millions and hundreds of thousands and tens of thousands and thousands and hundreds and tens of years; bread, ale, oxen, wild fowl, all good and pure things and clear water shall be offered to him in abundance...'

This spell was to be recited over a figure of Horus made of lapis-lazuli and placed near the neck of the mummy; it would give him power on earth over men and the gods, and if recited in the underworld it would be most beneficial.

Perhaps the most interesting spell is the one that accompanies the vignette of the Weighing of the Heart. Part of it today is called the Negative Confession. In it the deceased addresses the members of the tribunal one by one and declares his innocence of wrong-doing. It starts like this:

'Hail, you whose strides are long, who comes forth from Ammu, I have not done iniquity. Hail, you who are embraced by flame, who comes forth from Kheraba, I have not robbed with violence. Hail, Fentiu, who comes forth from Khemennu, I have not stolen. Hail, Devourer of the Shade, who comes forth from Qernet, I have done no murder, I have done no harm...'

Always the greeting comes first, then the statement of lack of guilt. It is still interesting today to see what was deemed to make up a life free from sin in ancient Egypt. Some of the sins enumerated in the negative confession include:

I have not defrauded offerings, I have not

Ani and his wife are shown as two soul-birds representing their bas. On their heads are thought to be perfume cones, but it is not known for certain what they are.

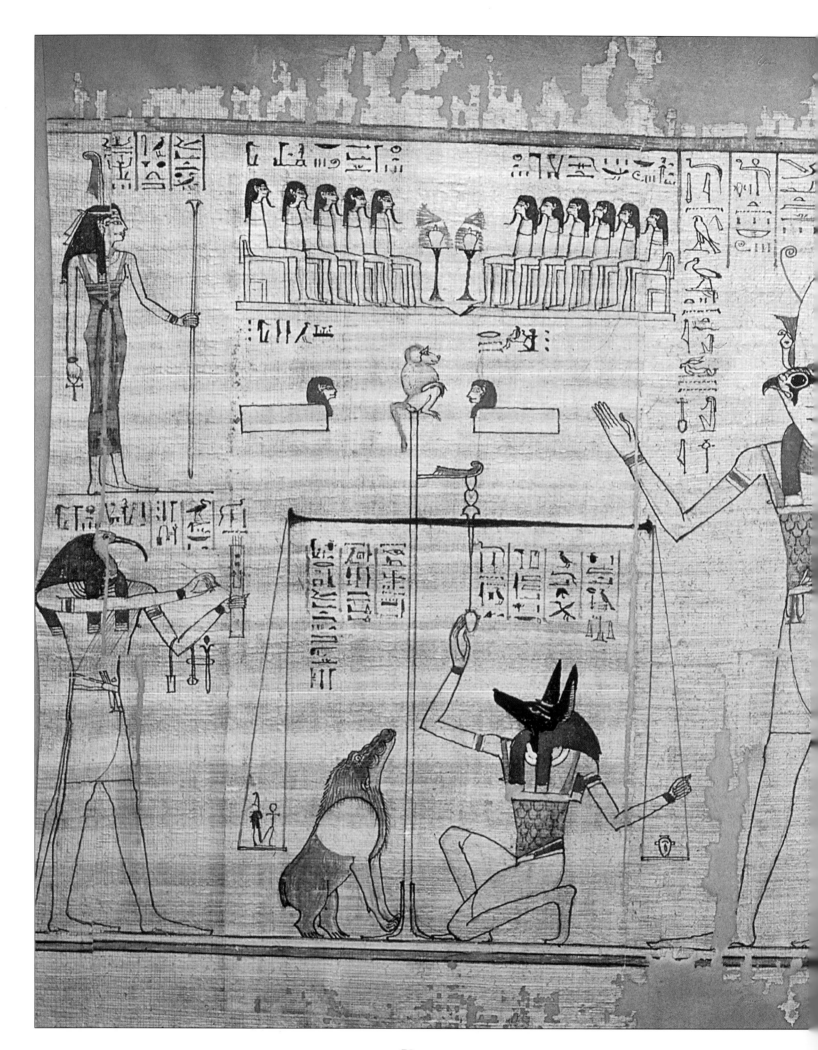

diminished oblations, I have not plundered the god, I have spoken no lies, I have not snatched away food, I have not caused pain, I have not committed fornication, I have not caused shedding of tears, I have not dealt deceitfully, I have not transgressed, I have not acted guilefully, I have not laid waste the ploughed land, I have not been an eavesdropper, I have not spoken evil against anyone, I have not defiled the wife of any man, I have not been angry without just cause, I have not polluted myself, I have not stopped my ears against words of right and truth, I have not acted with insolence, I have not stirred up strife, I have not judged hastily, I have never cursed the king, I have never fouled the water, I have never cursed God, I have not stolen, I have not plundered the offerings of the blessed dead, I have not filched the food of the infant nor have I sinned against the god of my native town, I have not slaughtered the cattle of the god, I have not behaved with arrogance, I have never magnified my condition beyond what was fitting.

Here we seem to have an insight into the moral aspirations of the ordinary person at the time, and a closer understanding of the values and practical requirements that controlled behaviour at the time. Even here, this section ends, in some of the texts at least, with an invocation which brings back the sense of magic in naming that occurs in many myths in all parts of the world. The dead person has to pass through the Hall of Two-fold Maat:

'I will not let you enter over me,' says the bolt of the door, 'unless you tell me my name.' 'Weight of the Place of Right and Truth is your name.' 'I will not let you pass by me,' says the right post of the door, 'unless you tell me your name.' 'Weight of the Labours of Right and Truth is your name.' 'I will not let you enter in by me,' says the left post of the door, 'unless you tell me my name.'

'Judge of Things is your name.' 'I will not let you pass,' says the threshold of the door, 'unless you tell me my name.' 'Ox of Seb is your name.' 'I will not open to you,' says the bolt-socket of the door, 'unless you tell me my name.' 'Flesh of His Mother is your name.' 'I will not open to you,' says the lock of the door, 'unless you tell me my name.' 'The Utchat of Sebek, the Lord of Bakhan Liveth is your name.' 'I will not open to you and I will not let you pass over me,' says the dweller at the door, 'unless you tell me my name.' 'Arm of Shu that Protects Osiris is your name.' 'We will not let you pass by us,' say the posts of the door, 'unless you tell us our names.' 'Serpent Children of Rennut are your names.' 'You know us, pass by us.' 'You shall not

Horus leads Anhai to the judgement where the ceremony of the Weighing of the Heart is taking place. Anhai's heart is in a small container on a balance, being weighed against Truth in the form of a small effigy of Maat, goddess of truth, distinguished by the feather on her head. Anubis supervises the weighing, and the monster Ammut waits to devour any heart which fails the test and is therefore unworthy of proceeding to the afterlife. Thoth, ibis-headed, stands to the left, recording the result, and the baboon sitting above the scales is also symbolic of Thoth. Beyond Thoth stands Maat, goddess of order and truth wearing the Feather of Truth and holding an ankh. Above the scales sit eleven gods who are witnesses to the judgement.

tread on me,' says the floor of the hall, 'unless you tell me my name.' 'I am Silent, I am Pure.' 'I know not the names of your two feet with which you would walk upon me; tell them to me.' '...before Amsu is the name of my right foot and Grief of Nephthys is the name of my left foot.' 'Tread upon me, because you know me.'

The vignettes shown here are also mostly taken from the Book of the Dead of the scribe Ani, from Thebes, dated about 1250 BC. Other illustrations are taken from the Papyrus of Anhai, who was a priestess-singer of Amun-Ra at Thebes, dated about 1150 BC, and from the Papyrus of Hunefer, who was an overseer and royal scribe in the palace of Seti I in the 14th century BC. These two papyri appear to have been made specially for each person. Later examples come from the Saïte period, when the Book of the Dead was extensively revised and the sequence of the spells, or chapters, was regularized. This form was popular from the 26th Dynasty until the end of the Ptolemaic period. The Papyri of Ani, Anhai and Hunefer are all now in the British Museum.

Other funerary texts were also used, both on the walls of pyramids and tombs and on papyri. The texts are called by such names as 'What is in the Underworld', 'The Book of Gates', 'The Book of Caverns', and 'The Book of the Secret Dwelling'. Even as late as the Ptolemaic period, new works of a similar nature were being produced, designed to protect the dead person and help him on his journey to the underworld. These include 'The Book of Spending Eternity' and 'The Book of Breathing'. They demonstrate a remarkable continuity of thought over centuries, but also show an increasing reliance on individual righteous behaviour as a qualification for attainment of the afterlife.

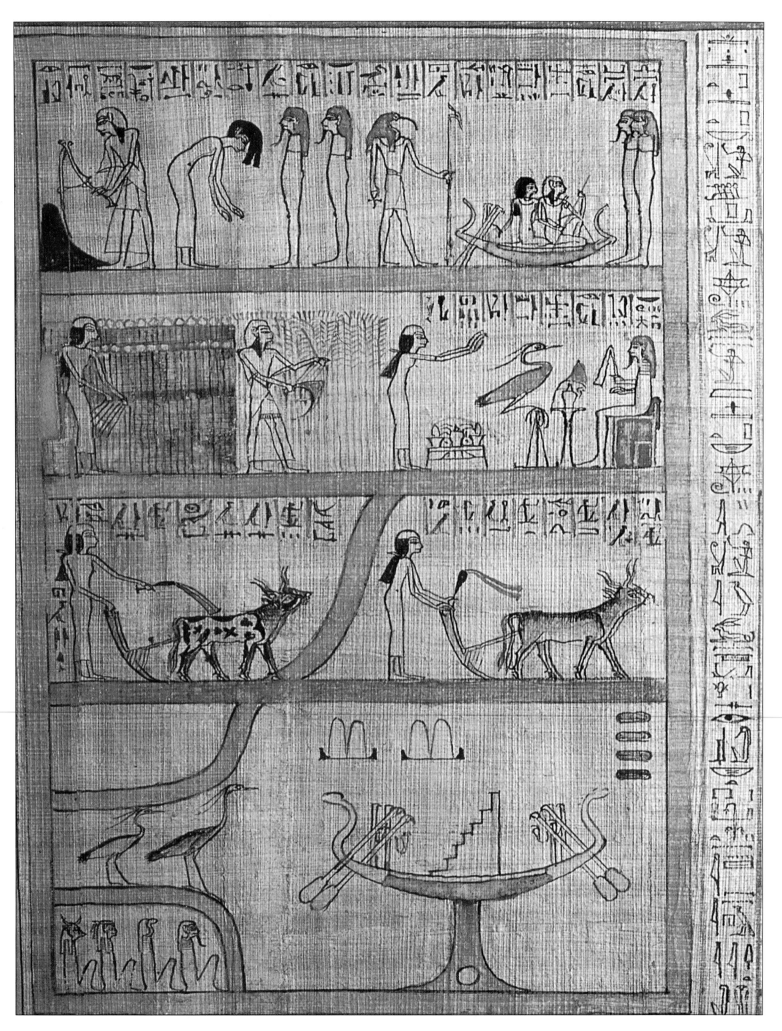

CHAPTER SEVEN
THE GODS OF ANCIENT EGYPT

*RIGHT
(British Museum) Ahmose Nefertari.
Wallpainting from a Theban tomb,
18th Dynasty, 16th century BC.*

AHMOSE NEFERTARI (c.1575-1505 BC)

Queen, wife and sister of Ahmose I and mother of
Amenhotep I, she outlived her husband and was
regent during her son's reign, and apparently outlived him too. She was later deified as one of the
divine guardians of the necropolis of Thebes, and
was especially revered at the village of Deir el-
Medina, where the workmen of the royal tombs of
the Valley of the Kings lived, and which was founded by Ahmose Nefertari and Amenhotep I.

AKER

An earth-god who controlled the junction of the
western and eastern horizons in the underworld, he is
usually shown as two lions seated back-to-back.

AMENHOTEP I (Amenophis I) (1525-1504 BC)

Second ruler of the 18th Dynasty, son of Ahmose
Nefertari and, like her, he was later deified as a
guardian of the Theban necropolis.

**AMENHOTEP SON OF HAPU
(c.1430-1350 BC)**

He was Scribe and Chief-of-all-the-Works of
Amenhotep III. He had cult chapels in temples at
Deir el-Bahri and Deir el-Medina, and was worshipped for his wisdom, as a scribe and for his powers of healing.

AMMUT

Underworld goddess with the head of a crocodile,
foreparts of a lion andrear of a hippopotamus. Known

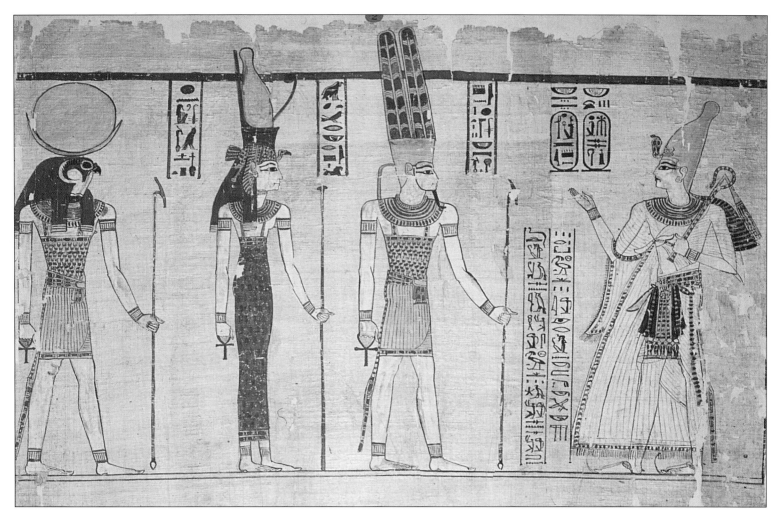

as the Devourer of the Dead, she is usually shown in the Book of the Dead beside the scales in the ceremony of the Weighing of the Heart, waiting to devour the hearts of those who fail the test and are not fit to pass into the afterlife because of their past deeds.

AMUN (Amen), Amun-Ra,

Originally a local deity at Thebes, usually shown in the form of a ram, he became the major deity of Egypt when the Theban kings of the 11th Dynasty rose to power. His position as the supreme god of Egypt was strengthened by assimilating with the sun-god Ra to become Amun-Ra. As Amun Kanutef he was a fertility god like Min, and was portrayed as an ithyphallic figure. He was the father of the Theban triad of gods, his wife being Mut, a local goddess, and their son the moon-god Khons. The great Temple of Amun at Karnak was his main centre, administered by a rich and powerful priesthood and visited by many pilgrims. The cult of Amun lost power temporarily when Akhenaten transferred his capital to El-Armarna and worshipped Aten. The supreme position was soon regained but declined when the Assyrians destroyed Thebes in AD 664 and the cult of Osiris became more popular and influential. Regarded by the Greeks as the equivalent of Zeus, the cult of Zeus

Ammon spread to Greece, and then as Jupiter Ammon his cult spread to the Romans.

ANUBIS

A god of the dead in the form of a dog or jackal. The jackal was an animal of the Western Desert, and so became associated with the domain of the dead, in the west. Later, the cult of Anubis became associated with that of Osiris, and Anubis was then said to be the son of Osiris and Nephthys. Anubis embalmed the body of Osiris and carried out the funerary rites for him. In the Book of the Dead, Anubis is the god who supervises the embalming and mummification process, who protects the mummy, is present at the ceremony of the Opening of the Mouth, and who performs the Weighing of the Heart. Anubis is also associated with the Imuit fetish, which is a headless, stuffed animal skin hanging from a pole standing in a pot. The Imuit fetish is often illustrated on stelae or papyri, and a model of it was found in the tomb of Tutankhamun, but its function is not known.

ANUKET (Anukis)

Goddess from Nubia whose cult centre in Egypt was in the region of the First Cataract. Khnum, Satis and Anuket formed the Elephantine triad.

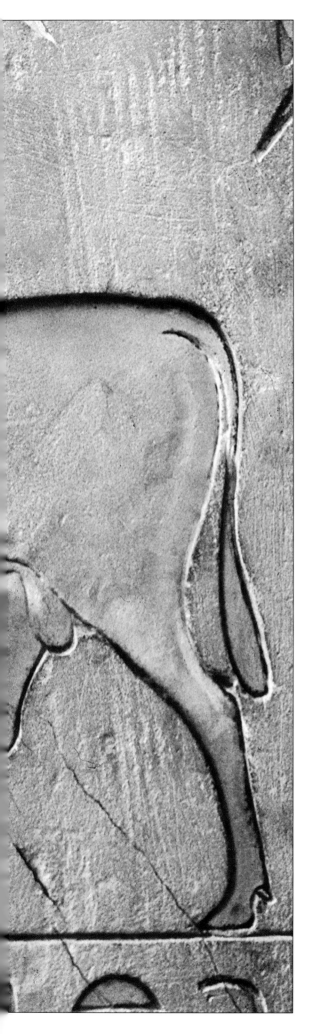

APIS

A sacred bull who was regarded as a manifestation of Ptah. At intervals a new Apis bull was born, black and bearing special markings that included a white mark on the forehead and the image of a vulture on its back. The new bull would be brought to his cult centre near that of Ptah at Memphis and the old bull would be ceremonially drowned in the Nile. The body of the old bull was mummified and buried in a splendid granite sarcophagus in an underground cat-acomb known as the Serapeum at Saqqara, a short distance from Memphis. The dead bull became iden-tified with Osiris, and was known as Osiris-Apis or Osorapis.

APOPHIS (Apep)

An underworld snake deity, personifying darkness, evil and chaos, Apophis attacks the boat of Ra as it travels through the Underworld each night, and is defeated, but never destroyed. Seth protects the boat of Ra and subdues Apophis, using force and magic to do so. Although Seth is shown as the enemy of Apophis, he later became identified with him, as a symbol of forces hostile to the order of the gods.

ATEN

The deity represented as the sun's disc, and empha-sizing the beneficial aspects of the sun. It is shown as a disc with many rays stretching out like arms, end-ing in hands, some of them presenting the ankh, sym-bol of life, towards the king. Aten appeared in the record as a god around 1500 BC in the reign of Thuthmose I and slowly gained prestige during the 18th Dynasty. Amenhotep III favoured Aten, and priests of Aten became established at Heliopolis, the centre of the cult of the sun-god Ra. When Amenhotep IV became ruler, he made Aten the prin-cipal god and built the Per-Aten Temple at Karnak, close to, and in competition with, the Temple of Amun.

Five or six years into his reign, Amenhotep IV founded a new city to the north beside the Nile, about midway between Thebes and Memphis. He called this Akhetaten, meaning The Horizon of Aten, known today by its Arabic name of El-Amarna. At the same time he took the name of Akhenaten ('glory of Aten') in place of Amenhotep ('Amun is con-tent'). Akhetaten became the new capital. Two new temples were built, not roofed as in the traditional temple design, but open to the sun. Aten was made the supreme deity of the state, but it is not possible to prove that this was a a complete conversion to monotheism. The religion was also exclusive in that

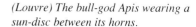
(Louvre) The bull-god Apis wearing a sun-disc between its horns.

only the king or his queen, Nefertiti, could have direct access to Aten. Akhenaten reigned for only 18 years, being succeeded briefly by Smenkhkare (Nefernefruaten) and then by Tutankhaten, who may have been the younger brother or the son of Akhenaten. Tutankhaten was married to Ankhesenpaaten, one of the daughters of Akhenaten, but the couple changed their names to Tutankhamun and Anhkesenamun, and dissociated themselves from the cult of Aten. The capital was moved back to Memphis and within a few decades the city at El-Amarna was abandoned. Many reliefs showing Akhenaten or Nefertiti were defaced, to erase them and their heresy from the record.

ATUM

The creator-god of Heliopolis who 'came into being of himself' among the primeval waters of Nun. He created Shu (air) and Tefnut (moisture), who became the parents of Geb (earth-god) and Nut (sky-goddess) whose children were Osiris, Isis, Seth and Nephthys. These were the family of the nine gods (or Ennead) of Heliopolis. Atum is usually shown in the form of a man, wearing the double crown.

BASTET (Bast)

Cat-goddess whose cult centre was Bubastis; as a daughter of the sun-god she personified the beneficial aspects of the sun's power, contrasting with the savage aspects attributed to Sekhmet. Bastet was shown with the attributes of a lion in the early period, but after the Middle Kingdom she was shown as a woman with a cat's head, and took on a more protective, friendly aspect. As a mother-goddess she is often accompanied by kittens. She is also often shown carrying a sistrum, which suggests association with Isis and Hathor.

(British Museum) Head of Hathor from Thebes. Faience. C.1000 BC.

BES

Bes was usually shown as a dwarf-like figure, with a grotesque bearded face. He may originally have been a lion-god, because he has a lion's tail, ears and mane, although it is not clear whether they are his own members or part of a lion-skin which he may be wearing. He was a protective spirit, helpful in keeping snakes away from houses, and generally warding off evil spirits. He would be present at a birth, dancing, singing and playing a tambourine or drum to frighten away evil. Bes became increasingly popular in the later period, and many domestic items such as mirrors, toiletry items, perfume jars, and beds bear his image. He acted also as a protector of the dead, as his image often appears on the disc-shaped head-rests of mummies.

His consort was Beset, depicted as a female dwarf, or as a snake, but he was also thought to be married to Taweret, a goddess of childbirth. Unlike other Egyptian gods, who are nearly always shown in profile, Bes is usually shown full-face. This may be because he could have originated outside Egypt, in the Sudan.

DUAMUTEF – see Sons of Horus

EDJO (Udjat)

The cobra-goddess of the Delta, with a cult-centre at Buto, Edjo was shown as a snake or a woman wearing the red crown of Lower Egypt. She was represented as the *uraeus* cobra worn on the forehead of the Pharoah in a menacing attitude to defend the king against his enemies.

GEB

The earth-god who appears in the creation myth of Heliopolis, the brother and husband of Nut, the sky-goddess, and the son of Shu, god of air, and Tefnut, goddess of moisture. His children were Osiris, Isis, Seth and Nephthys. Geb judged between Horus and Seth and made Horus, as the rightful heir of Osiris, ruler of the living, and from this came the pharoah's right to rule. Geb as the god of earth is a vegetation and fertility god: water and plants spring from him.

But for the dead he was a malevolent god, imprisoning the buried ones within his body. One ancient myth makes Geb and Nut the parents of the sun, and therefore the ancestors of all the gods. Geb is also seen as a goose, the Great Cackler, which laid the cosmic egg from which the sun was born.

HAPI (HAPY)

The god of the inundation of the Nile and one of the Four Sons of Horus, Hapi is portrayed as a man with pendulous breasts to emphasize his fecundity, and with papyrus or lotus plants on his head. His body is often shown coloured green or blue. He lived among the caverns in the rocks at the First Cataract and one of his main cult centres was near Aswan. Some temples show many figures of Hapi bearing offerings, again an indication of his role as fertility god.

HARPOCRATES

Horus as a child appears as a young boy with the sidelock of youth and his finger to his mouth. He is also shown gaining mastery over serpents, scorpions and crocodiles, and in the Greek and Roman periods images of him were set up in houses to protect the family from these creatures, and to ward off evil spirits. In the Osiris-Isis-Horus myth he was attacked as a child by snakes sent by Seth but overcame them.

HATHOR

Goddess of joy, love, fertility, music and dance, and daughter of Ra, Hathor was a sky-goddess like Nut, with whom she was often confused or assimilated. She appears in the form of a cow, usually bearing the sun-disc in her horns, or as a woman with the ears of a cow. As goddess of music and dance she carries a sistrum, a rattle-like musical instrument. Besides being regarded as the daughter of the sun-god, she was also regarded as the mother of Horus the Elder by Ra, and as the wife of Horus of Edfu. As the mother of Horus she was also regarded as the mother of the reigning king, and has been shown as a cow suckling the Pharoah. Her main cult centre was at

(National Archaeological Museum, Florence) The goddess Isis wearing the cow's horns and sun-disc associated with Hathor.

Dendera, where a huge temple was dedicated to Hathor in Ptolemaic times. From this temple at Dendera Hathor would make an annual journey by boat up the Nile to visit her husband Horus at Edfu, and this became a popular and joyous festival and pigrimage.

She was known as the Lady of the Sycamore in Memphis, and appears on many funerary objects as a cow-headed lady leaning out of a sycamore tree supplying food and drink to the deceased person. In a funerary context she was called the Lady of the West and received the setting sun each evening, protecting him on his nightly journey through the underworld. The dying therefore sought her protection, and in the Book of the Dead she stands as a cow on the slopes of the Western Mountain to protect and nurture the dead.

Hathor, as a benevolent deity, was popular at all levels from king to common person, and the great temple at Dendera, which was built in Ptolemaic times and continued to be enlarged in Roman times up to the reign of Trajan, shows that her popularity continued until late times. However, as the Osiris-Isis cult gained prestige and popularity, Isis usurped many of the features of the cult of Hathor and often appears as a combined Isis-Hathor figure.

HEH

One of the Ogdoad (group of eight primeval deities) of Hermopolis, Heh is the god of infinity, and by extension of this concept he appears on royal regalia as a charm to ensure longevity.

HEKET (Heqat)

A goddess in the form of a frog, associated with birth and re-birth. In the Pyramid Texts she helped the dead king on his journey to the sky. As the consort of Khnum (who made the first humans on his potter's wheel) she gave life to the figures which he fashioned, and as a goddess of childbirth it was believed that she shaped the child in the womb and gave it life.

HORUS

From earliest times the falcon was worshipped as a god of the sky and as a sun-god. As a sky-god, his eyes were the sun and moon. As the emblem of victorious leaders in predynastic times, the falcon became associated with the king, who was regarded as the earthly manifestation of Horus. As the sun-god Ra was also a powerful symbol of the king's might, Horus became identified with the sun too. The falcon must have been a popular symbol of power in early

times as there were many independent cult-centres dedicated to the falcon as god of the sky. With time, the different cults were brought into the cult of Horus, but remained as variants of the main Horus cult. Consequently the mythology of Horus is very complicated, and as with other Egyptian deities, their stories can be confusing and sometimes contradictory.

IMHOTEP

A historical figure, he was a courtier who held high office under King Djoser, or Zozer, in the 3rd Dynasty. He is credited with designing the Step Pyramid at Saqqara, the first stone building on such a scale. So great was his reputation that, very unusually, he was deified about 2,000 years after his death. Bronze figurines of him show him seated with a papyrus scroll open across his lap. He became credited with healing powers, which caused the Greeks to identify him with their healing god, Asklepios. He was also thought to be the son of the god Ptah, and was thus the focus of prayer by those who hoped he might be able to transmit his father's creative force.

IMUIT FETISH SYMBOL

This took the form of the skin of a headless animal that had been stuffed and hung on a pole. The pole stood in a pot. Although it is recorded as early as the 1st Dynasty, it became particularly associated with the worship of Anubis, and is sometimes thought of as his fetish or as one of his attributes.

IMSETY – see Sons of Horus

ISIS

A very powerful and popular goddess, Isis was one of the children of Nut and Geb and the devoted sister and wife of Osiris. The hieroglyph of her name represents a throne, and her name might actually have meant that. She became particularly associated with the throne of Egypt because she and Osiris were the first rulers in a golden age, and she became the mother of Horus, and therefore of all subsequent Egyptian kings. She breathed life into Osiris after his murder by Seth, and is often shown in the form of a kite, whose wings hover protectively over her husband. She protected her son, Horus, from the machinations of Seth until he was able to take his rightful place on the throne.

Isis was credited with particularly magical powers and great tenacity. She became closely associated with cures for children's ailments, especially

those caused by the bites and stings of snakes and scorpions. From the period of the New Kingdom, the *tyet* amulet became particularly associated with her. This was a girdle knotted in a certain way, which possibly has some connection to the *ankh*.

Because of her strongly maternal qualities, she could be presented as a sow. She was also sometimes shown as a cow, which perhaps accounts for her occasional confusion with the goddess Hathor. Her cult became extremely popular beyond the confines of Egypt in the Roman period.

KHENTIAMENTIU

Both Osiris and Anubis are described as Khentiamentiu which means 'foremost of the Westerners' to show their status over the necropolis, which was usually to the west of the Nile. An earlier canine deity at Abydos was called Khentiamentiu, but his cult was superseded by Anubis.

KHEPRI

The sun god as a creator, represented in the form of a scarab beetle. This was the name given to the sun-

god as he appeared above the horizon in the early
morning at the start of his daily journey, presumably
an analogy with the beetle that rolled a ball of dung
before him all day. The dung beetle was also an
appropriate image for the creator and sun god, Atum,
because from the ball of earth, containing its eggs, a
new beetle appeared to emerge spontaneously.
Although he is a comparatively early god, amulets in
the form of a scarab appear most frequently from the
Middle Kingdom.

KHNUM

A ram-headed god whose cult was centred mainly on
the island of Elephantine at Aswan from about 3000
BC. He was strongly associated with the annual
inundation of the Nile, which he was thought to
supervise. This, together with his powers as a ram,
made him one of the creator-gods. His creativity was
expressed through the pottery he made, and he is
sometimes represented sitting before a potter's
wheel on which he is turning a newly-created human
figure. His aspect as a potter was particularly evident
in his cult centre at Esna, where he was celebrated as
creator of gods, people, animals and fish.

KHONS

His name means the 'traveller' because he was a
moon god, who travelled across the sky. He is usually shown in mummy-like clothing that binds his legs
together, and wears on his head the full moon held
within the crescent of the new moon. Like other
moon gods, he was associated with the baboon, and
his early character was fierce. Later, at Thebes, he
was seen as the son of Amun and Mut, and sometimes shown as a child wearing the sidelock of
youth. In this aspect he shared the characteristics of
a protector against violent animals with Horus in his
aspect as a child.

MAAT

A goddess who personified the laws of ordered existence, harmony, justice and truth both in a cosmic
sense and among the society of men. She wears an
ostrich plume on her head, which was sometimes
used on its own to signify her. The hieroglyph used
for her name shows the plinth on which her seat rested, and it may also have signified the primeval
mound where life began. As well as order on earth,
she represented the order in the universe that resulted from the moment of creation. Quite late in
her development she became known as 'Daughter
of Ra'.

In funerary papyri she is often shown at the

judgment of the dead when the deceased's heart was balanced in a pair of scales against her feather to determine his suitability to enter the afterlife. It has been said that her effigy was worn by officials when they presided in Egyptian law-courts.

MENTU

A falcon-headed god of war. He is usually shown wearing a headdress formed from a sun-disc and two plumes. His cult centred on Thebes from about the 11th Dynasty, when some of the kings used the name Mentuhotep, meaning 'Mentu is content', but his cult there gradually gave way to that of Amun. His strength lay in fighting the enemies of the gods and he saw to it that the kings of Egypt were victorious over their enemies. Therefore he came to symbolize the more agressive aspect of the pharaohs. In the later period he was associated with a black-faced white bull called Buchis, who came to be regarded as an earthly manifestation of the god.

MERETSEGER

A local cobra-goddess of the mountain overlooking the Valley of the Kings at Thebes. Her name is usually translated as 'She who loves silence', which seems appropriate for one who watched over a great necropolis. She was particularly venerated by workers in the valley, who have left inscriptions on stones

(British Museum) Funerary stela showing the fertility goddess Qadesh, standing on a lion between the fertility god Min and Reshuf, an Amorite war-god.

attesting to her power to strike down with blindness or snake poisoning all those who committed crimes, and indicating that she could also offer cures to the repentant.

MESHKENT

Goddess of childbirth, identified with the kind of birth brick that Egyptian women squatted on to give birth. Sometimes she is shown as such a brick with a female head, at others as a woman with a brick on her head. As a funerary goddess, she helped the deceased to be reborn into the afterlife, and she was therefore present at the judgment of the dead. She was also thought to have had a hand in determining the destiny of a child at birth.

MIN

God of male potency and of fertility. His early emblem, somewhat resembling a bolt of lightning, has proved impossible to interpret. His representation as a man cannot, however, be mistaken. He is shown standing with his legs together and with an erect phallus protruding at right angles. In his right arm, which is held up away from his body and bent at the elbow, he holds a flail that rests on the fingertips of his right hand in a way that has been thought possibly to suggest sexual penetration. On his head he wears a crown surmounted by two very tall plumes, and a long ribbon from the crown hangs down his back. He seems to have been an early agricultural god who retained his characteristic of ensuring prolific harvests and fecundity in general by means of his sexual potency. He is sometimes shown with offerings of cos lettuces, which appear to have been a symbol of potency, perhaps because of their shape but more possibly because of the milky sap that is reminiscent of semen. Pharaohs in the New Kingdom took part in festivals in honour of Min as part of the ritual intended to celebrate the fruitful renewal of the kingship.

MUT

A Theban goddess who is shown as a woman, usual-ly wearing a brightly-coloured dress. On her head she wears a headdress shaped like a vulture, above which is placed the combined crown of Upper and Lower Egypt. She carries the papyrus or lily sceptre of Upper Egypt. She was so important at Thebes that she replaced Amunet as the wife of Amun, and thus became, like the other important mother-goddesses, Isis and Hathor, the symbolic divine mother of the earthly king. The child of Mut and Amun was Khons. When Amun was perceived as the sun-god Ra, she became the eye of Ra and was presented as a lion-headed goddess because that is how the eye of Ra was normally manifested. Because of this she began also to be associated with the cat and was therefore fused with the cat-goddess Bastet as Mut-Bastet.

NEFERTEM (NEFERTUM)

The god of the primeval lotus blossom that rose from the waters of Nun at the beginning of creation and from which, in one version of the myth, the sun first rose. He is described in the Pyramid Texts as the bloom 'held to the nose of Ra'. He is some-

(British Museum) Head of the goddess Nut wearing the headdress of Hathor. Faience.

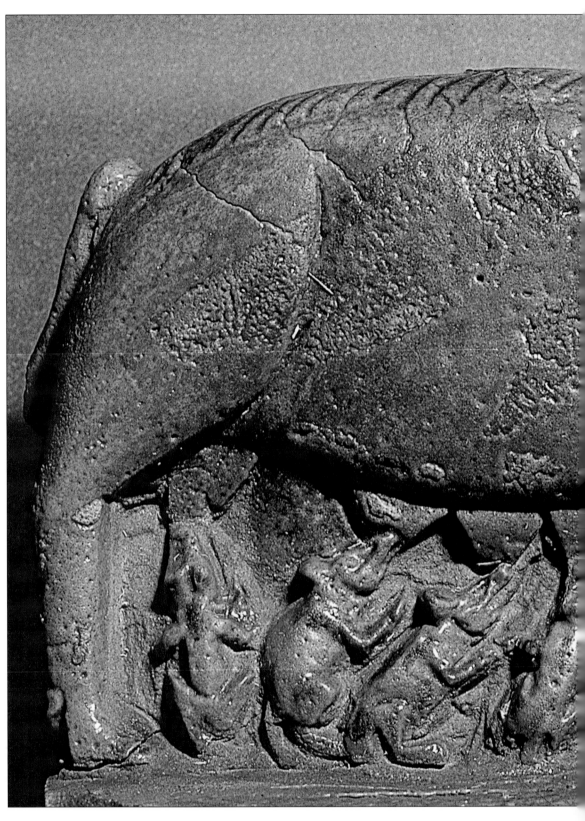

times equated with Horus as the child of the sun. He is usually presented as a man wearing a lotus-shaped headdress, sometimes decorated with two plumes. At other times he is shown with a lion's head, and at Memphis he was thought to be the son of the lioness goddess, Sekhmet.

NEITH

A very ancient creator goddess, whose cult was centred on Saïs in the Delta. Her earliest emblem was a shield with crossed arrows, and she is commonly shown wearing the red crown of Lower Egypt. By the period of the Old Kingdom she had become the consort of the god Seth and their son was the crocodile god Sobek. At various periods her important role as a creator was stressed, and she was even said to have invented birth. She was one of the four goddesses who watched over the bier of Osiris. Her funerary role centred on the linen coverings of the mummy, for she was thought of as

the mythical inventor of weaving.

NEKHBET

A vulture goddess whose local importance grew so that she came to represent Upper Egypt in the same way that Wadjet, the snake-goddess represented Lower Egypt. The vulture and the snake came to symbolize the two halves of the country, and were used in the royal insignia for that purpose. Nekhbet was often shown as a vulture with spread wings who clasps the symbols of eternity in her claws. She can also be a protective symbol, when she has one wing stretched out before her. Her chief function was as a mother-goddess and as a protective nurse to the king.

NEPHTHYS

A goddess of the Ennead of Heliopolis, one of the four children of Geb and Nut. To balance the marriage of Osiris and Isis, she is said to have married her brother Seth. In the Osiris myth she nevertheless

(British Museum) A painted pottery figure of Osiris shown as a mummy and holding the crook and flail, the symbols of royalty.

supports Isis sympathetically in her struggle against Seth. She accompanied Isis when she escorted successive monarchs to the underworld, weeping for them as she had done for her brother Osiris.

NUN

The god who contained within himself the waters of nothingness from which the creator-god emerged in the creation myths. Although he was known as 'father of the gods', this stresses his antiquity rather than his real position. Once Atum, the sun-god, had risen from the waters of Nun, Nun himself had no role to play except in his continued existence that implied the possibility that he could overwhelm the cosmos once again. He was also thought of as beneficent when his name was given to the sacred lakes within temple enclosures.

NUT

The sky goddess of the Heliopolitan creation myth. She was the sister of Geb, the earth, with whom she had four children: Osiris, Isis, Seth and Nephthys, before being separated from him by Shu, the air. She is shown arched across the earth, with her hands and feet at its four cardinal points, and thereby she holds at bay the chaos from which the cosmos had evolved. She was also thought of as the mother of Ra, the sun-god, because she swallowed him every evening and he travelled through her body at night to be born again from her body in the morning. She was also therefore perceived as a funerary deity, receiving the body of the king into her embrace. She came to be represented on the underside of coffin lids, where she arched her body over the deceased who might hope to be born again from it after re-enacting the sun's journey.

ONURIS

A god of hunting who was also a sky god sometimes identified with Shu, the air. He is usually shown as a bearded man holding up a sword and wearing four tall plumes.

OSIRIS

One of the most important gods of Egypt. He was probably an ancient god of fertility, who was associated with corn and with the cycle of its burial in the earth as seed, its resting time in the dark beneath the earth and its germination or resurrection to life. As his importance grew, he assimilated characteristics of other gods whom he displaced. He was strongly connected with kingship and is usually shown carrying the royal insignia of crook and flail. He was the son of Nut and Geb and the first king of Egypt. He was killed by his envious brother Seth, but restored to life by his wife Isis for long enough to impregnate her with a son, Horus, who eventually recovered his kingdom. The skills of Isis preserved him so that he was restored to life in the underworld. He ruled there, supervising the entry of the newly-deceased into his kingdom, and there he represented the sun in its night-time aspect. He became a symbol of the resurrection into life and was seen as such by the many followers of his cult.

PTAH

The creator god whose cult centre was Memphis. He is usually portrayed as a man dressed in a close-fitting garment; his head is shaven and he wears a tightly-fitting skull cap. In his hands he holds a staff that is a combination of the ankh sign and the sceptre of straightness and stability. From the period of the Middle Kingdom he is shown with a straight beard. He was above all the god of craftsmen, and was thought to have created skills in metal-work and sculpture. Consequently, Imhotep, who created the Step Pyramid, came to be thought of as his son. In the creation myth devised at Memphis, perhaps in rivalry to that of Heliopolis, he is said to have created the world by the thoughts coming from his heart and the words from his tongue. During the Old Kingdom his cult merged to some extent with another deity of Memphis, the hawk-god Sokar, and from this combination emerged the funerary god Ptah-Sokar. Naturally enough, this deity gradually assumed the attributes of Osiris, the god of the dead, and emerged as Ptah-Sokar-0siris, images of whom were often included among the funerary objects of private people.

QADESH

A goddess of Middle-Eastern origin who was introduced into Egypt in the New Kingdom and became part of a triad with the gods Min and Reshep. She was a goddess of sexual pleasure, and is usually shown as a naked woman holding out flowers while she stands on the back of a lion.

QEBEHSENUEF – see Sons of Horus

RA (RE)

The creator sun-god of Heliopolis, which was his chief cult centre. He is usually represented as a falcon wearing the sun's disc on its head, which in its turn is surrounded by the body of the snake-goddess that symbolizes his death-dealing powers. When he

is in the underworld he is shown as a ram-headed god. His worship became very important in the 4th Dynasty, and from the 5th Dynasty rulers sometimes incorporated his name into their own, as did Sahure, Menkheppere and Rameses, for example. He became so important that many of the most important gods were subsumed into the cult of the sun, for example Amun-Ra. He combined with the creator god of the Heliopolitan creation myth to become Atum-Ra. During the reign of Akhenaten, the sun-god was conceived as a universal deity to the extent that his worship almost approached monotheism. Ra travelled the sky by day in a boat called the *mandjet* and the underworld by night in a boat called the *mesektet*. Gradually, a synthesis was evolved between Ra and Osiris while Ra was in the underworld, 'Ra in Osiris and Osiris in Ra'.

SEKHMET

A lioness goddess whose name means 'the powerful one'. She was thought to be the daughter of Ra and was therefore considered to be 'the eye of Ra', and was closely linked with the threatening *uraeus*. At Memphis, she was the consort of Ptah. She is shown as a woman with the head of a lioness and her character was violent and destructive; pharaohs regarded her as a symbol of their courage in battle. Because of her lion shape she became linked to certain other deities, especially to the goddess Mut.

SERAPIS

A god originally associated with the Apis bull of Memphis, but then artificially developed under Ptolemy I as a god acceptable to the Greek and Roman world. He is usually shown with a corn measure on his head to emphasize his connection with the grain supply. He was also a god of the underworld and acquired the mixed characteristics of Osiris and certain Greek gods. His cult travelled throughout the Roman Empire, but was less popular finally than that of Isis.

SELKET (SERKET)

A scorpion goddess, usually shown as a woman; on

ABOVE
(British Museum) Lid of a bronze receptacle for the body of a scorpion. The figure represents the goddess Selket (Serket). She is one of the protector-goddesses who guard coffins and canopic jars.

OPPOSITE
(British Museum) Falcon wearing the aegis (broad neck-decoration) of Ra and carrying a solar disc. Bronze, painted and inlaid with gold, c.590 BC.

(British Museum) Bronze figure of the crocodile-god, Sobek, Ptolemaic period.

her head is a scorpion poised to strike and her name refers to her ability to enable the throat to breathe, presumably after a scorpion attack. She was the protector of the hawk-headed canopic jar deity and was one of the four goddesses responsible for guarding the royal coffin.

SETH (SET)

The god who brought chaos and disorder. He was represented as a bizarre animal with a long nose, upright, squared-off ears and an erect, forked tail. He was one of the four children of Nut and Geb, and murdered his older brother, Osiris, in order to seize his rule of the kingdom of Egypt. After a long contest with Horus, the son of Osiris, Seth was forced to resign his claim to the throne. He had the support of Ra during much of his struggle because he alone was

able to control the serpent Apophis, who nightly threatened the boat of the sun.

SHU

With his sister, Tefnut, he was one of the first deities created by Atum, the sun-god of Heliopolis. He was born either from Atum's semen or from his sneeze. He was a god of the air through which the sun shone. He supported his daughter, Nut, as she held the sky away from the earth.

SOBEK
(SEBEK, SUCHOS)

A crocodile god who is sometimes presented as a crocodile, sometimes as a man with the head of a crocodile. In the Old Kingdom he was thought to be the son of Neith. His cult was particularly strong in the Fayum. In the course of time he became assimilated into the cult of Amun and worshipped as another manifestation of the sun-god.

SOKAR
See Ptah

SONS OF HORUS
These were the four deities who were responsible for protecting the internal organs of the deceased once they had been put into canopic jars. Their roles became defined over time and the stoppers of the canopic jars were then made in the forms of the heads of each of the gods. Human-headed Imsety was responsible for the liver; ape-headed Hapi was responsible for the lungs; jackal-headed Duamutef was responsible for the stomach, and falcon-headed Qebehsenuef was responsible for the intestines.

TAWERET (TAURT, THOERIS)
A hippopotamus-goddess who protected women in childbirth. She was said to have been the concubine of Seth but to have gone over to the side of Horus in the dispute between them, thus showing her kinder nature. She can be shown with the head of a hippopotamus, the legs and arms of a lion, the tail of a crocodile and the pendulous breasts of a mature woman – an appearance that was meant to deter malevolent forces from harming women in labour, and one that did not prevent her from being a very popular goddess with the ordinary people of Egypt.

TEFNUT
The sister of Shu. They were the first gods produced from the body of Atum.

THOTH
A moon-god who was responsible for knowledge and writing, and who was particularly venerated by scribes. He had two forms – a baboon and an ibis – probably because at some stage he had become assimilated with another god. In papyri he is sometimes shown in his ibis-headed form recording the results of the weighing of the heart of the deceased, but he was also thought of as guardian of the dead, helping them to find their way in the underworld.

TRIADS
The word triad is used to describe a group of three gods. The three are usually perceived as forming a divine family of father, mother and son, who were all venerated as a group at a particular cult centre. The constitution of the triads sometimes seems forced as it was clearly a convenient way of bringing together gods who had earlier had an independent existence in an area. Among such triads were Amun, Mut and Khons at Thebes, Ptah, Sekhmet and Nefertem at Memphis, Khnum, Satis and Anuket at Elephantine. Osiris, Isis and Horus formed the most familiar triad, but each was actually worshipped at an independent centre.

WEPWAWET
A jackal-headed god whose name meant 'opener of the ways', which could refer both to the conquests of rulers and to the entrance to the underworld, for he sometimes helped the king in battle, but he also performed the ceremony of the Opening the Mouth of the king at his burial and lead him into the underworld.

CHAPTER EIGHT
GREEK, ROMAN AND COPTIC EGYPT

RIGHT
(Musée Boreley, Marseilles) The god
Bes dressed as a warrior. Painted
terracotta, Roman period.

OPPOSITE
(Sopron Museum, Hungary) Bronze
jug with gold decoration of the Roman
period found in Sopron, Hungary.
The inlay shows the frog-goddess
Heket between Isis and Thoth. This
would have been used in the Isis cult
which spread through the Roman
Empire in the early 1st millenium AD.

Under the Ptolemies the city of Alexandria, on the Mediterranean coast, became established as the capital and grew to be an important centre of trade and learning. There had already been a significant population of Greeks in Egypt before Alexander the Great, and during the rule of the Ptolemies more Greeks came to Egypt, to trade and to settle, and their influence increased, particularly in the Delta and in the Fayum.

The Ptolemies encouraged Greek culture, so that Alexandria became the major centre of learning in the Mediterranean world during Hellenistic times. At the same time, however, as pharaohs they encouraged the Egyptian priesthood, restored many temples and founded a number of new ones.

Ptolemy I introduced the cult of Serapis, combining Egyptian and Greek gods into one deity, and he established the main cult centre, the Serapeum, at Alexandria. Serapis was formed from the fusion of the Egyptian gods, Osiris and Apis combined with the Greek gods Zeus, Hades, Asklepios and others. This was brought about as a deliberate attempt to retain the elements of Egyptian religion while adding those of Hellenistic Greece, and was largely successful. Not only was the cult popular in Egypt, but it spread to other parts of the Hellenic and Roman world, and a cult centre to Serapis was even set up on the sacred Greek island of Delos in the 3rd century BC. Serapis was a god who could be all things to all people and nations, for he represented the solar, fertility, healing and funerary aspects of divinity. Usually he is shown with a corn measure on his

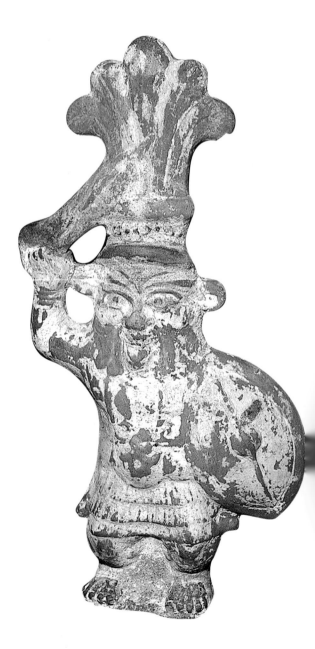

1052

HPAKMAC ΩCLMᴍ LTRAΘΥΡ

ΘΥΥΧΙ

head, which represents an aspect reminiscent of Osiris as a god of corn and fertility.

The Greek influence on Egyptian culture is further demonstrated by the adoption of mainly Greek script for writing the Egyptian language, so that the use of demotic, hieratic and hieroglyphic forms of writing gradually diminished.

Under the Ptolemies, the Greek language was used for official business, for much trade and many literary works. Under the Romans, Latin became the language for administration, but Greek remained the important language for intellectual uses in Egypt.

The Roman emperors did not reside in Egypt as the Ptolemies had done. Instead, the Romans treated Egypt as a province to provide food and taxes for Rome. Emperors did visit Egypt, and are shown on temple reliefs as Egyptian kings, claiming Hathor or Isis as their divine mother. Some emperors, notably Hadrian and Trajan, restored temples and took an interest in Egyptian culture and religion.

There had for a long time been a considerable Jewish population in Egypt, and in the 1st century AD, during the reign of Nero, St. Mark the Evangelist brought Christianity to Egypt. Christianity spread through Egypt, but there were persecutions under some of the Roman emperors. Some Christian leaders took to a life of meditation in the desert, partly to avoid persecution. So the traditon of monasticism and of ascetic hermits developed.

At first, funerary customs continued the ancient Egyptian tradition, and even the early Coptic funerary art retains references to Anubis, the *ankh* and other symbols. Mummification was still practised during the Roman period and mummy portraits show a delightful fusion of traditional Egyptian art with the Hellenistic style.

The cult of Isis had increased in popularity in the later dynasties of ancient Egypt, and continued to do so during Ptolemaic times. Under the Romans it spread throughout the empire. A temple of Isis was found under the ashes which covered Pompeii, and artefacts relating to the Isis cult have been found in many parts of the Roman world.

When the Roman Empire became Christian, the old religions of Egypt declined. Many temples were taken over to become monastic centres. Others had Christian churches built within them. Christian burial customs differed from the earlier ones in tending to include fewer grave goods with the burial. A few centres of the old Egyptian religion carried on. The Temple of Isis at Philae near Aswan continued the cult of Isis in Egypt until the reign of Justinian in the 6th century AD, and the closing of this temple may be considered to mark the end of the last phase in the practice of the religion of ancient Egypt.

TABLE OF EGYPTIAN RULERS

Many of the dates before the 27th Dynasty are approximate

EARLY DYNASTIC PERIOD 3100-2686

1ST DYNASTY 3100-2890
Narmer
Aha
Djer
Djet
Den
Queen Merneith
Anedjib
Semerkhet
Qaa

2ND DYNASTY 2890-2686
Hetepsekhemwy
Raneb
Nynetjer
Weneg
Sened
Peribsen
Khasekhemwy

OLD KINGDOM 2686-2181

3RD DYNASTY 2686-2613
Sanakht
Djoser (Zozer)
Sekhemkhet
Khaba
Huni

4TH DYNASTY 2613-2494
Sneferu	2613-2589
Khufu (Cheops)	2589-2566
Djedefre	2566-2558
Khafre (Chephren)	2558-2532
Menkaure (Mycerinus)	2532-2503
Shepseskaf	2503-2498

5TH DYNASTY 2494-2345
Userkaf	2494-2487
Sahure	2487-2475
Neferirkare	2475-2455
Shepseskare	2455-2448
Neferefre (Raneferef)	2448-2445
Nyuserre	2445-2421
Menkauhor	2421-2414
Djedkare	2414-2375
Unas	2375-2345

6TH DYNASTY 2345-2181
Teti	2345-2323
Userkare	2323-2321
Pepi I	2321-2287
Merenre	2287-2278
Pepi II	2278-2184
Nitiqret	2184-2181

FIRST INTERMEDIATE PERIOD 2181-2055

7TH AND 8TH DYNASTIES 2181-2124

9TH AND 10TH DYNASTIES 2160-2025
(Capital at Herakleopolis)
Meryibre (Khety)
Wahkare (Khety)
Merikare
Ity

11TH DYNASTY 2125-2055
(Capital at Thebes)
Mentuhotep I
Intef I	2125-2112
Intef II	2112-2063
Intef III	2063-2055

MIDDLE KINGDOM 2055-c.1700

11TH DYNASTY 2055-1985
Mentuhotep II	2055-2004
Mentuhotep III	2004-1992
Mentuhotep IV	1992-1985

12TH DYNASTY 1985-1795
Amenemhat I	1985-1955
Senusret I	1965-1920
Amenemhat II	1922-1878
Senusret II	1880-1874
Senusret III	1874-1855
Amenhemhat III	1855-1808
Amenhemhat IV	1808-1799
Queen Sobekneferu	1799-1795

13TH DYNASTY 1795-after 1650
Many rulers, including:
Hor
Khendjer
Sobekhotep III
Neferhotep I
Sobekhotep IV

14TH DYNASTY

SECOND INTERMEDIATE PERIOD c.1700-1550

15TH DYNASTY 1650-1550
Hyksos kings, ruling in the Delta
Salitis
Khyan
Apepi
Khamudi

16TH DYNASTY 1650-1550
Hyksos kings ruling in the Delta at the same time as the 15th Dynasty

17TH DYNASTY 1650-1550
Rulers at Thebes, including:
Intef
Taa I
Taa II
Kamose

NEW KINGDOM 1550-1069

18TH DYNASTY 1550-1295
Ahmose	1550-1525
Amenhotep I (Amenophis)	1525-1504
Thutmose I	1504-1492
Thutmose II	1492-1479
Thutmose III	1479-1425
Hatshepsut	1473-1458
Amenhotep II	1427-1400
Thutmose IV	1400-1390
Amenhotep III	1390-1352
Akhenaten (Amenhotep IV)	1352-1336
Smenkhkare	1338-1336
Tutankhamun	1336-1327

Ay	1327-1323
Horemheb	1323-1295

19TH DYNASTY 1295-1186

Rameses I	1295-1294
Seti I	1294-1279
Rameses II	1279-1213
Merenptah	1213-1203
Amenmessu	1203-1200
Seti II	1200-1194
Saptah	1194-1188
Tausret	1188-1186

20TH DYNASTY 1186-1069

Sethnakhte	1186-1184
Rameses III	1184-1153
Rameses IV	1153-1147
Rameses V	1147-1143
Rameses VI	1143-1136
Rameses VII	1136-1129
Rameses VIII	1129-1126
Rameses IX	1126-1108
Rameses X	1108-1099
Rameses XI	1099-1069

THIRD INTERMEDIATE PERIOD 1069-747

21ST DYNASTY 1069-945

(Capital at Tanis)

Smendes	1069-1043
Amenemnisu	1043-1039
Psusennes I	1039-991
Amenope	993-984
Osorkon the elder	984-978
Siamun	978-959
Psusennes II	959-945

Priest-kings at Thebes contemporary with Tanite Dynasty above:

Herihor
Paiankh
Pinudjem I
Masaherta
Menkheppere
Pinudjem II

22ND DYNASTY 945-715

(Capital at Bubastis)

Sheshonq I	945-924
Osorkon I	924-889
Sheshonq II	c. 890
Takelot I	889-874
Osorkon II	874-850
Takelot II	850-825
Sheshonq III	825-773
Pimay	773-767
Sheshonq V	767-730
Osorkon IV	730-715

23RD DYNASTY 818-715

Various ruling groups centred on Heracleopolis, Hermopolis, Tanis etc.

24TH DYNASTY 727-715

LATE PERIOD 747-332

25TH DYNASTY (KUSHITE)

(Capital at Thebes)

Piy	747-716
Shabaqo	716-702
Shabitqo	702-690
Taharqo	690-664
Tanutamani	664-656

26TH DYNASTY 664-525

(Capital at Sais)

Psamtek I	
	664-610
Nekay II	
	610-595
Psamtek II	
	595-589
Apries	
	589-570
Ahmose II	
	570-526
Psamtek III	526-525

27TH DYNASTY (PERSIAN RULE) 525-404

Cambyses	525-522
Darius I	522-486
Xerxes I	486-465
Artaxerxes I	465-424
Darius II	424-405
Artaxerxes II	405-359

28TH DYNASTY 404-399

(Capital at Sais)

Amyrtaios	404-399

29TH DYNASTY 399-380

(Capital at Mendes)

Nepherites I	399-393
Hakor	393-380
Nepherites II	c. 380

30TH DYNASTY 380-343

Nectanebo I	380-362
Teos	362-360
Nectanebo II	360-343

PERSIAN RULERS

343-332

Artaxerxes III	343-332
Arses	338-336
Darius III	336-332

MACEDONIAN AND PTOLEMAIC PERIOD 332-32

MACEDONIAN DYNASTY 332-305

Alexander the Great	332-323
Philip Arrhidaeus	323-317
Alexander IV	317-310

PTOLEMAIC DYNASTY

Ptolemy I Soter I	305-285
Ptolemy II Philadelphus	285-246
Ptolemy III Euergetes I	246-221
Ptolemy IV Philopator	221-205
Ptolemy V Epiphanes	205-180
Ptolemy VI Philometor	180-145
Ptolemy VII Neos Philometor	145
Ptolemy VIII Euergetes II	170-116
Ptolemy IX Soter II	116-107
Ptolemy X Alexander I	107-88
Ptolemy IX Soter II (restored)	88-80
Ptolemy XI Alexander II	80
Ptolemy XII Neos Dionysos	80-51
Cleopatra VII Philopator	51-30
Ptolemy XIII	51-47
Ptolemy XIV	47-44
Ptolemy XV Caesarion	44-30

ROMAN AND BYZANTINE PERIOD 30 BC-AD 642

Ruled by the Roman and Byzantine Emperors from 30 BC until the Arab conquest in AD 639-642.

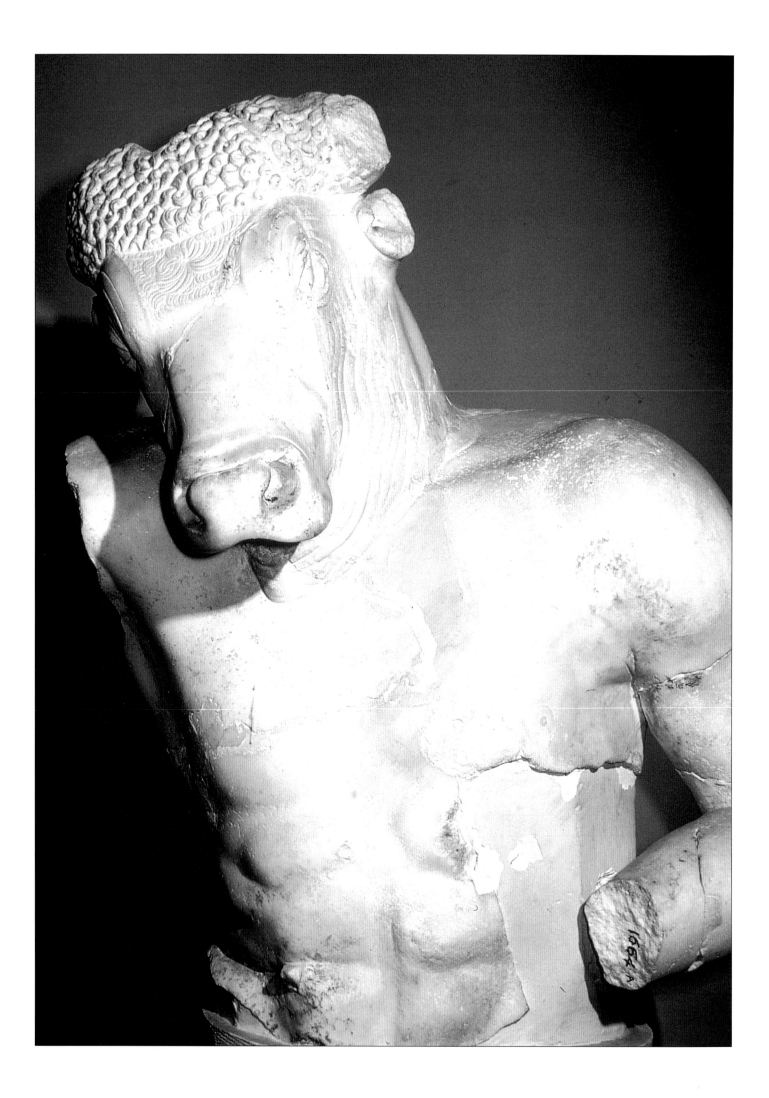

Greece

INTRODUCTION

The gods and myths of Ancient Greece still have a significant place in Western culture. The thunderbolt of Zeus, the trident of the sea-god Poseidon and the staff of Hermes are still recognizable and evocative images. We speak familiarly of the constellations of Orion, Cassiopeia and Andromeda. Modern writers can conjure up the futile heroism of war and the destruction of civilizations by mention of Troy. The heroes Heracles and Odysseus still exemplify strength and wily resourcefulness respectively, and we all know how Freud made use of the Oedipus myth. The stories of the Greek gods and heroes have been retold, reinterpreted and alluded to in the painting, sculpture, literature and music of the Western world for centuries.

This book sets out, in images and words, to familiarize the reader with some of the most important myths. It introduces the chief gods of Ancient Greece with the attributes by which they can be recognized. Then it outlines the stories of some of the most popular heroes of myth, and recounts briefly the tale of the Trojan War and the return of Odysseus. It ends with an account of the mythical stories of two of the ruling dynasties of Ancient Greece, showing how the dramatists of Classical Greece found inspiration in stories that were already ancient, and used them to explore both human morality and the relationship between gods and men.

Before exploring the myths themselves, however, the book gives a brief account of the changing civilizations from which they emerged. Myths might be described as traditional tales that have significance for the people they belong to. They are sometimes connected with early religious or social practices or ceremonies; they sometimes attempt to explain the origins of a group of people or celebrate their victory over another group; they are occasionally explanations of natural phenomena or allegories for the subordination of savage forces to rational order. Above all, they are good stories that give some shape to human experience and help people to talk about why things are as they are.

The origin of the myths is usually unknown and lies in the very distant past, long before the people who told them could read or write. Because they are stories that one generation of people told orally to another, they developed and changed in the telling according to the customs, tastes and needs of the tellers. We know them only in the form they had attained at the moment when they were written down and only in the versions that happen to have survived. The very act of writing the stories, which usually happened long after they had first been told, probably changed them yet again.

The Greek myths developed over a long period, during which a number of different groups of people inhabited the land we now call Greece. The myths include stories that probably originated in Asia, the Middle East and other parts of Europe, and to see why this is so it is necessary to begin with some account of the land, its changing population and the religion that gradually developed there before the eighth century BC.

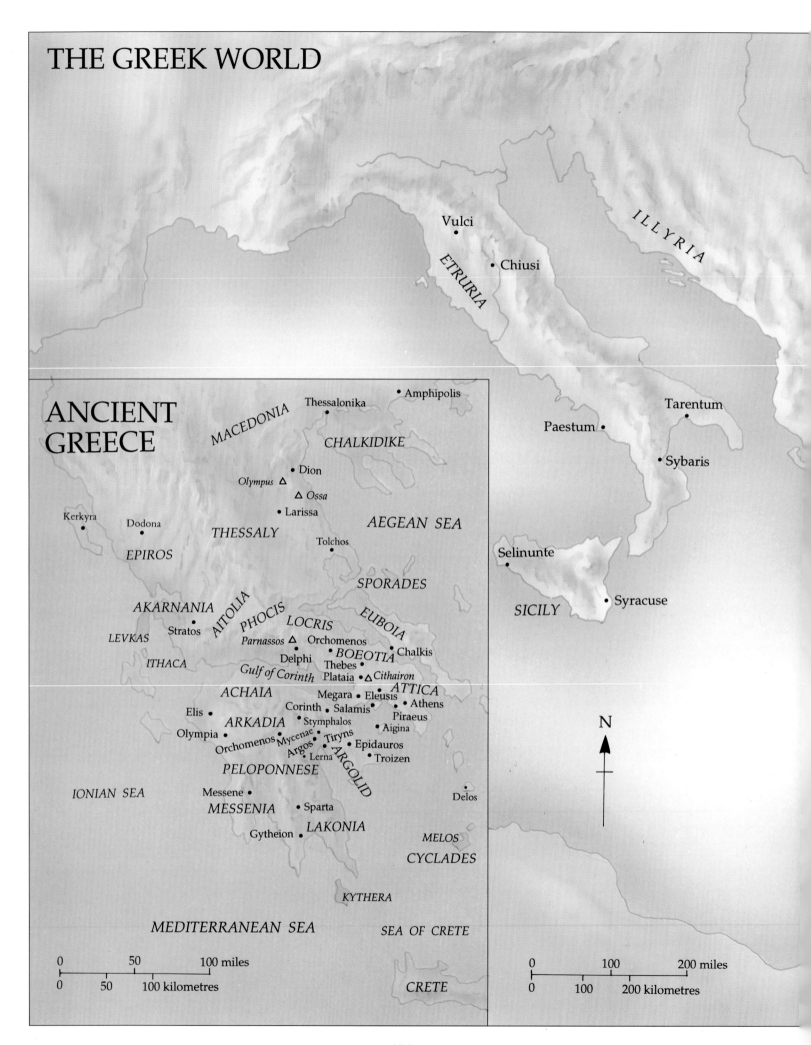

THE GREEK WORLD

ANCIENT GREECE

MACEDONIA
Thessalonika • • Amphipolis
CHALKIDIKE

• Dion
Olympus △
△ *Ossa*
• Larissa

Kerkyra •
Dodona •
THESSALY
AEGEAN SEA

EPIROS
Tolchos •

SPORADES

AKARNANIA
Stratos •
AITOLIA
PHOCIS
LOCRIS
EUBOIA

LEVKAS
Parnassos △ Orchomenos •
ITHACA
Delphi •
BOEOTIA
Chalkis •
Thebes •
Gulf of Corinth Plataia • △*Cithairon*
ACHAIA
Megara • • Eleusis
ATTICA
Corinth • • Salamis
• Athens
Elis •
ARKADIA
Stymphalos •
Piraeus •
Olympia •
Orchomenos •
Mycenae •
Tiryns •
• Aigina
Argos •
• Epidauros
Lerna •
ARGOLID
• Troizen
PELOPONNESE

IONIAN SEA
Messene • •
Delos •

MESSENIA
• Sparta

Gytheion •
LAKONIA
MELOS

CYCLADES

KYTHERA

MEDITERRANEAN SEA
SEA OF CRETE

CRETE

• Vulci
ILLYRIA
ETRURIA
• Chiusi

Tarentum •
Paestum •
• Sybaris

Selinunte •
SICILY
• Syracuse

N

| 0 | 50 | 100 miles |
| 0 | 50 | 100 kilometres |

| 0 | 100 | 200 miles |
| 0 | 100 | 200 kilometres |

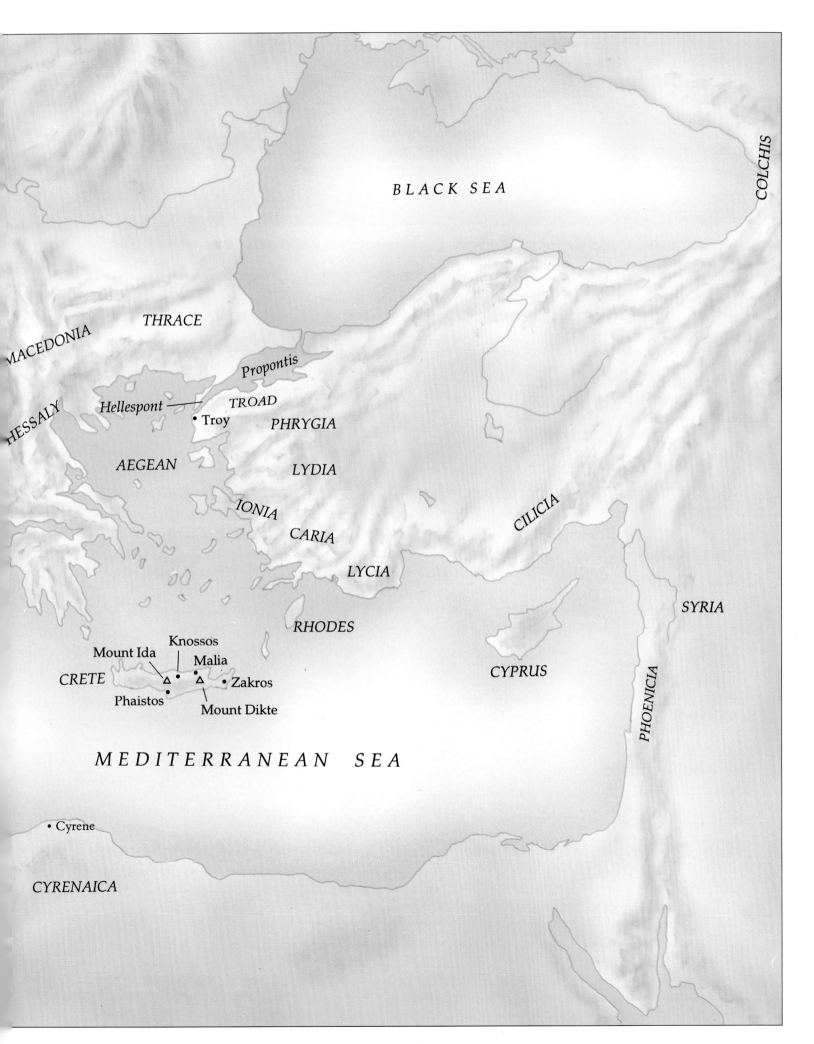

BLACK SEA

COLCHIS

THRACE

MACEDONIA

Propontis

HESSALY

Hellespont

TROAD

• Troy

PHRYGIA

AEGEAN

LYDIA

IONIA

CARIA

CILICIA

LYCIA

SYRIA

RHODES

CYPRUS

Knossos

Mount Ida

Malia

CRETE

△ •

△

• Zakros

Phaistos

PHOENICIA

Mount Dikte

MEDITERRANEAN SEA

• Cyrene

CYRENAICA

CHAPTER ONE
GREECE: THE LAND AND THE PEOPLE

ABOVE
Sunrise behind the mountainous Isle of Hydra.

OPPOSITE
A typical sheltered, fertile area edged by mountains. Mount Parnassus, once sacred to Dionysus, is in the background.

The geographical position of Greece in the ancient world was probably a crucial factor in the development of its richly varied mythology, which absorbed elements from a number of different cultures. Because Greece lies towards the eastern end of the Mediterranean, it is a stepping stone between west and east, between Europe and western Asia; groups of islands in the Aegean form a bridge between Greece and Asia Minor, and the land mass itself stretches southwards into the Mediterranean basin, towards Egypt and Libya.

Four-fifths of Greece is mountainous, or semi-mountainous, but from the mountains the sea is usually visible. From early times, the rugged nature of the terrain encouraged its inhabitants to travel more easily by sailing round the coast and from the mainland to nearby islands and other Mediterranean coastal areas. The deeply indented coastline, sheltered bays, gulfs, and archipelagoes, together with the tideless Mediterranean and unusually clear light made sea travel comparatively easy, so trade and cultural contacts with nearby maritime civilizations were established early.

Yet the cultural diversity that such contact brought to Greece was balanced by an intense and proud localism largely caused by the nature of the land itself. Since agriculture was by far the most important activity for almost everyone, population was necessarily concentrated in the scarce fertile areas: in the coastal plains, estuaries, and river valleys edged by mountains, on isolated plateaux and on the islands. It is not surprising that there was compe-

tition for these areas and that, from time to time, groups of people migrated from less favoured to more favoured land, where they formed relatively isolated but close communities. There are no great navigable rivers, and roads have to find their way round mountains. Thus when incomers brought their stories and their gods to a new area, the stories and the gods were likely, over time, to be assimilated into existing ones, to be given local significance and to be subjected to local interpretation.

Ancient Greek civilization developed with man's ability to make and use metal. In the Aegean area, the effects of the new technology of the Early Bronze Age were most obvious at first in the Cycladic Islands, but from about 2500 BC they seem to have spread throughout the area and reached parts of mainland Greece. Higher civilizations that were both urban and literate had, of course, already come into being by this time in favourable areas, to the East in Mesopotamia – in the fertile plain of the Tigris and the Euphrates – and, slightly later, to the south in Egypt – in the Nile Valley. These cultures were influential in the Eastern Mediterranean throughout the Early Bronze Age.

In the Middle Bronze Age, about 2000-1450 BC, the first European high civilization developed gradually in Crete. The archaeologist, Sir Arthur Evans, who excavated and reconstructed the Palace at Knossos on Crete, named this the Minoan civilization because of memories, preserved in the Greek myths, of stories of the great King Minos of Crete, his palace and its labyrinth.

(British Museum) A bronze stand from Cyprus (c.1600-1100 BC) shows a man carrying a copper ingot. Copper was mixed with tin to produce bronze.

Crete became the unchallenged and dominant naval power in the Aegean. In about 1900 BC, Minoan power within the island seems to have been centralized in a number of newly constructed palaces, some built on the sites of older ones, each of which became the focus of its surrounding area. The palaces were important administrative centres and also clearly centres of wealth and therefore of artistic and technical achievement. This period of Minoan administrative centralization and cultural growth in Crete paralleled the rise of the Hittite civilization in Asia Minor. Surviving artefacts from Crete suggest that, while the Minoan civilization was influenced by the East, it possibly had a more humane religious and artistic tradition of its own that found much of its inspiration in nature.

Its power was ended by natural disaster. Archaeologists have shown that when, in about 1500 BC, an earthquake, followed by a huge volcanic eruption, tore the island of Thera apart, submerging

LEFT
The Throne Room in the Minoan Palace of Knossos (c.1700-1450 BC) contains one throne, carved in gypsum, perhaps in imitation of an earlier wooden chair. The beaks of the two griffins painted on the wall would have flanked the head of the occupant of the throne in a manner typical of oriental art and found occasionally in Cretan and Mycenaean art.

BELOW
Detail of the remains of a Minoan town excavated at Akrotiri on the island of Thera (Santorini). The town was preserved under a layer of volcanic ash that covered it during the eruption that destroyed the heart of the island in about 1450 BC.

BOTTOM
Grave Circe A, the Royal Cemetery, at Mycenae (c.16th century BC). Six shaft graves were found in the enclosure, in which 19 skeletons were buried with rich grave furnishings.

half of it, the resultant tidal waves, which carried masses of exploded pumice, battered many islands in the southern Aegean, including Crete. Sometime just before 1450 BC there seems to have been another major natural disaster, and the fires that followed it destroyed virtually all the important Minoan buildings on Crete. A generation later, the palace of Knossos was re-occupied by Greek-speaking Mycenaeans from the mainland, who continued there until its final destruction in about 1375 BC.

The Late Bronze Age on mainland Greece (c.1450-1200 BC) is actually often referred to as the Mycenaean Age in reference to the rise and subsequent expansion of the Greek-speaking civilization that had been developing there, and whose population is sometimes described as Achaian, a term used by Homer. The most important centre of this civilization was Mycenae, which is in the Argolid in the north eastern Peloponnese and was brought to light in modern times by Heinrich Schliemann in 1876.

Mycenaean culture, based on farming and stock-breeding, had long been comparatively austere. It is, incidentally, interesting in this context to note that Homer describes an early king, Odysseus, doing his own ploughing. Yet when Schliemann excavated the shaft graves of rulers at Mycenae, which date from about 1600 BC, he found evidence of great material wealth, partly in the form of golden objects. It is now thought possible that gold was brought back to Greece, in the form of wages, by Mycenaean soldiers who had fought as mercenaries for Egypt, and that the inclusion of precious objects in the graves was influenced by Egyptian burial customs.

Both the weapons and the warlike decoration of other objects found in the graves give a picture of a more aggressive civilization than that of the Minoans, and the fact that some of the skeletons were almost two metres tall adds to the impression that their owners were taller and stronger than the Mediterranean people.

After the destruction of the Cretan centres, Mycenaean influence increased in the Aegean. The Mycenaeans had assimilated certain elements of Minoan civilization, such as the method of conducting their administration from a number of powerful centres, and they learned to be sufficiently good sailors and merchants to overtake the Cretans' dominance at sea. They soon expanded their interests to the islands, to the west coast of Asia Minor and to trading posts in Cyprus. They exported their pottery, which was simpler and cheaper to produce than Minoan pottery, to southern Italy and Sicily and to

Egypt. They also extended the number of their settlements on the mainland, right up to the Thessalian plain, which was horse-breeding country.

Population increased, agricultural methods improved, and there was probably a rise in the standard of living. Palaces were built at Tiryns, Mycenae, Pylos and Thebes that fulfilled an administrative function for their surrounding regions similar to that adopted earlier in Crete. Some of these centres had strongly built, fortified walls that greatly impressed a later, less developed population who attributed almost supernatural powers to their dead builders. The Mycenaeans organized a road system that connected the centres of scattered kingdoms with their outlying regions and with each other, yet legends and poetry record memories of warlike conflict between the states.

Mycenaean civilization reached its peak towards the end of the thirteenth century BC. According to

tradition, it was in those years that its rulers and young warriors undertook an expedition against Troy; indeed, epic accounts of this expedition were so deeply embedded in oral tradition that it was accepted as an historical fact by later Greeks. Nevertheless, Mycenaean civilization had almost come to an end by that period. At the end of the thirteenth and the beginning of the twelfth centuries, for as yet unknown reasons, a number of its centres in Greece were destroyed by fire, and others were simply abandoned.

At the same time, across the sea in western Asia there was a period of great instability and confusion. A number of factors led to the break-up of the Hittite Empire and this had indirect but serious consequences for the Mycenaean world. For example, the destruction of the Canaanite trading cities on the coast of Asia Minor helped to destroy Mycenaean trade with the East, so that the Mycenaeans became reliant instead on what they could grow and make at home. This in turn lessened their need for the upper layer of palace administration that had controlled foreign trade and the distribution of goods.

The consequent falling standard of living persuaded some people to disperse from mainland Greece to familiar areas of the Near East and to the islands of Rhodes and Cyprus. In Greece itself there was a movement of population away from the difficult hinterland towards the more fertile eastern and western coastal areas. As a result, the great palace centres were replaced by less powerful, less wealthy, more dispersed centres of smaller regions. These, however, still maintained some indirect contact with the East, mainly through Mycenaeans living in Cyprus.

Gradually, less advanced people from the mountains and arid plains moved southwards down the Greek peninsula to take over newly-abandoned land that was nevertheless preferable to their own. There was a consequent slow but comprehensive resettlement of population throughout Greece. Soon after 1100 BC there were no more attempts to revive foreign trade; the last acropolises were abandoned and so were some settlements that had formerly lived chiefly off trade. The Mycenaean world sank into the period of adjustment that is, perhaps unfairly, called the Dark Ages.

The migratory movements of various groups in this period, roughly between 1125 BC and 800 BC were far too complex to detail here, but they had a profound effect on the development of religion and culture in Greece. The migration, which used to be called loosely the Dorian invasion, was not a single movement as this suggests but a gradual change:

sometimes groups split up; sometimes they moved swiftly, stayed in a new area for a few decades, then moved on again. Quite large groups crossed over from the mainland to the western coast of Asia Minor, for example to the area that became known as Ionia.

The migrating groups gradually settled down and, in spite of emerging inequalities between groups and individuals, the Greek people began to share certain common beliefs and cultural standards. When the 'Phoenician' alphabet was adopted to Greek use it initiated the possibility of literacy throughout the Greek world. Although the new states and political units were smaller than those of their Mycenaean predecessors, many of them survived for centuries.

During this period, we move from prehistory to history, and the use of written records adds a new dimension to our knowledge. The written myths suggest that migrating Greek-speaking tribes had memorized early catalogues of their genealogies and explanations of their origins and that they handed down traditional stories about their settlements and their feuds from one generation to the next. Once these stories were collected and written down, they came to be treated as distant but authentic history. The so-called 'Dark Ages' were, therefore, actually crucial to the restructuring and formation of the Greek world, and it was during this period that many of the myths must have developed.

The period between about 800 BC and the Classical period that shone particularly brightly in the fifth century BC is usually called the Archaic period. One of the most significant new developments at this time was social and political. The immigrant groups had preserved their ancient organization into 'tribal states', although in many cases these no longer corresponded to specific tribes. In these states the ruler's power was derived from an assembly of warriors who supported him as long as his good fortune and physical strength assured them that he was favoured by the gods. This is the kind of state that seems to form the background of most of the myths. In the eighth century a new kind of social and political organization called the *polis* began to emerge, which moved the emphasis away from the power of the ruler towards a more collective and public responsibility.

The Greek term *polis* is difficult to define because examples of it were so variable. It is usually translated into English as 'city state', but this gives a somewhat false impression. In general terms, the *polis* was a self-ruling, autonomous community that could consist of a group of villages and some scattered settlements or might include a town. It functioned in those areas of communal life that demanded collective action, and in time it usually developed a focal point such as a town with a market and a place of assembly.

Greater stability and gradually improving agricultural methods at this time meant that some small landowners began to prosper and, as heads of families, some of them now became citizens, eligible to join local councils, which now met at stated regular intervals and made real decisions. Clearly this shifted the balance slightly between rulers and ruled. Local aristocrats, usually from a limited number of well-established families, nevertheless monopolized official positions, such as the magistracy, and so increased their political influence.

Gods and myths must have played a significant role in the establishment of these newly structured communities that were so dependent upon their members' shared sense of place and kinship. The practice of local religious cults and the telling of traditional local legends helped to define a *polis*, and loyalty to its cults would be expected of all its citizens. Archaeological evidence supports this view by suggesting that the sort of items that had normally been buried with rich individuals were from this time more commonly dedicated at civic sanctuaries, which were often sited outside the main settlement and probably maintained by communal expenditure.

These successors of the Mycenaeans, who included descendants of some of the earlier Mycenaean inhabitants of their localities, gradually caught up with the more advanced people of the Mediterranean area and, as they did so, seem to have become more consciously Greek. An important focus for this consciousness were the works of the poet we know as Homer, which were probably written down in the eighth century BC, or even a little earlier. The *Iliad* and the *Odyssey* celebrated the achievements of earlier, greater, probably Mycenaean, heroes in stories that had clearly been told and developed over several centuries before they were finally written down. For the Greeks of the Archaic and Classical periods they had historical rather than legendary or mythical significance, and aristocrats would recount genealogies that demonstrated their direct descent from one or other of the heroes who had fought at Troy. From Homer and subsequent writers the Greeks also derived a common pantheon of gods with which they were able, in many cases, to assimilate their local gods.

The development of athletic competitions formed further links between Greeks. Aristocrats dedicated much of their time to achieving and maintaining healthy and beautiful bodies through exercise. Men of this period inherited a tradition of athletic contests, which had sometimes been held originally to mark an important event such as a victory or the funeral of a hero. Such games became displays of physical superiority. In this period of the development of communal institutions, the contests became closely linked with religious festivals and holidays and could be seen as each individual's pious offering of his best efforts to the gods. Several of these games became pan-Hellenic events, notably the ones held at

(Capitoline Museum, Rome) Roman copy of a Greek imaginary portrait of the poet Homer. No authentic image of Homer exists, but this is typical of ancient perceptions of him.

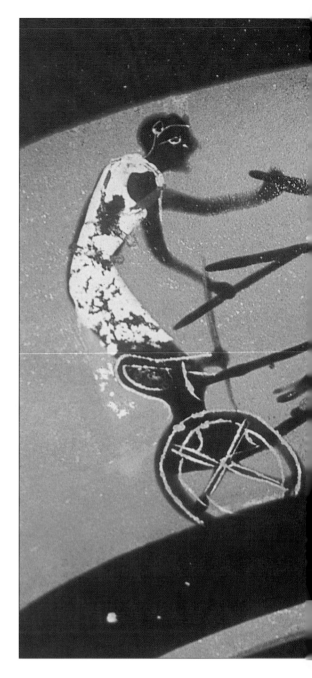

Olympia. The origins of the Olympic games are unknown, but the conventional date of the first games is 776 BC, and the four-yearly event soon served as a dating system for the whole of Greece.

This period is one of expansion, when Greeks, having already settled in the East, founded colonies to the west, in southern Italy and Sicily, and this period of exploration and settlement is also reflected in some of the myths. It was also a period of great diversity among states and races, and of turmoil and revolt as men fought for a greater share of power.

Some states made notable advances: Sparta greatly increased its extent and population through military conquest, while Athens flourished economically and produced goods, such as pottery, of increasing interest and accomplishment. Sparta moved towards a democratic system of rule, but was held back by its inflexibility. In the sixth century,

however, Athens began to achieve something closer to a true democracy when it allowed small local units to control their own affairs without the interference of the aristocracy, yet to be grouped into larger units so that they felt part of the state for other purposes.

Fifth-century Athens, during the flowering of the Classical period, is the time and place most people imagine when they think of Ancient Greece. By that period the gods and myths were not only established in the popular consciousness but celebrated and recalled in writing, in dramatic festivals and in the arts of architecture, jewellery and pottery. Stories were sometimes elaborated deliberately and with artistic intent, but they were still reworkings of the mythical narratives that concern us here, which had been formed, then developed, merged, systematized and transmitted by word of mouth through the preceding centuries.

ABOVE
(Old Corinth Museum) Greek vase painting (6th century BC) shows a competitor taking part in a chariot race, an important event at the Olympic Games.

OPPOSITE TOP
(British Museum) Black figure dish from Attica (c.550 BC). The lively depiction of a hunter and his dog is typical of the fluidity of design achieved in the area around Athens at this time, when pottery was increasingly often decorated with scenes from everyday life.

OPPOSITE BOTTOM
The vaulted entrance to the Stadium at Olympia has been restored to its form of the 4th century BC. Excavation of the stadium unearthed votive offerings that had been found buried respectfully by men who had made repeated alterations in much earlier times.

CHAPTER TWO
RELIGION: FROM PREHISTORY
TO HISTORY

Cycladic marble female figure (third millenium BC). This is characteristic of the flattened, schematic figures that were laid in tombs beside the dead. Their significance is not clear.

The changes in population, outlined in the previous chapter, naturally brought changes in religious belief. The religious beliefs of people in prehistory cannot be recovered with any certainty, but archaeological evidence sheds some light on their religious practices. If we begin once more in the Aegean Early Bronze Age (c.2800-1900 BC), no building has been found on the Greek mainland that can be said certainly to have been intended for a sacred purpose, whereas such buildings have been found in more Eastern civilizations dating from much earlier periods. On the other hand, graves found in the Cycladic islands at this period suggest that great care was taken over the burial of the dead, who were surrounded with personal belongings as though they were expected to need them in a life that would continue after death. It has been suggested that some of the apparently simple figurines found in the Cyclades both in settlements and graves may have represented goddesses, but there is no proof of this. Somewhat later, however, in the Middle Bronze Age (c.1900 BC-1500 BC), there is evidence for the worship of a female deity in a special sanctuary on the island of Keos.

In the Early Bronze Age, in parts of Crete, the dead were buried in small, stone, vaulted 'beehive' tombs with doorways, a long-lasting style, which later developed into the monumental *tholos* tombs that were also found in Mycenaean Greece. The care taken over such tombs again suggests belief in the after-life but perhaps more importantly a desire to honour the dead who had been important in life.

In the Middle and Late Bronze Ages (c.1900 BC-1100 BC) most evidence of the worship of deities and the particular importance of certain symbols comes from the Minoan civilization of Crete. Our ideas about Minoan religion have been deduced partly from the unusually fine objects and paintings found in Crete by archaeologists and partly from what appear to be memories of Minoan beliefs that were assimilated into Greek myths.

The number and variety of representations that have been found of a female figure suggest that the chief deity was a goddess, or a number of different goddesses. Early deities are often represented as female, and this was certainly the case in many Asian cults. The Cretan goddess appears in association with mountain peaks, with a sacred tree, with snakes, poppies and doves. Sometimes she is shown as 'The Lady of the Animals', with lions and panthers, just as the goddess Artemis was, later, in Greece. This manifestation indicated both her power over wild nature and her protective attitude towards it, as opposed to her connection, suggested by her association with trees, with the vegetation and cultivation upon which people depended for daily life. Her female nature is usually stressed in early figurines by her nakedness and later by her dress and her full breasts, which are usually shown uncovered. A young god seems to have been associated with her, possibly sometimes as her son, sometimes as her partner. It has been suggested that he was a particular representation of the vegetative aspect of nature, since he was born, died and came to life again each

year. He too has parallels in earlier Asian cults.

Minoan worship and art seem to have been intimately connected with the natural world, which is scarcely surprising at a time when agriculture and the capture of wild game were obviously the basis of life. Joy at bringing in the harvest is expressed so vividly by the singers engraved on the vessel known as the 'Harvester's Vase' that it cries out to us today. At some of the palaces, such as Malia and Zakros, a type of circular altar called a *kernos* with hollows all round the rim and a larger hollow at the centre has

been found. It is thought that such altars were used to make multiple offerings, probably of cereals, with oil in the centre hollow, and that they might have represented the 'first fruits' of the land.

There is a good deal of evidence to suggest that caves and mountain peaks and certain trees, pre-eminently the useful olive, were treated as sacred. For example, in the Cave of Eileithyia near Amnisos, named after a goddess of reproduction, a large and a smaller stalagmite were apparently perceived as representations of the goddess and her child, since their

votaries, or worshippers, built a low wall, which still exists, round the stalagmites, and left vessels there. These were likely to have been filled with oil or honey since tablets inscribed with Linear B script have shown that the Cave of Eileithyia was one of the places to which olive oil and honey were distributed as religious offerings by the Palace of Knossos.

Small figurines, representing the votaries themselves, have been found in the Diktean Cave, which was thought by the Greeks to be the place where their goddess Rhea hid her new-born son Zeus. Bronze double axes, an important symbol to the Cretans, were found with swords in a cave near Arkalochori, which was presumably felt to be the home of a warlike divinity. Sanctuaries were also built on some mountain peaks.

Rooms that appear to be shrines have been found in houses and palaces, and in late Minoan times what seem to be communal sanctuaries began to appear. It is possible that the king and queen themselves represented the deities at palace shrines, and received offerings in their place. Some memory of royal participation in religious ritual is perhaps suggested by the stories in Greek myths of King Minos of Crete and of his wife Pasiphaë.

The bull occupied a central place in Cretan culture, its original importance presumably being simply that it supplied meat, leather and dung, and inseminated the dairy herds. In some Eastern religions the bull deity is identified with the heavens and the sun, while the sacred cow is associated with the moon. Cretan art presents us with numerous lively representations of bulls, especially in the public sports where athletes appear to have seized the bulls' horns and somersaulted the length of their backs. There are images of bulls being sacrificed, and bulls' horns had symbolic significance for the Minoans, apparently being used to mark off certain areas of the palaces.

ABOVE
(Archaeological Museum of Heraklion) Detail from a sarcophagus from the Minoan Villa of Aghia Triada (c.14th century BC). This is a unique illustration of Minoan rites connected with the death of a king. A bull has been tied down and sacrificed, and its blood is being collected in a pail while two goats wait their turn beneath the altar. Meanwhile, a male figure plays the double flute. On the right a priestess, wearing a sheepskin skirt, presents a bloodless offering of fruit and wine at the altar in front of a column crowned by a double axe, on which a bird sits.

LEFT
A kernos, or offering table, still in its original position at the Minoan palace of Malia, Crete (c.1700-1450 BC). This vessel, in which small quantities of agricultural produce were probably blessed then offered to a god, is situated conveniently close to the store-rooms of the palace.

OPPOSITE
The Cave of Eileithyia, showing the low wall that was built round the stalagmites. It was a shrine in Neolithic times and, during the Minoan civilization, was sacred both to the goddess of nature and to Eileithyia, the goddess of childbirth. It was still remembered in Homer's day, since he makes Odysseus claim that his ship once put in at Amnisos 'where the cave of Eileithyia is'.

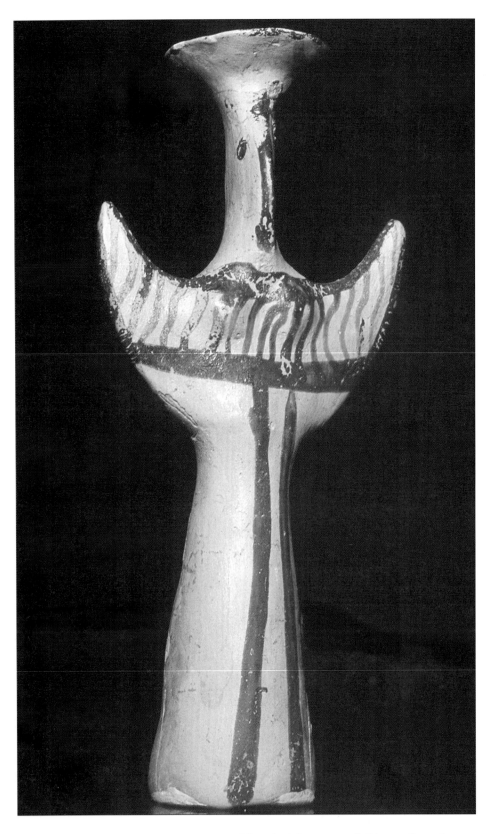

From such evidence it seems likely that early Mycenaeans had also adopted a goddess of vegetation and fertility and there are images of a goddess as 'The Lady of the Animals', who would have been important to the Mycenaeans who were hunters and stockbreeders. Some clay figurines show a stylized goddess with her arms raised in an attitude of benediction. There is no evidence that the Mycenaeans adopted the Cretan snake goddess, however. As a more warlike civilization, they made images of a goddess of war, not as a woman but in the form of a palladion, or shield-like standard made in the familiar figure-of-eight shape of early Mycenaean shields, with a female head projecting from the top of it and a spear from its side. It seems likely that the early shield was itself the significant symbol of a cult connected with war.

Engravings on jewellery suggest that the Mycenaeans, like the Minoans, regarded the tops of hills and mountains as sacred places and built small cult shrines there, decorating their façades with bulls' horns, which were an important symbol for them also. Although Mycenaean religion borrowed some elements from Crete, it is likely that it actually originated elsewhere and that its tradition was essentially closer to the Greek religion of historical times that we shall examine next.

The centuries that followed the end of Mycenaean palace civilization are 'dark' in the sense

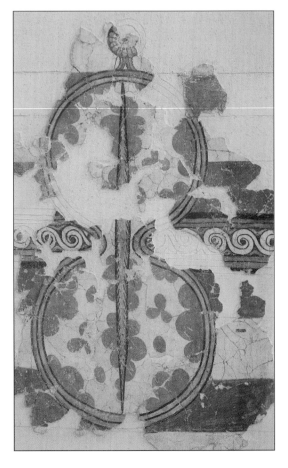

ABOVE
(Argos Museum) A terracotta figure typical of the last period of the Mycenaean Age whose attitude of benediction may originate from the posture of earlier Minoan goddesses.

RIGHT
(National Archaeological Museum, Athens) A Mycenaean fresco showing a figure-of-eight shield.

The decipherment of Linear B script on Mycenaean tablets from Knossos has shown that some Olympian gods, including Zeus, Poseidon, Hera and Hermes, were already being worshipped by the Mycenaeans in the fourteenth and thirteenth centuries BC and had been taken by them to Crete at the end of the Minoan period. It is, however, difficult to discover much about the beliefs of the Mycenaeans, and knowledge comes chiefly from small statues and from carvings on jewellery and seal stones.

that so little is known about them, yet they were crucial in forming the religion that we now recognize as Ancient Greek. The gods of this religion emerge to clear view in the works of Homer and Hesiod sometime in the eighth century BC (although some people now place Homer in the second half of the ninth century BC) and they will be described in detail in the following chapters.

The gods who lived on Olympus had, in some respects, a recognizable family life, although in most respects an extremely irregular one. The structure of the Olympian pantheon was probably a simplification and reduction of belief as it actually existed among the population at large in the eighth century, yet it was important in that it served to give some sort of uniformity and consistency to Greek religion right through to the Classical period and beyond.

Its polytheism implied that different gods had different spheres of influence and that all of them could be worshipped by a pious person because each god had influence over a different aspect of human life. At the same time, it was perfectly possible to pay particular attention to one god. Worship of one god did not exclude worship of the others. There was no single correct belief, only correct religious practice.

Neither was there a single origin of this religion, as has been demonstrated. The only god whose name it seems possible to reach back to with any certainty

is that of Zeus himself, the sky god, whose name probably originates from an Indo-European word. Since the language of the Greeks suggests that they were once Indo-European speaking, such an origin for their most important god seems obvious. The origins of the other deities cannot be determined simply. It must be remembered that the Bronze Age inhabitants of Greece had contacts with the ancient civilizations of the Near East. Then, after the end of the Mycenaean palace period, new Indo-European speaking tribes, probably having beliefs of their own, moved southwards into Greece. Some earlier inhabitants moved away and resettled on the west coast of Asia Minor, where they were subject once again to new influences because Asian cultures had also undergone change over time. These influences had an effect, in their turn, on the population of mainland Greece.

During the period of the settlement of new tribes and the resettlement of the existing population in Greece it seems that both groups were broadly tolerant in religious matters. As incomers settled into new areas, they seem to have accepted the deities that already existed there as well as sometimes importing new ones. The long period between the ending of Mycenaean civilization and the clarification of belief we see recorded in the works of Homer was therefore one of adjustment, of assimilation of new rituals to old ones, of the merging of different but often probably closely related deities. In time, the local gods became subsumed into the Olympian pantheon, possibly because the Olympians carried more prestige.

It is because of this readjustment that the gods often have more than one name, are described by different epithets, are shown with different attributes and have so many myths associated with them. Many of their epithets and attributes demonstrate local claims on a god of the pantheon, or encapsulate memories of an earlier god who has been assimilated with one of the Olympians. Sometimes an epithet merely indicates the aspect in which the worshippers wish to appeal to the god on a particular occasion, thereby encouraging an important generalized deity to focus on a small, particular need that might once have been served by a special, local god. It was considered important to address a god correctly by the name that would best enlist his help in a particular function.

The number of female partners attributed to some of the male divinities probably reflects the need to subordinate powerful, early, local female deities to newer, male gods.

The new settlers in Greece would have been

introduced to existing sacred places where divinity was felt to be present, where cults were practised, offerings made, or perhaps shrines or sanctuaries were built. Sometimes these were the sites not of major divinities but of some minor supernatural figure, such as a local spirit of nature, a nymph, or a hero. As on Crete, sometimes stones or trees were themselves felt to be sacred.

Hero cults tended to be particularly localized, and were often focused on an early tomb or a place where some event of local importance, such as a vic-

(British Museum) Greek terracotta seated figure from Boeotia. Such terracotta figures were produced in large numbers and usually had a votive function, representing the deity of a specific sanctuary. Boeotia was particularly active in their production.

135

RIGHT
The impressive landscape surrounding
the Sanctuary of Apollo at Delphi.
In the foreground is a marble tholos,
or rotunda, built in the early 4th century BC.
Its dedication is unknown and it is one of the
many buildings that accumulated over
the centuries at this particularly sacred site.

tory in battle, had occurred. It is important to remember that the telling of myths and stories of heroes provided a history for people who had no recorded past, and that aristocrats, in all seriousness, charted their descent from gods or heroes. The migrations of people meant that it became particularly important to be able to establish divine authority for a group's presence in and rule over their new locality, and this was sometimes achieved through stories of a local, tribal god who was said to have emerged from the earth itself. Yet in spite of population changes, there was often continuity of worship at ancient shrines. There were sometimes changes in the identity of the deity being worshipped, but respect was usually shown by the incoming group to the beliefs of those who had gone before.

Once the Olympian theological system had been established it became possible for groups all over Greece to share it, at least at the level of common public belief. Places that had long been held as particularly sacred became accessible to everyone. Among these were the great sanctuaries whose remains we can still see. What impresses the visitor to Greece today is the beauty of many of these sites. It is easy to understand how divinity could have been felt to inhabit their very rocks and trees.

The sanctuary at Delphi was already the most important religious centre in Greece, and was in fact regarded in antiquity as the centre of the world. It was originally sacred to Gaia, or Ge, the earth mother, but it later adopted the cult of Apollo, and was later still also associated with Dionysus. Like other cult areas it would originally have been just an open precinct with an altar and perhaps a simple, representational statue of the cult figure. Later, a large temple was built to house a statue of the god and gradually other buildings clustered on this uniquely important site. From the eighth century BC it was normal for a religious site of any importance to have a temple with a cult image inside it – a home for the god rather than a place for communal worship; the sacrificial altar would stand in front of the temple.

The great sanctuaries were unusual in maintaining a priesthood, and it was to the Delphic priesthood that city states turned for advice on religious matters, such as the acceptance of foreign cults. Rulers of states and individuals all approached the Delphic oracle for advice.

There were many sanctuaries where methods of divining the future were practised and to which people turned for advice and guidance. There are numbers of myths concerning the Delphic oracle, but in historical times prophecies seem to have been given by a series

ABOVE
The theatre built in the 3rd century BC at the remote, northern Sanctuary of Zeus at Dodona. Buildings arrived late at this very ancient sanctuary where Zeus continued to be worshipped in the open air until the end of the 5th century BC. His cult goes back at least to the 14th-13th centuries BC there, and was probably preceded by an earlier earth cult. The sanctuary is mentioned in the Odyssey *and in the myth of the Argonauts.*

OPPOSITE PAGE
TOP LEFT
(Louvre Museum) Roman replica of a 5th-century Greek relief showing Hermes taking Orpheus to the Underworld to meet Eurydice. The names above the figures were added in medieval times and are now known to be incorrect.

TOP RIGHT
The Tholos (c.360-320 BC) at the sanctuary of Aesclepius at Epidauros. This once-impressive building had a colonnade of 26 columns; beneath its central pavement lay circular passages reminiscent of a labyrinth. Their function is unknown; it has been suggested that religious rites were held there or that they housed the sacred serpents of the healing god.

BOTTOM
(Ioannina Museum, Epirus) One of the lead tablets, inscribed in Greek boustrophedon *writing, left by a supplicant to the oracle of Zeus at Dodona (c.214 BC). It says 'Hermon asks to which god he should pray to have useful children by his wife Kretaia, apart from those he already has'.*

of venerable women, each called the Pythia, as they sat on the sacred tripod inside the temple of Apollo. The sanctuary at Dodona long remained simply an open-air precinct, where the priests heard the oracles of Zeus in the sounds of the wind-blown leaves, or the metal cauldrons that they hung in the branches of the trees. Small tablets have been found there on which people inscribed their questions for the god, and these show how directly and intimately religion and daily life were connected.

The sanctuary at Epidauros gave revelation in a different way. People who were sick visited this shrine dedicated to Asclepius, a healing god, and spent the night in special rooms at the sanctuary until the god sent them a curative dream. Inscriptions have been found there that tell the stories of specific cases of dreams that induced healing.

Each city probably had its own cult, and some of these attained a pan-Hellenic importance. A few became popular mystic cults whose celebration was more personal and intense than usual and which differed from the normal forms practised on behalf of the people by their rulers and aristocratic magistrates in being more concerned with death and the after-life than the here and now.

One of the most important of these was the cult of Demeter at Eleusis. This was probably a very early rural cult in origin, celebrating the corn-goddess, Demeter, and her daughter, Kore – 'the maiden' – later called Persephone. Demeter is said to have rested at Eleusis during her search for her lost daughter,

who was being held in the Underworld. Her cult developed into the Eleusinian Mysteries, to which men were initiated by means of secret teachings, and which were said to offer great consolation and revelations about life, death and the after-life.

In about the sixth century BC, another cult arose that attached little importance to earthly life but suggested that men must prepare themselves for greater happiness in an after-life. Followers of this cult were called Orphics, probably after Orpheus who went down to the Underworld to bring back his wife Eurydice from the dead, but had her snatched from him again when he turned to look at her as they neared the entrance to the world of the living. Orphics saw the body as a prison in which the soul, which had once been happy, was confined for some fault that the owner of the body was unaware of. At death, the soul had atoned for its fault, and was free to return to the blessed land – unless the owner of the body led an unjust life, in which case the soul was imprisoned in another body until full atonement was made.

Another rural cult that became a popular ecstatic cult and moved into cities was that of Dionysus, which is thought to have come from Asia through Phrygia and Thrace. Dionysus was a vegetation god, but one associated with trees and the vine, sap and wine, rather than cereals. There are many myths about celebrations of his festival by women who took to the mountains, where, in a trance-like state, they ate the raw flesh of animals. It is possible that the festivals did in fact provide rare occasions for women to leave their husbands

and their confinement to home and duty for a brief period and to take part in celebrations, which often seemed to involve dancing.

Ecstatic cults and those that emphasized the importance of the after-life were criticized in the Classical period. In a sense they looked forward to a different kind of religious sensibility that we perhaps recognize today. They were departures from the religion that was normally practised in public in Greece at this period.

Normally a cult was observed by acts rather than beliefs. The practice of worshipping a deity, bringing votive offerings to it, being present at a sacrifice, meant that the head of a household publicly displayed his membership of his community and culture. Festivals celebrated what was important to people: the events of the agricultural year, the founding of a city or a state, the death of a hero, the right order of society – including conflict between the sexes and rites of passage from one stage of life to the next. Gods had to be propitiated, given gifts in exchange for favours, so that they would withhold their potentially harmful powers and work on man's behalf. They could be asked for guidance and for healing. They loved beautiful things and noble deeds, and these things could be dedicated to them. It is clear that religion was a social cement and an occasion for pious observance, celebration and public demonstrations of right living.

The myths about the gods set down by Homer and Hesiod and other poets and prose writers were, then, inherited stories that had for a long time provid-

ed a way of talking about human experience through enjoyable narratives. They dealt with supernatural experience, human emotion and the functions of the natural world in a poetic way, through the use of metaphor and allegory. Once they were set out in writing and organized into a commonly accepted system of belief, the myths provided a pattern for this belief,

139

a succession of examples. It was natural, as time went on, that this system should be challenged.

Some commentators on the myths write about a change in Greek thinking from *mythos* to *logos* between the seventh and the fourth centuries BC, to suggest a move from mythical thinking to a more rational explanation of the world. This was, however, a very slow and complex process and one that probably did not affect most people in ancient times. It is interesting to note that one of our best sources for the myths is Apollodorus, who did not set them out until the second century AD, when they were clearly still popular. There were, however, a number of individuals who struggled to find alternative ways to think about the world and how it was formed.

Among the earliest were a group who lived in Miletus in Ionia on the west coast of Asia Minor (now Turkey) at various times in the fifth century BC. Throughout the seventh and sixth centuries BC there had been a coming together in Ionia of knowledge about other cultures and this had led to the realization that both Eastern and Greek myths of creation had certain features in common, so some men began to feel that the basis of their own beliefs was probably purely conventional and that they might therefore be questioned.

Between the end of the sixth century and the beginning of the fifth, Heraclitus began to talk about one central force that directed nature, an intelligence 'that does and does not want to be called Zeus'. Thus he removed himself to some extent from the habitual dependence on thinking by means of concrete examples. Gradually the importance of argument for its own sake asserted itself, as evidenced by Plato's fourth-century accounts of Socrates's fifth-century dialogues. Plato objected to the mythical gods and heroes on moral grounds, but in his powerful literary style he created something very like myths of his own to express those things that cannot be said in ordinary speech.

Perhaps the complexity of these matters is best illustrated by the opening of Herodotus's Histories, which he calls his 'Researches', and which are often based on his own careful observation. These were written some time in the fifth century, and he begins with accounts of how certain peoples came into conflict, quoting as examples the clearly mythical stories of the abductions of Io, Europa, Medea and Helen. He then dismisses these accounts with 'So much for what Persians and Phoenicians say ... I prefer to rely on my own knowledge'. So he passes on to what he perceives as a historical account of King Croesus of

Lydia, which actually sounds similarly mythical to us.

It is important to remember that the heroic world presented by Homer represented the historical truth to its original audience, that his heroes were their forbears, and his gods their gods. His poetic works were taught in school to the children of aristocrats, many of whom would be the future rulers and magistrates of cities. It is difficult to overestimate the influence of his works on the ancient Greeks. It is also difficult to exaggerate the richness, detail and interconnectedness of the myths by his period.

CHAPTER THREE
THE BIRTH OF THE GODS

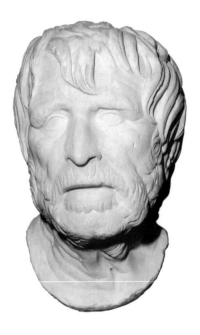

(British Museum)
Portrait bust of the poet Hesiod who wrote about the Creation of the Gods.

We are dependent upon writers who lived in or after the ninth or eighth centuries BC for our knowledge of ancient Greek myths and have to accept the fact that we cannot know who told these stories for the first time nor how they had changed over the centuries before the writers set them down. We can gain some idea of certain scenes and narrative events from the works of sculptors, engravers and painters, but we still have to refer such scenes back to written accounts to identify them with any certainty.

Surviving visual images and works of literature preserve comparatively few versions of the group of myths that concerns the beginning of things, the creation of the world and the gods. It is an unusual phenomenon, as in many cultures creation myths are both popular and important. The natural tendency of the Greeks seems to have been to shape their gods in as human and beautiful a form as possible, rather than in the inhuman or grotesque forms found in some other mythological systems. They also seemed indifferent to deities who were merely personifications of abstractions or of natural phenomena, and who did not make good stories.

Shortly after the heroic epics of Homer were written down in Ionia, a poet called Hesiod, from Boeotia on the mainland of Greece, wrote didactic epics, poems whose aim was to teach. One of these, written some time in the eighth century, is called Theogony, or the Creation of the Gods. It is actually also a cosmogony, for in it the poet recounts the story of the creation of the world as well as the birth of Zeus and 'the holy race of gods'. In this poem it seems likely that he collected up a number of myths on these subjects that were current in his day, some of them probably dating from centuries earlier and originating in different cultures; it is also likely that he made embellishments and additions of his own. Because it is the single most comprehensive text we have on the Greek creation myths, it is worth looking at it in some detail to provide an introduction to the subject.

Chaos was there at the beginning, says Hesiod; by Chaos he did not mean confusion but a kind of yawning void. Next came Gaia, or Ge (Earth), and Tartarus (a dark place below the earth) followed by Eros (Love). Then Night and Erebos (Darkness) came from Chaos; Night gave birth to Day and Ether (the air above us), having conceived them with Erebos through the power of Eros. After this, without the help of a mate, Earth produced Ouranos (Heaven) to be her equal and her comforter and to provide a home for the gods who would come later; then she gave birth to the mountains and the sea. She then mated with her self-created consort, Ouranos, and gave birth to Oceanus. The name Oceanus, or Ocean, did not imply the sea but the great river the Greeks imagined as perpetually eddying and circling round what they perceived as the flat disc of the known earth, and beyond which lay mysterious lands. From this union came other children also: Koios, Kreius, Iapetos, Hyperion, Theia, Rhea, Themis, Mnemosyne, Tethys, Phoebe and Kronos.

These children were known collectively as the

Titans and seem to be figures from an extremely remote past who feature very little in familiar Greek myths. The general view is that they perhaps represent distant memories of pre-Greek spirits of the natural forces exerted by the sky and the earth. Mnemosyne is, however, simply an abstract personification of Memory. We later discover that three males among the group of Titans – Kronos, Oceanus and Iapetos – mated with three females – Rhea, Tethys and Themis. Kronos and Rhea play an important part in later events.

Earth next gave birth to three monsters, the unpleasant but skilled and energetic Cyclopes, so-called because each had only one round eye set in the middle of his forehead, and to three unspeakable hundred-armed and fifty-headed sons, called Kottos, Gyes and Briareus. After this catalogue of births, the poem now springs into action. Ouranos hated the sons he and Gaia had created and hid them back inside her body. She suffered huge pangs as she

LEFT
(National Archaeological Museum, Athens) Bronze statue, 5th century BC, found in the sea off Cape Artemision, thought to be either Zeus holding his thunderbolt or Poseidon wielding his trident.

BELOW
Petra Tou Romiou: the rock on this shore in Cyprus marks the legendary birth place of the goddess Aphrodite when she rose from the sea. Her cult is thought to have arrived in Greece from Cyprus.

144

strained to eject them, and she devised a plan to free herself of the torment.

She shaped a mighty sickle and called upon her Titan sons to help her. The only one who volunteered was the youngest, Kronos. She hid Kronos, who waited until he saw Ouranos come to Gaia at night, stretching himself over and around her, in the way that Heaven always embraces Earth. At that moment Kronos moved; he cut off his father's genitals and threw them away from him. Drops of blood fell from them on to Earth and, as a result, a year later she gave birth to more children: the Erinyes (Furies), the Giants, and certain nymphs. Ouranos's severed genitals fell into the sea, where they floated for a long time, surrounded by white foam. From this foam emerged a beautiful girl who was carried on the foam first to Kythera and then to Cyprus, where she came to land. As she walked ashore grass sprang beneath her delicate feet. This was the goddess Aphrodite. Love and Desire followed her and became her constant companions.

Hesiod then gives the names of the children born to Night; some of them were simple abstrac-

tions, but among them were the Hesperides and the Destinies. Pontus (the Sea) fathered Nereus, a sea-god, who has become most familiar to us as the father of the Nereids, or sea nymphs. Another of the sons produced by the Sea and the Earth later married the daughter of Ocean and fathered Iris, the goddess of the rainbow, and the Harpies, female winged creatures who appear in various guises in different myths. Hesiod associates them primarily with the force of the wind, but we shall find them behaving like evil and aggressive birds elsewhere.

According to Hesiod, two of the children of the Sea and Earth married and produced the sisters called the Graiai (Grey Ones) and also the Gorgons, one of whom, Medusa, was mortal.

When Perseus killed Medusa, in a myth that will be recounted later in this book, two creatures sprang from her: the flying horse, Pegasus, and Chrysaor. Pegasus later flew up to live with the gods on Olympus, but Chrysaor fathered some monsters: Geryon (later killed by Heracles) and Echidna, half-woman and half-snake. She in turn produced monsters familiar to us through myths: Cerberus (the

(Terme Museum, Rome) Relief showing the birth of Aphrodite, who is being helped from the sea by two nymphs, c.460 BC. The relief forms the front of the so-called 'Ludovisi throne' which may be part of an altar. It was the work of a Greek sculptor and was found in Rome.

(Delphi Museum) Detail from a frieze showing the battle between the Gods and the Giants, from the north side of the Siphnian Treasury at the Sanctuary of Apollo at Delphi, 526-525 BC. The gods fight from the left of the illustration, as victors usually do in Greek representations of battles.

BELOW

(Berlin) Charon poles his ferry across the River Styx to carry a soul to the Underworld. The figure on the right is Hermes, who escorted souls to the Styx after death. These white-ground funerary vases were fairly common and were often filled with oil as grave offerings.

hound of Hades), the Hydra of Lerna (another victim of Heracles), the Chimaera who had the heads of a lion, a goat and a snake (killed by Bellerophon), the Sphinx (defeated by Oedipus) and the Nemean lion (also subdued by Heracles). Scholars suppose that these creatures have their origins outside Greece and may be oriental. In Greek myths, as we shall see, some are associated with the underworld. Most of them are perceived as being dangerous foreign creatures, in the sense that they live outside the natural order of things and threaten peaceful society; heroes have to destroy them in order to restore normality. They may once have been deities in distant countries, but they have been incorporated into Greek mythology as grotesque monsters.

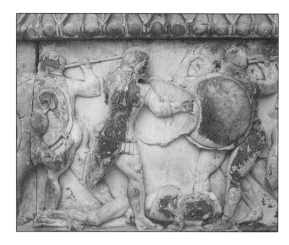

Hesiod next describes the children of Oceanus and his wife: they are all the rivers of the world and all the river nymphs, among them Styx, the river across which souls were ferried to the Underworld by Charon. Hesiod says Oceanus has so many roaring rivers among his sons that it is hard for mortal men to name them, 'but they are known to those who live nearby'. The phrase reminds us that all Greeks perceived their local streams and rivers as being sacred, however obscure they were.

The poem then describes the offspring of a number of the Titans, few of whom have an important place in popular mythology until we come to the children of the youngest son, Kronos, who forced a union with his sister Rhea. Their children were Hestia, Demeter, Hera, Hades, Poseidon and Zeus, who were to become major figures among the gods of Olympus. Kronos had learned from his parents, Ouranos and Gaia, that he would one day be overcome by one of his sons. Therefore, in a reversal of his father's action when he pushed his children back into their mother's womb Kronos swallowed each of his sons as he was born. Their mother, Rhea, suffered great grief, just as Gaia had suffered great physical pain. When Rhea was about to bring forth her last son, Zeus, she appealed to her parents, Ouranos and Gaia, to help her conceal the birth. They sent her to Crete, where Gaia agreed to nurture the child. When Zeus was born, at Lyktos on Crete, according to Hesiod, Rhea hid him appropriately, deep under the earth in a vast cave on Mount Aigaion. Meanwhile, Rhea took a giant stone, wrapped it in swaddling clothes and gave it to Kronos, who swallowed it down, assuming it was his last son.

The young Zeus grew quickly in strength and beauty. By some means Rhea persuaded Kronos to vomit up the children he had swallowed. The first to emerge was the stone, which had been swallowed last, and this was set at 'holy Pytho' (Delphi) in a cleft beneath Mount Parnassus, to be a wondrous

(Corfu Museum)
This relief on the pediment of a Temple of Artemis in Corfu, c.580 BC, shows Zeus striking a Titan during the great battle between the Gods and the Titans.

sign to men. Once his brothers had been freed from Kronos's stomach, Zeus returned and freed his uncles, the monster-like children of Ouranos, from the bonds with which Kronos, in envy of their strength, had earlier bound and imprisoned them. In binding the Cyclopes and the monsters, who were his brothers, Kronos had lost their allegiance forever.

War now broke out between the young gods and the Titans. The young gods based themselves on Mount Olympus and the Titans on Mount Othrys. The savage battle raged on for ten years; it blasted the earth with storms, earthquakes, floods and droughts. In an effort to end it, the Olympian gods fed the six monstrous brothers of Kronos with their own food of nectar and ambrosia and appealed to them for help. The Cyclopes, in gratitude for their freedom, gave Zeus the thunderbolt and lightning that became his characteristic weapons ever afterwards. Their three many-armed brothers used their strength to hurl huge rocks at the Titans. At last the Olympian gods and their allies defeated the Titans and imprisoned them in Tartarus, as far beneath the earth as heaven is above it.

In order to avenge the Titans, Gaia's brood of Giants revolted against the gods in another fierce struggle, known as the Gigantomachy, in which the mortal, Heracles, came to the help of the gods, who finally won the battle. Gaia then mated with Tartarus and, as her last child, bore mighty Typhoeus, a monster with a hundred dragon heads, which all breathed out fire so that the earth groaned and the sea boiled. Zeus attacked the monster with his thunderbolt and finally maimed and defeated him, hurling him down to Tartarus. This episode may, of course, recall memories of early, violent volcanic activity that certainly took place in the Aegean area.

As it can be seen, there are various puzzling inconsistencies in the story of the birth and succession of the gods and it is also uncharacteristically grotesque and savage. Many scholars suggest indeed that it includes stories from different cultures, and they find in the castration of Ouranos episode parallels with a Near-Eastern tale, extant in Hittite texts, but possibly spread by the Hurrites and originating in Babylon. Certain elements seem to come from nearer home. For example Gaia and Rhea, whose fertility is inexhaustible and who put care for their children above care for their husbands, seem to have a good deal in common with the female deities of Minoan Crete. Neither is it surprising to find that in this story

147

Zeus was born in a cave on a mountain in Crete, which was exactly the sort of place where cults had been practised since early times.

The Titans are difficult to explain since they figure so little in Greek mythology as a whole, apart from Kronos who ruled, in a myth at least as old as this one, over an innocent and happy golden age. The most common explanation is that they represent a poetic way of dealing with an earlier order of belief that gave way to a new one. The gods who defeated the Titans were the gods of current belief in Hesiod's day; in winning the war, they seized power, restructured belief and buried old ideas forever. The movement from one set of beliefs to another can be seen in action by the way in which the cult of Gaia, the earth goddess, gave way to that of Apollo, the Olympian god, at Delphi.

It is worth noting that Chaos, Gaia and Eros – the Void, the Earth and Love – were the first things to come into existence, and that there was no single divine principle that created everything. The gods who emerge as rulers in this story are, apart from Aphrodite, descended from Gaia, or the earth itself.

CHAPTER FOUR
THE GODS OF OLYMPUS

The Olympian gods make their presence felt throughout Greek literature. In the *Iliad* and the *Odyssey* Homer allows gods and goddesses to concern themselves with individual heroes and to favour one side rather than another in conflicts. More can be learnt about the gods from thirty-three poems that are known as Homeric Hymns or Preludes because they are written in a metre characteristic of Homer's epic verse, although they actually date from a number of different periods. The plays of the Classical period demonstrate the powerful influence of the gods on men and women, and there are accounts of the myths concerning the gods in a number of prose works dating from later than that.

Pictorial images of the gods alter with changes in contemporary artistic styles, but also in accordance with their varying popularity at different times and in different places. Some account will be given here of each of the Olympian gods, beginning with the greatest of them.

Mount Olympus, part of the highest mountain range in Greece, rising to 2917m (9570 ft), and the traditional home of the gods. It lies in the north of the country, on the borders of Thessaly and Macedonia.

ZEUS

Although the last-born of his brethren, he was always the first in importance. The root meaning of the early form of his name, Dies, (also found in Latin *dies* 'day'), is 'bright' or 'shining', and he was clearly associated with the sky. He parallels gods from other Indo-European speaking races, for example the Indian Dyaus and Roman Jupiter, who are also sky gods. Homer calls him 'father of gods and men', and this reflects the word pater, 'father', that is found in Sanskrit Dyaus-pitar.

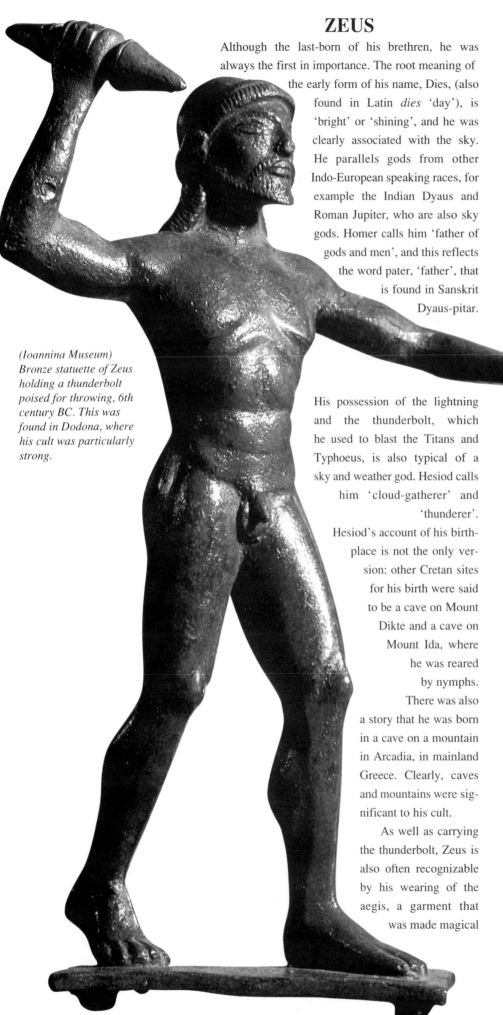

(Ioannina Museum)
Bronze statuette of Zeus holding a thunderbolt poised for throwing, 6th century BC. This was found in Dodona, where his cult was particularly strong.

His possession of the lightning and the thunderbolt, which he used to blast the Titans and Typhoeus, is also typical of a sky and weather god. Hesiod calls him 'cloud-gatherer' and 'thunderer'. Hesiod's account of his birthplace is not the only version: other Cretan sites for his birth were said to be a cave on Mount Dikte and a cave on Mount Ida, where he was reared by nymphs. There was also a story that he was born in a cave on a mountain in Arcadia, in mainland Greece. Clearly, caves and mountains were significant to his cult.

As well as carrying the thunderbolt, Zeus is also often recognizable by his wearing of the aegis, a garment that was made magical by his power. It is often shown as fringed, probably because it would originally have been a goat-skin, worn as a protection against bad weather, as they sometimes are by Greek shepherds today. The god often has an eagle with him, whose associations with the sky are obvious. The tree that was especially sacred to him was the oak, which once grew abundantly in Dodona where he was particularly worshipped, and which is, of all trees, most susceptible to lightning.

Once established as the chief of gods, Zeus lived in a palace on the highest peak of Olympus, as an early king would have lived on the summit of a hill. He was clearly conceived by people to whom rule by a king and a noble family was the natural order of things. He emerged from battle as permanent ruler of the world, since he was immortal, and he avoided the jealous fears of his predecessors by sharing his rule with his brothers and establishing his family around him.

Zeus and his brothers, Poseidon and Hades, agreed to hold Olympus and the earth in common, but cast lots for dominion over the sky, the sea and the underworld, dividing the three areas between themselves in a version of the system of inheritance we now know as partible that was common enough in antiquity, and indeed later. Zeus drew the sky as his portion, Poseidon the sea and Hades the underworld. For this reason, although Hades continued to be an immortal god, he seems never to have been thought of as an Olympian.

Zeus now turned his attention to women and to the extension of his family. The liaisons of the god are puzzling to us, and were objectionable to some people who worshipped him, because they break the normal customs of the time concerning monogamy and incest. It seems clear that they arose as a way of explaining two things. First, they brought the female deities of existing native cults into submission, or at least partnership, with the premier male deity of an invading people. Secondly, they are sometimes a purely allegorical way of explaining the god's acquisition of certain qualities. In any case, after a number of early marriages, Zeus settled down to a permanent marriage with one divine wife, straying thereafter to human mistresses in a manner that would have been found fairly normal and that will become clearer in the retelling of some of the myths.

The first wife chosen by Zeus was Metis, whose name means 'wisdom' or 'good advice'. He was advised that any son born of this union would over-

power him so, in an action reminiscent of his savage father, he swallowed his wife. Thus, allegorically, the god can be said to have swallowed wisdom, which was to be his innate quality thereafter. The story is more complex than that, however. Some time later Zeus suffered from a violent headache and Athena, his warrior daughter, sprang, fully armed, from his head. Vase-painters often illustrate this by showing Hephaestus assisting the birth by taking an axe to the head of Zeus. Here we can see the assimilation of an old cult to a new one. Athena seems to represent a goddess who had been worshipped in Greece at least since Mycenaean times and who therefore could not be born as a child from a newer god. By springing complete from her father's head, she remains herself and retains her importance, yet she is no longer supreme.

Zeus then married the Titan Themis, whose name means Custom or Law, and whose children were the Seasons and the Moirai (Fates). A similarly allegorical union with Eurynome, a daughter of Oceanus and Tethis, resulted in the birth of the Graces. He next married his powerful sister Demeter, an early divinity of grain and fruitfulness,

and their daughter was Kore, the Maiden, who is usually known as Persephone. The marriage of Zeus to Mnemosyne resulted in the birth of the nine Muses; thus the arts sprang from the union of divinity with memory. Two new Olympian gods resulted from Zeus's next union with the Titan Leto: the twins Artemis and Apollo became important members of the pantheon.

Finally, according to Hesiod, Zeus married Hera, who became his permanent, immortal wife. Homer, however, says that she was his first wife. She was also his sister, and in this and their marriage we may perhaps see a double attempt to rationalize the assimilation of the very powerful and well-established cult of Hera that had long been celebrated in the Argolid to the cult of the new chief god. Their children were Hebe and Eileithyia, representing youth and childbirth, and Ares, the rather blundering god of war. Without the help of any partner, Hera then gave birth to Hephaestus, the

god of metal-work and fine craftsmanship.

The Olympian pantheon now, therefore, consisted of Ouranos's daughter Aphrodite; Kronos's children: Hestia, Demeter, Hera, Hades, Poseidon and Zeus; Zeus's children: Athena, Artemis, Apollo, and Ares, and Hera's son Hephaestus. To these were later added Hermes, son of a liaison between Zeus and Maia (the daughter of Atlas, a Giant who had been sentenced eternally to support the earth on his shoulders), and Dionysus, the son of Semele, who is a mortal woman in Greek mythology, but was probably an adopted Phrygian earth-goddess. Busy, quiet Hestia, goddess of the hearth and home, seems gradually to have yielded her place in the ruling group to Dionysus. Hades remained in the Underworld but, with this exception, Zeus now had his complete family about him on Olympus.

Something should be said of the relationship between Zeus and humankind. It has already been seen that he was wise and that he controlled the weather, and thus the earth's fertility. He has an almost inexhaustible list of epithets, which suggest that he was perceived as being involved in every sphere of human activity. He was known, for example, as Zeus 'Polieus', that is 'of the city', and was thus the god of civic leaders as well as farmers. Above all, he was thought to rule with justice. When Greek thought began to move towards monotheism it moved towards his powerful figure as the principle god.

Nevertheless, Zeus had had problems with mankind. It is interesting that Hesiod, who relates these, does not say how mankind was created; men were simply present in his newly made world, although women were not. Among the children of Iapetos, the Titan, was Prometheus 'the foreseeing', who was permanently at odds with Zeus. There is a story, not told by Hesiod, that this demi-god made the first men out of clay figures, into which Athena breathed life. Zeus did not love the first men and, among other deprivations, took fire from them. Prometheus therefore stole fire from heaven and took it back to men in a dry fennel stalk. In doing this he angered Zeus once again.

A popular story, retold by Hesiod, explains that Prometheus had already angered Zeus by his decision about how a sacrificed animal should be shared between men and the gods. Having killed an ox, Prometheus butchered it, separating the meat from the bones and the fat. He parcelled up the bones and fat, reconstructing the animal by wrapping them in its skin; then he squeezed the meat into the animal's stomach and asked Zeus to choose between the two parcels. The god chose the attractive-looking bulky parcel, full of fat and bones, and was naturally angry. Most scholars think this tale is merely a comfortable rationalization of the fact that when the Greeks sacrificed an animal they were simply butchering it for food, and it made sense to offer the inedible parts to the gods, especially since the fat would send a savoury smell more speedily up to Olympus.

The creation of women formed part of Zeus's revenge for this action. He persuaded Hephaestus to form a female figure out of clay; she was dressed and given beauty, charm, guile and deceit by some of the other gods, and for this reason called Pandora, 'all gifts'. Zeus sent her to Prometheus's dull brother, who accepted her as a wife, despite warnings from Prometheus that he should accept nothing from the gods. From rash curiosity, she opened a closed and prohibited jar, and so set free its contents – all the evils and illnesses that have since plagued the human race; only Hope remained, under the lid of the jar. From Pandora descended women, who have ever

since been a torment to men, says Hesiod. This episode led to the terrible punishment of Prometheus by Zeus, from which he was released by Heracles, as we shall see. Once again, it seems likely that the story actually shows Zeus assimilating the power of an ancient god into his family; Prometheus perhaps represents the traces of an ancient fire-god, who was superseded by the Olympian god Hephaestus.

When Prometheus's son, Deucalion, married Pyrrha, Zeus sent a flood to destroy the human race, but Prometheus advised his son to build a wooden ark, in which he and Pyrrha survived the nine-day inundation. Deucalion made a sacrifice to Zeus for saving them and, pleased by this, Zeus showed them how to repopulate the earth by casting stones behind them, which then became men and women. This is clearly also an imported story, coming from a Middle-Eastern culture in which floods were important to agriculture, but it establishes the power of Zeus over the human race.

(Nicosia Museum) This early vase of the Mycenaean period, found in Cyprus, shows Zeus and Hera riding in a chariot, c.14th century BC.

153

POSEIDON

The brother of Zeus, is much less clearly defined in myths. He was primarily a sea-god, but was also associated with fresh water. He is usually shown carrying a trident that he sometimes used to release springs of water from the earth. His blows could also bring earthquakes of the kind that are still experienced in the area. He is usually presented as a violent and unruly deity.

Most of his children were also strong and violent, the Cyclops Polyphemus being a good example. Poseidon's constant enmity to Odysseus, described by Homer int the *Odyssey*, resulted from the maiming of Polyphemus by the hero. Poseidon also held a long grudge against the Trojans because the king of Troy did not pay him, as promised, for the strong walls he built round the city, and in the *Iliad* Homer shows how Poseidon supported the Achaian (Greek) side in the Trojan war.

Poseidon was also associated with horses, and sometimes called Poseidon Hippios (Poseidon of the Horse). In Arcadia, where both he and Demeter were worshipped as horse-headed deities, presumably in memory of some very ancient cult, there was a local story that she turned herself into a mare to escape his advances, but he then became a stallion and overcame her. One of the results of this union was Arion, a wonderful horse.

Another local story relates to Attica, land which both Athena and Poseidon wanted to rule. They held a contest in Athens, the chief city: Poseidon struck the rock of the Acropolis with his trident and produced a salt spring. Athena produced a growing olive tree, however, and was judged the winner.

DEMETER

Was the corn-goddess and the mother of Persephone. We know her story from the Homeric Hymn to Demeter. Demeter took her young daughter to Sicily to protect her from the attentions of Hades, the god of the Underworld, who wanted her as his wife. One day while Persephone was in the fields gathering flowers her attention was caught by one that was rare and fine. As she picked it, the earth opened and Hades drove out from beneath it in his chariot. He seized the girl and carried her off to his gloomy kingdom. Demeter was inconsolable at her loss and sought through the world for her daughter. Because she was the goddess of cereals and grains, while she was absorbed in her unhappy search famine struck the earth. When the sun told her that he had seen the abduction she was furious with the other gods for what they had allowed to happen. During her wanderings, she passed some time at Eleusis, where she was received hospitably and in return taught the rites that later became famous there.

Finally, Hades and Demeter were reconciled, and Persephone returned to the earth, although she had to live in the Underworld, in the house of Hades, for a third of each year because she had eaten some pomegranate seeds during her captivity there. Demeter then revived the earth's fertility. She chose Triptolemos, a son of the royal house of Eleusis, to take seeds and the skills of growing corn to the

places on earth where men did not yet know them. The importance of the story lies in its theme of the rebirth that follows death, the natural sequence of the seasons for an agricultural people, but a theme that was taken up on a different level in the Eleusinian Mysteries.

HERA

The wife of Zeus, was also his sister. She was chiefly seen as a goddess of women, in the role of bride and wife rather than mother. Perhaps for this reason, the children Zeus had with her are the least impressive of the gods. Hera had important early cults of her own, notably in Argos, and her chief significance to humans lay in her government of marriage. A number of local marriage rites, some involving wedding processions, were gradually associated with her marriage to Zeus. The fertile nature of their union is suggested by Homer in the *Iliad* when, as they make love on Mount Gargaron, the earth breaks lavishly into flower-embellished grass beneath them.

Myths about Hera are chiefly tales of her jealous

hounding of the women to whom her husband made love. She was also a relentless enemy of some of his love-children, particularly Heracles. Her vindictiveness pursued the Trojan, Paris, after he chose Aphrodite, not her, as the most beautiful goddess and she acted against his people during the Trojan war.

Some examples of her jealousy against the women impregnated by Zeus must suffice. When Leto was expecting Artemis and Apollo, Hera pursued her so vengefully that no country dared to take her in, until she was given shelter on the island of Delos. When Semele was pregnant with Dionysus, after visits by Zeus during which he had concealed himself, Hera advised her to make Zeus swear to grant her any wish and then to ask him to appear before her. He was thus obliged to do so, but the power of his divine presence and the lightning that accompanied it burnt everything in the room to ashes, except for the embryonic Dionysus.

When Zeus turned the pregnant Io into a cow to escape Hera's attentions, Hera first tethered her under the watchful gaze of many-eyed Argos and, when she escaped, pursued her through the world. There is a story that when Io reached Egypt she regained her human shape in order to give birth and that she then became the Egyptian goddess Isis. Io had been Hera's priestess and her story perhaps conceals a primitive reason for Hera's usual association with the cow, and with the peacock, whose tail is many-eyed like Argos.

ATHENA

Was a virgin goddess, uninterested in love. Her probable Mycenaean past is reflected in her warrior qualities, and she is usually shown with a spear and an aegis in the form of a shield that bears the Gorgon's head given to her by Perseus. When she sprang from her father's head, holding her spear, Olympus shook and a loud shout arose from the earth.

She was particularly associated with the city of Athens but it is not known which took the name from the other. There is a myth that helps to explain the connection. Hephaestus struggled to make love to Athena, and as she resisted him his sperm fell to the ground and fertilized the earth. Nine months later Erichthonius was born. Athena put the baby in a lidded casket, and gave him to the daughters of King Kekrops of Athens to care for, telling then not to open it. Two of them did so, however, and threw themselves over the Acropolis in terror at the serpents they saw inside. Athena then brought him up on the Acropolis herself and when he was an adult he

ABOVE
(British Museum) An early terracotta goddess from the Argolid, possibly representing Hera, 6th century BC.

LEFT
The Heraion of Argos. From early times Hera was the most popular deity throughout the Argolid. Her sanctuary, set above the fertile plain of Argos, reveals complex ruins on different levels. The site was first occupied in prehistoric times.

(National Archaeological Museum, Athens) Athena Promachos, the goddess in her manifestation as a warrior champion. Bronze statuette from the Acropolis in Athens, her home, c.500 BC.

became the king of Athens. This is a kind of myth that was frequently constructed to give legitimacy to an immigrant people's right to claim a particular city or state as their own. Greek names containing the element *chthon* are used to suggest that people are autochthonus or native to the place, that they sprang from the earth. In vase-paintings Erichthonius is sometimes shown with a serpent's tail, again suggesting that he came from the earth itself.

Athena was worshipped in her city for her introduction of the olive tree in the contest with Poseidon that has already been described. She has other qualities that make her an appropriate goddess for city-dwellers. She was a craftswoman, who was particularly skilled at spinning and weaving, as she demonstrated in her spinning contest with Arachne, who was turned into a spider for her temerity in challenging the goddess. It is claimed that she invented the flute, but threw it aside in disgust when she saw how ugly she looked as she played it. She was also interested in making chariots and warships, and she is said to have had a hand in building the ship called the Argo for Jason. Her popularity among the skilled vase-painters and boat-builders of Classical Athens is not surprising.

Athena's familiar creature is the owl. She is described as wise and as moral and righteous. Homer often refers to her shining grey eyes. She is sometimes known as Pallas Athene. Some people think this might be a reference back to the palladion or shield-shaped goddess of the Mycenaeans, others see in it the ghost of the story of her accidental killing of her friend Pallas, with whom she was brought up. Neither of these may be the reason. She was also often described as Promachos (Champion). For the same reason as Hera, she favoured the Greeks in the

Trojan war, but unlike Hera she was a friend to Heracles and dealt tenderly with Odysseus.

ARTEMIS

Was another virgin goddess, but of a very different kind. She was a young huntress who also defended wild game, particularly young creatures. Perhaps because of her interest in young things, women called upon her in childbirth. Her name is not Greek and, although she was Apollo's twin sister and born with him on Delos, they were not worshipped in the same places. Her connection with wild animals is reminiscent of the Cretan goddess, described in *Chapter Two*, in her manifestation as The Lady of the Animals.

She was attended by a number of young women who defended their virginity fiercely. Among them was Britomartis, who had a Cretan name and a Cretan story. It was said she was pursued by Minos and leaped off a cliff to avoid him, but was safely caught in some fishermen's nets and later went to live quietly in Aigina where she was worshipped as Aphaia, which means Invisible. Another follower of Artemis was Callisto, who was raped by Zeus who tricked her by disguising himself as Artemis. Artemis was so incensed when she noticed Callisto's pregnancy that, in spite of the girl's innocence, she turned her into a she-bear and sent her away.

These stories suggest that some of the followers of Artemis might once have been deities similar to Artemis herself. Anthropologists today see in her roaming band of young virgin followers indications of a rite of passage, when a group of girls of almost marriageable age live together for a time outside the constraints of normal society.

Artemis was implacable in the defence of her own honour, and of that of her family. Niobe, the

happy mother of many children, foolishly boasted of her superiority to Leto, whose only children were Artemis and Apollo. At this, Artemis and Apollo seized their arrows; Artemis killed all Niobe's daughters and Apollo all her sons. Niobe, whose tears would not cease, and who turned into a stone that still wept, has become a permanent image of maternal grief. Artemis was responsible for the death of some men too, notably Actaeon who, while he was hunting in the mountains, watched her and her nymphs as they bathed in a pool. She caused him to be torn to pieces by his own hounds.

She was much worshipped in wild, mountainous places and this accords with her untamed nature.

APHRODITE

The goddess of love, is by no means virginal. We have already recounted Hesiod's story of her birth, but there is another. In this version Zeus was married to Dione, whose name is the feminine form of Zeus, and Aphrodite was their daughter. Homer also describes her as the daughter of Zeus. It seems likely that

Hesiod was reflecting the way in which eastern myths were slowly adapted to Greek ways of thought, for Aphrodite seems certainly to be eastern in origin, entering Greece from the islands of Kythera and Cyprus, where her cult was particularly strong at Paphos. Scholars see in her parallels with Sumerian, Akkadian and Canaanite love goddesses.

In the way of powerful goddesses, she had a comparatively insignificant husband, the lame metalworking god Hephaestus, who probably also originated in the east. She fell in love, however, with Ares, the war god. Hephaestus, who was a cunning craftsman, contrived a strong and fine-meshed net with which he entrapped them in the act of love and displayed them to the other, laughing gods.

Another of her adulterous unions was with a mortal, Anchises, who was the cousin of Priam of Troy. The son she bore from this union was Aeneas, who grew up to become a hero and the leader of the Trojan people after their expulsion from Troy. He eventually founded another city, which was later claimed to be the precursor of Rome. It was quite usual for great

heroes to have one divine parent.

The most powerful myth about Aphrodite probably followed her from the east and tells of her love for Adonis. This is thought to be a version of the eastern myth of the great mother and her divine lover, which was also probably current in Minoan Crete. The story begins when Aphrodite caused a young princess to fall in love with her father and deceived him into making love to her under cover of darkness. When he discovered what he had done and threatened to kill his daughter, the gods turned her into a tree called by her name, Myrrh. In time, a beautiful boy was born from the tree. He was named Adonis, and because he had no mother he was given a choice of guardian. He chose Aphrodite, but was allowed to spend only two thirds of the year with her, being sent to spend the remaining months with Persephone in the Underworld. Adonis was killed by a boar when he was hunting, and flowers sprang from his blood. His myth can be compared with the Babylonian story of Tammuz, who was also a god who disappeared for part of the year and whose reappearance coincided

with the return of fertility. The seasonal festival marking the coming of winter, when women mourned for the death of Adonis, continued in Greece into historical times.

APOLLO

Was one of the most important gods, and his qualities and characteristics continued to be developed by writers right through to Classical times, when they were particularly appreciated. He was the god of music and poetry and of all kinds of inspired arts. He had some ability to heal, having probably assimilated the role of an earlier healing deity. He was also sometimes an aggressive archer, particularly in concert with his sister, Artemis. He is usually shown with a lyre and a bow, and sometimes with the birds that were particularly associated with him – swans, kites, vultures, and the crows used by seers as omens. In late periods he was sometimes identified with the sun, but this is not part of his early mythology.

He was close to Zeus and because he knew his father's will he was highly regarded as a prophet. The playwright Aeschylus, in the *Eumenides*, makes him say: 'I never lie. In my role as prophet I have never made a statement concerning man, woman or city that was not prompted by Zeus.' That play also demonstrates his highly developed morality as he pleads for mercy rather than vengeance for Orestes, who is on trial before the gods.

The birth of Apollo and Artemis on the island of Delos has already been mentioned. That story may have originated in a desire to account for the otherwise surprising fact that the Ionian cities chose to meet regularly on that small, rocky island for the Panionian festival, and Apollo had an important sanctuary there. His most famous sanctuary was, however, the one at Delphi. The story goes that he went to Delphi shortly after his birth and there slew a female serpent called Python, the terrible guardian of the place, so that he could establish himself there. Since it seems likely that there had long been a shrine to an earth goddess there, her representation as a serpent, who comes from the earth, and Apollo's defeat of her both serve to explain how an early cult was ousted by a later one.

The Terrace of the Lions, 7th century BC, on the Island of Delos, leading to the precinct of Leto, whose cult was observed on the island and who is said to have clung to a palm tree there as she gave birth to Apollo and Artemis. Delos is the smallest of the Cyclades but was once a religious centre of the Aegean. Its oracle was next in importance to that of Delphi, and there was a great temple to Apollo there.

He is usually represented as a beautiful young man. Like the other gods, he pursued mortal women, but the women often met disastrous fates. Daphne, fleeing from his advances, turned into the laurel tree that bears her name. Marpessa, given the choice between Apollo and an insignificant human husband, chose the latter because he would age along with her, unlike an immortal god, and so be less likely to leave her as her youth vanished. Apollo attempted to seduce Cassandra of Troy by teaching her the skills of prophecy, but when she still refused him he modified the gift, which he could not withdraw, by making sure that no one would ever believe her prophecies, in spite of their truth.

Apollo loved Koronis, another mortal, but she deceived him with a human lover. When a crow, which was then a white bird, told him of this, Apollo shot Koronis with his bow and, in grief at his loss, turned the crow black. This story had a good outcome, however, for Apollo saved the child Koronis was bearing, and sent him to the Centaur, Cheiron, to be brought up. Cheiron was the greatest and gentlest of the Centaurs, creatures who were half-man and half-horse, and he educated a number of famous heroes. He was very successful in teaching Apollo's child, Asclepius, the arts of healing. The success of Asclepius in bringing dying men back to life disturbed Zeus, who sent him down to Hades with a thunderbolt.

Apollo, in his anger at this, killed the Cyclops who had made the thunderbolt. For this crime, Apollo was banished from Olympus for a year and sent to be serf to a mortal king, whose cattle flourished under his divine care. Happily, Asclepius raised himself from the dead, and later took his place among the immortal gods.

When Apollo fell in love with Cyrene, he took her in a chariot to Africa, to the land that was named after her. There she gave birth to Aristaeus, who later became a deity of such rural occupations as bee-keeping, hunting and olive-growing. As well as other affairs with women, Apollo was also attracted to young men, such as Hyacinthus, whom he killed acci-

dentally with a discus, and who became the flower of that name. This incident might well represent the assimilation into Apollo's worship of an earlier young and beautiful god.

It was said that Apollo was a Hyperborean, that he came from a land beyond the north wind, and it seems likely that this deity actually arrived in Greece from the north. An annual ritual procession at Delphi always moved northwards, as though towards the land from which the god had come. It was said also that in the winter he handed the sanctuary over to Dionysus and withdrew to the blessed lands of the Hyperboreans, where the climate was always moderate, the crops good and the people just and happy.

(Epidauros Museum) Statue of Asclepius with a sacred serpent found at the sanctuary at Epidauros that was earlier sacred to his father, Apollo. As the healing cult of Asclepius grew more popular at Epidauros, he was said to have been born there.

HERMES

Was the younger brother of Apollo, and is usually shown by later artists as young. He often wears winged shoes, carries a golden staff and wears a hat, which is sometimes shown with the kind of broad brim that would keep the sun off a traveller's face. The Homeric Hymn to Hermes has a light tone, characteristic of this god. He was a native of Greece; his parents were Zeus and a nymph called Maia and he was both conceived and born in his mother's home, a cave on Mount Cyllene in Arcadia.

On the day of his birth he walked to the entrance of the cave, where he found a tortoise. He killed it and used its shell to construct a lyre, the first ever made. Then he took a long walk to Pieria, where he stole a herd of cattle that his brother, Apollo, was meant to be watching. Crafty Hermes made shoes for the feet of the cattle and drove them backwards to his cave, to confuse anyone looking for them. On the way home, he slaughtered two of them as a ritual sacrifice to the gods. He then returned to his cradle and played the part of an innocent baby.

In spite of his youth, he was summoned before Zeus, who ordered him to restore the cattle, which he did, together with Apollo's bow and quiver, which he had also appropriated. He soothed Apollo by giving him the lyre he had made, and in return Apollo gave him the golden staff he had used for driving cattle and also some lessons in minor divination. The incident is typical of Hermes, who did not share the moral grandeur of his brother, and who became patron of traders and thieves and all those who turn an honest or dishonest penny.

His chief function was to be herald, or messenger, to the gods. This task seems to have been based on his earlier experience as protector of travellers and god of roads and pathways. In his manifestation as Hermes Psychopompous, he also accompanied the dead to Hades. His name is similar to the Greek word used for heaps of stones that were used in the rocky country landscape to mark holy places and boundaries. He was a popular god, frequently worshipped, particularly by young athletes. At places of his worship people set up *herms*, simple pillars or stones that could be set up anywhere; these were often marked only by being topped by the representation of a human head and having male genitalia at an appropriate level.

Hermes is sometimes credited with fathering Pan, the rustic divinity, half-man and half-goat, who was the shepherd's god and who played the pipes, chased nymphs and grew ferociously bad-tempered if his afternoon rest was disturbed.

DIONYSUS

Was undoubtedly a foreign god. He was clearly felt to be a late arrival into the Pantheon, and may not have been absorbed into the system until sometime after 1000 BC. There are many myths about him, and the same myths have a variety of versions, as different writers and artists modified the narrative to suit their own purposes. Many of the myths concern the disasters that befell people who showed resistance to him or his cult, and it is possible that these reflect actual civic opposition to the spread of the cult, as well as individual doubts about the nature of the worship of Dionysus.

His birth has been touched on already. His mother was Semele, the daughter of Cadmus, King of Thebes, and his wife, Harmonia, who was the

ABOVE
(British Museum) Terracotta of Dionysus from Tanagra holding a cockerel and an egg, both symbols of rebirth, c.370 BC.

OPPOSITE
(National Archaeological Museum, Florence) Detail of the François Vase (called after its finder), painted by Kleitias in Athens (c.570 BC). It shows Hermes carrying the herald's staff and wearing his broad-brimmed traveller's hat.

daughter of a god. Semele's name is very close to that of a Phrygian earth goddess. It was in Thebes, however, that Semele was scorched to death by the visit from Zeus that Hera had persuaded her to request. Zeus took the embryo of his child from Semele's womb and stitched it into his thigh.

When Dionysus came to term and was born, Hermes took him to be nursed by Semele's sister, Ino, who was married to Athamas, King of Orchomenos. As a result of Hera's implacable pursuit of those who cared for her husband's love children, Athamas and Ino were driven mad; they killed their own children and Ino threw herself into the sea from a cliff-top. Dionysus was then given to the nymphs of Mount Nysa, who nursed him as a child and later became part of the group of followers who always accompanied him.

Once he had grown up, Dionysus somehow discovered the art of wine-making, which became one of his important attributes. This also enraged Hera, who sent him mad and caused him to wander for a long time through foreign lands such as Egypt, Syria and Phrygia. He was restored to sanity, some say by Rhea the mother goddess, who also taught him some of her mysteries. He then returned to Thrace.

This was the beginning of the god's travels through Greece and a number of hostile and violent encounters with his hosts. Euripides gives the most moving account of one of these in his play the *Bacchae*. When Dionysus returned to his birthplace, Thebes, the ageing former king Cadmus had given up his rule to his daughter Agaue's son, Pentheus. Pentheus was hostile to Dionysus and appalled by the behaviour of the women of his city, including his own mother and aunts, who left their homes and were 'gadding about' the slopes of Mount Cithaeron 'dancing in honour of this upstart god Dionysus.' Pretending to be a traveller, Dionysus advised Pentheus to disguise himself as a woman in order to see what they did on the mountain and put a stop to it. The women saw through the disguise and, in their wild frenzy, tore Pentheus apart. His mother Agaue lead the ferocious attack, and she did not discover the horror of what she had done until she recovered from her frenzy some time later and saw that the thing she was holding in her hands, which she had thought was a lion's head, was actually the head of her son. Euripides makes Cadmus reflect: 'If any man derides the unseen world, let him ponder the death of Pentheus, and believe in gods.'

When Dionysus arrived in Argos, the women wandered through the wild landscape and, in their possessed state, ate the flesh of their own children.

At Tiryns, the daughters of the king were hostile to the cult; they were punished by a frenzy which made them wander all over the mountainous country of the Peloponnese.

Dionysus also visited the islands and, in one version of a fairly common story about his sea journeys, he was captured by pirates. They found it impossible to keep him tied up, and the pilot of the ship realized that he was a god. The other men paid him no heed, however, and as the ship journeyed on, a vine grew from the mast, the ship ran with wine and their passenger turned into a lion. All except the pilot jumped over the side, where they were turned into dolphins.

Even the kindlier actions of the god resulted in distress. When he visited Attica, he was received with great kindness by a local ruler called Icarius. In return, Dionysus gave Icarius the gift of wine, which he shared with his people. When they felt the strange effects of this new drink, however, they imagined that they had been poisoned and killed Icarius, whose daughter then hanged herself for grief.

The cult spread, nevertheless, but its practices were clearly very different from normal civic, well-regulated processions and offerings made by the male heads of households. Something has already been said about the development of this cult in *Chapter Two*. The celebrants drank wine and, apparently, ate raw flesh in order to assimilate the god into themselves and they danced themselves into an ecstatic state. Dionysus is usually accompanied by a trail of women followers, the Bacchantes, together with a collection of obviously sexually active young satyrs, and usually at least one elderly, bloated, drink-sodden Silenus.

ARES

The god of war, is perhaps the least developed of the whole Pantheon, probably because Athena was a much more skilful fighter and he was, in a sense, unnecessary. Although a god, Ares was actually wounded on a number of occasions, by Heracles and by Diomedes. He is shown as crudely violent and not popular with the other gods, apart from Aphrodite. He had some affairs with mortal women, but most of his children were unpleasant and violent. He is usually shown dressed in armour and helmet, and carrying a shield, spear and sword.

HEPHAESTUS

Was the son only of Hera, according to Hesiod, but of Hera and Zeus according to Homer. This may suggest a reworking of the myth by Hesiod's day to account for the decreasing importance of this god.

169

(National Archaeological Museum, Florence) Detail from the François Vase, c.570 BC. Hephaestus rides to Olympus on a mule. Dionysus had made him drunk as the only way of persuading him to go home and free Hera from the throne in which he had imprisoned her. A Silenus, one of the drunken followers of Dionysus, follows him. Hephaestus's lameness is indicated by his feet that point in opposite directions.

He is connected with fire, with metals and metal-working, and he ruled over the volcanoes that were his workshops, where, it is said, the Cyclopes assisted him. It seems likely that he came originally from outside Greece, from Lemnos or one of the islands near it, for in early times Mediterranean people were better metal-workers than the Greeks.

His myths connect him with Lemnos because they say that on one occasion he crashed to land there and damaged his leg when he had been hurled from the heavens and spent a whole day falling through the air. Other writers say that he was congenitally lame, and history tells us that working at a forge was a more appropriate occupation than agriculture for lame men.

His skill was consummate. It was because of Hera that he had been thrown from Olympus and, in revenge, he constructed a wonderful throne for her, which closed about her when she sat on it. The gods could not free Hera, so Dionysus was sent to get Hephaestus drunk enough to be brought on a mule to release her. He also made the strong web that he used to trap his wife and Ares as they made love. It was he who constructed the first woman, Pandora, from clay, and he made the chains that fastened Prometheus to a rock in the Caucasus so that Zeus could punish him. Achilles' wonderful armour was also the work of Hephaestus and he used flame as a weapon in the Trojan war.

HESTIA

The sister of Zeus, has a name that means simply Holy Hearth. The hearth was the centre of the house or palace, providing heat, light and warm food. There are no myths about Hestia because she was a virgin aunt who stayed at home and looked after everyone else. Yet because her cult was a family cult it was important to ordinary people.

CHAPTER FIVE
THE HEROES

Just as different regions of Greece had their own cults, so they also had their own heroes, some of whom were claimed as ancestors of important regional families. The adventures of these heroes were gradually woven into a rich and complex pan-Hellenic pattern in which they entered one another's stories and made connections between ruling families; if a thread is pulled from one of these myths it unravels several others at the same time. The gods themselves participated in the lives of the heroes, sometimes even in their parentage in the case of the demi-gods who had one divine parent.

The areas from which the best-known of these myths spring are Argolis, the area once ruled from the great Mycenaean palaces; Boeotia, whose chief city was Thebes; Thessaly, further north, and later Attica, whose chief city was Athens. Myths about the tragic fate of the ruling families of Argolis and Thebes will be recounted in a later chapter, as will the exploits of the heroes of the Trojan war. Here we shall be concerned with those regional heroes whose parentage was sometimes ambiguous and who, as young men, were forced by circumstances to leave their homes and to go on quests that led them to encounters with dangerous, even monstrous, enemies. In the course of their adventures they discovered their true identity, and usually found a wife and even a kingdom.

Their stories were sufficiently interesting to become part of the common stock of Greek myths that would have been well known to everyone. Because of this shared cultural inheritance, there was no need for poets always to recount the myths in detail; they could simply refer to them to make a point. Vase-painters could conjure up a whole narrative by painting one scene from it. Similarly, after the Greeks had defeated a mighty Persian force, a sculptured *metope* was made for the Parthenon depicting the mythical battle between the Lapiths and the Centaurs; this celebrated the notion of victory by indigenous people over powerful intruders by alluding to a story that everyone would have recognized, without having to make a direct triumphal boast that might have offended the gods.

Myths were a way of talking about experience and of presenting a picture of the past, not as it actually had been but as a construct that could be shared as a reference point. They are enjoyable stories, but they can also be used to instruct, to explain why things are as they are and why society operates in the way that it does, to account for place names and give authority to the foundation of cities, to examine man's relationship with the gods and the results of his moral choices, and to explore the lengths to which heroic men can go – to the extent of having to cross the border between the living and the dead on some occasions.

The myths are set in the past, but not in any recognizable time. The heroes are part of a society that is ruled by kings, and they themselves are young warriors, although they have sometimes become kings by the end of their story. They belong in the period Hesiod describes as the fourth age of man. He sets out five ages of man: in the first a golden race lived in happy, healthy prosperity; in the second a silver race lived only until they were hidden away by Zeus as spirits of the Underworld because they injured each other and neglected the gods. In the third age a race of bronze lived, worse than the one before, great warriors who died by their own hands and went to Hades.

The fourth age is the one that concerns us. Then there was a race of god-like heroes. Some were killed in battle and lie beneath the earth, but others have been rewarded with a carefree life in the Blessed Isles. Hesiod laments that he lives in the fifth age, in a race of iron whose men praise the bad and despise the just and good. Our predecessors, who still had contact with the gods, established a world we have spoiled.

The myths about the heroes have certain narrative patterns that have made some people compare them with folk-tales, but they have proved capable of bearing more layers of interpretation at different periods than folk-tales have. Nevertheless, certain motifs recur in many of them: heroes are often unaware of their true parentage or are disappointed of an inheritance; they are given advice by an oracle that they misinterpret; they make rash boasts, are punished for impiety, go on quests, succeed in

impossible tasks that were intended to kill them, defeat violent enemies through strength or trickery; they often win a wife as a reward, kill a loved one by accident, inherit a kingdom and so on. They all travel, and by that means they gather up other stories into their own. The stories of five heroes will be recounted here; they are Perseus, Bellerophon, Heracles, Theseus and Jason.

PERSEUS

Was the son of Zeus and a mortal woman and was conceived in a strange fashion. A king of Sparta, Akrisios, had only one child, a beautiful daughter called Danaë. He longed for a son, but when he consulted an oracle he was told that, although he would have no more children, his daughter would have a son who would kill him. To avoid this outcome, he locked his daughter away, some say in an underground chamber of bronze, others say in a tall tower. Yet in spite of her father's care, Zeus found his way into Danaë's room in the form of liquid gold, which poured into her lap, and from which she conceived Perseus.

Fearing the consequences for himself of the birth of a grandson, Akrisios put Danaë and the baby into a wooden chest, which he abandoned to the sea.

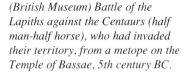

(British Museum) Battle of the Lapiths against the Centaurs (half man-half horse), who had invaded their territory, from a metope on the Temple of Bassae, 5th century BC.

172

They survived, however, and came to land on the island of Seriphos, where they were found by an honest fisherman called Dictys, who was the brother of Polydectes, king of the island. Dictys cared for them until Perseus was a young man. By that time Polydectes wanted Danaë for himself, and considered how to rid himself of Perseus, her young son and protector. When Perseus boasted that he could bring Polydectes the head of the Gorgon, Medusa, the king took him at his word and sent him to get it.

There were three Gorgons, of whom only Medusa was mortal. They were creatures with snaky hair, teeth like boars' tusks, bronze claws and golden wings. Anyone who looked directly into the face of a Gorgon was turned instantly to stone. They had three sisters called the Graiai, women who were born old and who shared one eye and one tooth between them. Athena and Hermes decided to help Perseus on his difficult quest, so they led him to the Graiai. Perseus held the sisters to ransom by stealing their eye and their tooth until they told him the way to some nymphs who could help him further. Perseus returned the eye and the tooth and went to the nymphs, who gave him three gifts: winged sandals that would enable him to fly, a helmet that would make him invisible and a pouch into which he should put the head of the Gorgon once he had cut it off. Hermes gave him a sharp knife.

Thus equipped, Perseus flew across the sea to find Medusa. When he arrived, Athena gave him a bronze shield that shone so brightly it acted as a mirror. The Gorgons were sleeping and Perseus approached Medusa, holding the shield before him so that he looked at her reflection, not her face, as he cut off her head. As soon as he had done it, two crea-

tures sprang from Medusa's body. One was Pegasus, a winged horse, whose seed had been placed in Medusa by Poseidon; the other was a monster called Chrysaor, who was to become the father of the three-headed monster Geryon whom Heracles later dispatched. Perseus saved himself by putting on his helmet of invisibility; then he took off over the sea in his winged sandals, carrying the Gorgon's head in the pouch he had been given.

As he flew over a lonely Ethiopian shore he saw a solitary young woman bound to a rock. He went to her help, and found that she was Andromeda, a princess of Ethiopia. She was there because her mother, Cassiopeia, had foolishly boasted that she was more beautiful than the Nereids, the sea-nymphs, and Poseidon had sent a sea-monster to punish the King and his people for his wife's impiety. The monster would ravage the country unless the king left his daughter tied up on the shore as a sacrifice to it. Perseus slew the monster and rescued Andromeda. The king then gave her to Perseus in marriage as a reward.

Perseus and Andromeda returned to Seriphos, where they found that his mother had had to take refuge with Dictys in order to escape the unwanted attentions of Polydectes. Perseus went to the king's palace, where he stood before the assembled court and, looking aside, held up the Gorgon's head. Polydectes and his companions were turned to stone and Perseus handed over the kingdom to Dictys. He later gave the Gorgon's head to Athena, who placed it on her shield.

On his return journey with his bride to Argos, his birth-place, Perseus stopped to take part in the athletic games at Larissa. Meanwhile, his grandfa-

ABOVE LEFT
(National Archaeological Museum, Palermo) Greek gold plaque showing a Gorgon in a typical running posture, from Sicily, 6th-7th century BC.

ABOVE
(Louvre Museum) Relief amphora from Boeotia, c.660 BC, shows Perseus beheading the Gorgon, Medusa, with the knife Hermes gave him; he wears his hat of invisibility and his magic sandals and carries a bag in which to put the head. Perseus turns his head away from Medusa in order to avoid being turned to stone. In this early representation, Medusa has the body of a horse, probably because her father was Poseidon and she would give birth to the winged horse, Pegasus, as she died.

ABOVE
(National Archaeological Museum, Palermo) On this metope from a temple at Selinunte, Perseus beheads Medusa, who is holding the winged horse, Pegasus, to which she has just given birth. Athena, who assisted Perseus in the enterprise, stands by, c.530 BC.

OPPOSITE
(British Museum) Bellerophon, holding the reins of the winged horse, Pegasus, is here incised on an Etruscan cista, or cylindrical box, c.300 BC. When Greeks colonized parts of central Italy in the 8th century BC they had a profound influence on Etruscan art, which already benefited from rich resources of metal.

ther, King Akrisios of Argos, having heard that Perseus was returning home, fled from Argos, fearful of the prophecy that his grandson would kill him. Ironically, he too chose to go the games at Larissa, where the prophecy was fulfilled when a discus thrown by Perseus killed him accidentally. Perseus was so distressed that he could not bring himself to return to his newly-inherited kingdom of Argos, but exchanged it instead for Tiryns, which is why his descendants, including Heracles, ruled there.

BELLEROPHON

The myth of Bellerophon has similarities to that of Perseus, and tells more about the horse Pegasus. Bellerophon repeatedly dreamed that he was trying unsuccessfully to capture a wonderful winged horse. At last, Athena appeared in his dream, offering him a golden bridle. When he awoke he found he actually had the bridle in his hands so he went to the spring at Peirene, where he had seen the horse, and captured it with ease. The horse helped him to success in many of his later adventures.

Bellerophon lived for a time with King Proitos of Argos, until Proitos's wife tried to seduce him. When Bellerophon refused her, she claimed he had assaulted her, so Proitos sent him to Iobates, the king of Lydia, with a sealed letter instructing that the bearer of the letter should be killed. Iobates therefore sent Bellerophon to fight the Chimaera, a fierce, fire-breathing monster that was shaped like a lion, a dragon and a goat. Bellerophon succeeded in killing the Chimaera and Iobates gave him his daughter and half his kingdom.

After a number of other successful heroic expeditions, Bellerophon succumbed to pride, and tried to ride Pegasus to the gods on Olympus. The horse threw him to earth and went on alone. Bellerophon, injured in the fall, spent the rest of his life as a solitary wanderer, hated by gods and men.

HERACLES

(Hercules in Latin) is the most important of the adventuring heroes, and was probably the most popular of them in the ancient world. He seems to have originated at least as early as the Mycenaean period, and perhaps earlier, but additions were made to his story over the centuries. The incident of his assumption to Olympus as a god after his death might have been added in about the seventh century BC. He is a hero of conflicting qualities; he has the strength, appetites and unthinking brutality of wild nature and is subject to occasional fits of madness, but he can also show a desire to right wrongs and perpetuate civilized ideals. He had strong links with the

(British Museum) Bellerophon, mounted on Pegasus, kills the monster Chimaera, here shown as part-lion, part-goat. Terracotta relief from Melos, probably used as a hanging decoration, c.475-450 BC.

Centaurs, who were themselves ambiguous creatures, and he actually entered the Underworld yet came back to earth. To add to this, he was also sometimes the butt of jokes.

Heracles has local connections with both Argolis and Boeotia. He was born in Thebes in Boeotia, but his stepfather, Amphitryon, was actually a prince of Tiryns who was temporarily exiled in Thebes. The consummation of Amphitryon's marriage to his wife, Alcmena, was delayed until his return from an urgent military expedition. Zeus also admired Alcmena and, on the night of Amphitryon's return, disguised himself as her husband and lay with her first. When Amphitryon arrived, his suspicions were aroused by Alcmena's knowledge of his recent campaign, which she had gained from the disguised Zeus. He had his wife placed on a funeral pyre, but Zeus created a downpour to quench the flames, at

which Amphitryon understood and forgave her. As a result of the two unions, Alcmena had twin sons: Heracles, the son of Zeus, and Iphicles, the son of Amphitryon, who was nevertheless descended from Perseus and therefore, indirectly, from Zeus.

Zeus had unwisely prophesied that the next-born descendant of Perseus would rule over other leaders. Hearing this, Hera determined that it would not be Alcmena's son by Zeus. She therefore sent her daughter, Eileithyia, the goddess of childbirth, to delay the birth of Heracles and hasten the birth of another child who was descended from Perseus. This was Eurystheus, who was born at seven months. He grew up to be the king of Mycenae, whom Heracles later had to serve. Ironically, Hera's name is preserved in that of Heracles, which means Fame or Glory of Hera.

Heracles showed the great powers of a demi-god

as a baby when Hera, in her jealous rage, sent two enormous snakes to his cradle. Heracles woke up and strangled them both, thus also saving the life of his brother Iphicles. Iphicles' son, Iolas, became a devoted companion to Heracles on some of his later adventures.

When Heracles was eighteen he killed a fierce lion that was roaming on Mount Cithaeron. The ruler of the region gave him great hospitality in gratitude. Heracles is said to have slept with his fifty daughters either all in one night or on fifty consecutive nights. On his return journey to Thebes, Heracles met messengers from the King of Orchomenos who were coming to collect the tribute due to Orchomenos from Thebes. He cut off their noses and ears and tied them round their necks. In the ensuing retaliatory war, Thebes defeated Orchomenos and received tribute in its turn.

In gratitude for his valour during the war, the king of Thebes gave Heracles his daughter, Megara, as his wife. They had children and lived happily together until Hera, ever vengeful, struck him with a fit of madness that caused him to kill all his family. Polluted by this deed, Heracles had to leave Thebes, go to Mycenae and submit himself to King Eurystheus for twelve years. During this time Eurystheus gave him twelve labours or tests that he had to complete.

The Nemean Lion. His first task was to bring back the skin of the Nemean lion, a skin that could not be pierced by weapons. Heracles choked the lion in his strong arms, then used its own claws to skin it, and returned to the city with the skin slung across his shoulders. Because of this, he is usually shown wearing a lion skin as well as carrying a club.

The Hydra of Lerna. He was next sent to Lerna to destroy the Hydra, a many-headed water monster that lived in a swamp. It often ventured on to dry land and destroyed crops and animals in the surrounding region. Every time Heracles cut off one of its heads with his bronze knife, two new ones replaced it, and while he was struggling with it Hera sent a large crab to bite his legs. Eventually his nephew, Iolas, scorched the stumps with a flaming

(National Archaeological Museum, Athens) Heracles fights the Nemean Lion, the first of the twelve labours imposed upon him by Eurystheus.

torch as Heracles cut off the heads, until he had cut off the last head and buried it. Before he left, Heracles dipped his arrows in the bile of the Hydra so that they would inflict deadly wounds.

The Erymanthian Boar. Then he had to capture and bring back alive a huge boar that ranged over Mount Erymanthos and devastated local crops and herds. He travelled further from home on this quest and, as he was on his way to the mountain, he was offered hospitality by a Centaur called Pholos. Centaurs, who were four-legged creatures, with a man's head, shoulders, arms and torso and the long back and hindquarters of a horse, seem to have been either very rational, humane creatures, or very wild and vicious ones, rather as Heracles himself combined a desire to do right with wild and violent behaviour.

Pholos was sensitive enough to Heracles' needs to roast meat for him, although he ate it raw himself. He had a large jar of wine, which Heracles urged him to open. The other Centaurs were drawn to the wine by its smell and threatened violence to get it. After fighting them off, Heracles chased the survivors to Cape Malea, where they sought refuge with the great, humane Centaur, Cheiron, who lived there alone. In earlier times he had nurtured and educated Asclepius, Achilles, Aristaeus and Jason. As Heracles shot at the fleeing Centaurs, he accidentally wounded Cheiron with one of his poisoned arrows. Although he was immortal and could not die, Cheiron was in great pain and Heracles was able to release him from his suffering only by arranging that he should be allowed to go to Hades in exchange for Prometheus, which is another story.

Heracles continued his search for the boar, which he cornered in a snow-drift. He caught it in a noose, then tied it up and carried it on his shoulders to Eurystheus, who took refuge in a large bronze jar as soon as he saw it.

The Ceryneian Hind. This was a marvellous creature, sacred to Artemis according to some sources, that had golden antlers. It moved swiftly and Heracles spent a year pursuing it until he caught it in Arcadia when it was exhausted. After some pleading, Artemis allowed him to take it back as proof to Eurystheus before setting it free again.

The Stymphalian Birds. Heracles had next to destroy some birds that were increasing in number on the shores of Lake Stymphalos, between Mycenae and Arcadia. They are sometimes said to have had metal feathers and claws, and they fed on animals and men. He found it difficult to shoot them while they were roosting in the trees but Athena, who unlike Hera was sympathetic to him, gave him a bronze rattle made by Hephaestus. The noise of the

rattle startled the birds into flight and Heracles shot them down as they rose from the trees.

The Augeian Stables. Heracles had to clean the stables, or possibly the cowsheds, of King Augeias of all the dung that had accumulated there over many years; the king agreed to reward him with one tenth of all his herds if he completed the task in one day, knowing it to be impossible. Thereupon, Heracles diverted two rivers and channelled them together in such a way that they flooded through the stables and cleaned them out in one day. Augeias refused his reward, however, and in a later expedition Heracles killed him. Some people think this story was told to account for the great drainage dykes that had been dug in earlier times in the Peloponnese, which later inhabitants thought only a man of superhuman strength could have made.

To undertake the next three labours Heracles was forced to go further afield, away from his native Peloponnese.

The Cretan Bull. A mad bull was loose on Crete and Heracles had to capture it and bring it back to Eurystheus. A number of earlier stories have become involved with this one, and they give the bull different identities: some versions say it was the bull that brought Europa to Crete; others that it was the bull loved by Pasiphaë, the wife of Minos and mother of the Minotaur, that had originally been sent from the sea by Poseidon for Minos to sacrifice. Minos had incurred Poseidon's anger by substituting an inferior bull for the sacrifice so Poseidon caused the bull to become ferocious and a menace to the islanders.

Heracles captured it nevertheless and brought it home. When Eurystheus prepared to sacrifice it to Hera, she refused it because Heracles had brought it, so it was turned loose and wandered off to the plain of Marathon, where it later became part of the story of Theseus.

The Horses of Diomedes. Heracles had to go far northwards to Thrace to capture the horses of King Diomedes, which the king fed on human flesh. There are at least two versions of this story; the most com-

mon one tells how Heracles slew Diomedes, fed his flesh to the horses, then drove them back to Mycenae.

The Girdle of the Amazon. It is not clear whether this was actually a girdle or a piece of bronze waist armour, but it belonged to Hippolyta, the Queen of the Amazons – a race of female warriors, and she had received it from her father for bravery. The daughter of Eurystheus longed to have it, so Heracles was sent to the shores of the Black Sea to get it. He

(National Archaeological Museum, Palermo) A metope from a temple at Selinunte shows Heracles fighting an Amazon, a female warrior, c.5th century BC. While she holds an axe, he fights like a wrestler, holding down her foot with his.The limestone figures have eroded more than the marble heads.

179

(Villa Giulia, Rome) On this vase, Heracles, wearing the skin of the Nemean lion and carrying his club, brings the three-headed dog Cerberus to King Eurystheus from its home at the entrance to the Underworld. Eurystheus takes refuge fearfully in a large storage jar.

brought the girdle back, but accounts differ as to whether or not he had to kill Hippolyta to do so. Some say she gave it to him, others that Hera stirred up a war between the Amazons and Heracles' followers, in which the Queen was killed.

Heracles now had to go to the western edges of the known world, and even to the Underworld itself.

The Cattle of Geryon. Geryon, or Geryones, was a giant who had three heads and shoulders all growing from one trunk. He therefore had six arms, all of which held weapons. Heracles was sent to get his herd of cattle, which grazed in the far West, beyond the river Oceanus. First, Heracles had to kill a guard dog, Orthus, with his club; then he killed the herdsman and finally shot Geryon with his arrows. His chief problem then was how to get the cattle home,

(National Archaeological Museum, Athens) Atlas brings the golden apples that he has picked in the garden of the Hesperides to Heracles, who has meanwhile taken his place in holding up the sky on his shoulders. White-ground vase.

and there are a number of tales about this. In one, he borrowed the cup that Helios, the Sun, used as a craft on the River Oceanus to make his return journey each night from west to east; in this Heracles transported the cattle across the river.

He then had a number of adventures on his way home, pausing to set up the Pillars of Heracles in the Straits of Gibraltar. His homeward adventures took place in what we now call France, Sicily and Italy, and the stories of these adventures became popular with the Greek colonists who had settled in those areas and who were thus able to identify the hero with their own localities.

Cerberus. Heracles was told to bring the dog Cerberus up to earth from Hades. Cerberus had been set in the Underworld precisely to guard it against

181

(British Museum) Heracles and Apollo struggle for the sacred tripod after Heracles had seized it on being refused advice by the oracle at Delphi. Zeus later separated the half-brothers with a thunderbolt and punished Heracles for his impiety. Athenian Vase found in Etruria, c.490 BC.

intruders not just to stop people escaping; he had three dogs' heads, a mane of snakes' heads and a serpent's tail. So dangerous was the task of capturing him, that Zeus sent Athena and Hermes to accompany Heracles.

While he was in the kingdom of Hades, Heracles rescued Theseus, who had been sent there for trying to help a friend capture Persephone and marry her himself. Heracles then found himself moved to tears by the story told by Meleagros, who had died recently, and he set Meleagros' mind at rest by promising to marry his unprotected sister, Deianeira, on his return to earth. He overcame Cerberus by squeezing him round the neck. When he presented the hound to

Eurystheus, the terrified king told him to return it to Hades immediately.

The Golden Apples of the Hesperides. Heracles was next sent to gather golden apples from a tree that was guarded by the Hesperides, nymphs who cared for the garden of the gods on the western edge of the world. The apples grew there on a tree that Gaia, the Earth, had given Zeus and Hera as a wedding present.

A number of stories are told about Heracles' adventures on his journey to the distant garden. In Libya he had to fight the giant Antaeus, who challenged, and defeated, all visitors. Heracles realized that because Antaeus was a son of Gaia he drew his

strength directly from contact with the earth so he overcame him by lifting the giant up so that his strength evaporated. In Egypt he had to kill King Busiris and his son, who had intended to sacrifice him to Zeus. While he was in the Caucasus he found Prometheus, whom Zeus had chained to a rock in order to punish him for his impiety. Each day an eagle devoured his liver; each night a new one grew. Heracles killed the bird and freed Prometheus from his torment.

Prometheus then told him that no mortal could enter the garden of the Hesperides. Heracles therefore persuaded the Giant, Atlas, to go and collect the apples for him, while he relieved him of his perpetu-al task of holding the heavens on his shoulders. When Atlas returned with the apples, it took all Heracles' ingenuity to persuade him to take up his burden again. Eurystheus feared to keep the golden apples that belonged to Hera, so Heracles gave them to Athena who had helped him.

After this, Heracles was free, but his life was no more straightforward. He won Iole, the daughter of a king, by beating her father at an archery contest, but lost her when he murdered her brother who was staying at Tiryns as his guest. This act broke all the sacred laws of hospitality, and Heracles was once more polluted.

He went to consult the oracle at Delphi, but was

(National Archaeological Museum, Palermo) Metope from a Temple at Selinunte, early 6th century BC, shows a simple representation of Heracles' punishment of the Cercopes, who nevertheless laughed at his hairy bottom which they could see while they were hanging upside down from a yoke over his shoulders.

(British Museum) This Roman relief shows Theseus as a young man raising the stone beneath which his departing father left a pair of sandals and a sword before Theseus was born. His mother, Aethra, who has judged him ready to perform the deed, encourages him.

refused advice, so he angrily wrestled with Apollo himself for the tripod. Zeus separated his two sons with a thunderbolt and then forced Heracles to sell himself as a slave for a number of years. He was bought by Queen Omphale of the Lydians, and there are stories of how they sometimes exchanged both their roles and their clothes.

During further travels, probably after his release from Omphale, he captured the Cercopes, two notorious criminals and murderers. He slung them upside down from a yoke across his shoulders, from which point they could see his hairy bottom, about which

they made so many jokes that he laughed and let them go. But he slew the owner of a vineyard who used to force strangers to dig his vineyard and then murder them.

Heracles took part in many military expeditions, which are too numerous to detail here. During this period he married Deianeira, as he had promised her brother he would, and stayed with her father for a time. After he had again accidentally killed a man, this time one of her father's kinsmen, he and his wife went into voluntary exile. During their travels they came to a river and Heracles asked the ferryman, who was the Centaur, Nessus, to take his wife across. Her screams alerted him to Nessus' assault on her, and he killed the Centaur by shooting a poisoned arrow into his heart. The dying Nessus, in apparent remorse, told Deianeira to mix his spilt sperm with the blood from his wound and to keep the liquid as a love philtre in case Heracles ever fell in love with another woman.

Later, Heracles went on an expedition against the king whose daughter, Iole, he had formerly won and lost. He defeated the king and returned with Iole. When Deianeira heard of his imminent arrival with another woman, she anxiously prepared fresh clothes for him, and dipped his tunic into the love philtre that she had taken from Nessus. She did not realize that because Nessus had been killed by one of Heracles' poisoned arrows, the philtre itself was a corrosive poison. When Heracles put on the tunic, it clung to his body and began to sear his flesh agonizingly.

He asked for a pyre to be made, then mounted it and persuaded a shepherd to set light to it. As the flames licked through the pyre, a cloud descended, caught up the hero and carried him to Olympus. Once there, he was reconciled with Hera, and given her youthful daughter Hebe as a bride. The gods then granted him the gift of immortality.

Further myths explain in great detail how the descendants of Heracles – the Heracleidai – came to rule over the Peloponnese, so that later rulers were descended from him. His three great-great-grandsons divided the area between them. In a later generation two brothers shared the rule of Sparta, which explained why Sparta had two kings down to historical times.

THESEUS

Is an Athenian hero, more polished than Heracles, but strongly associated with him in some of his exploits. Parts of his story must be very old, as they are set in a period when Athens was subservient to Knossos in Crete, but it seems clear that in sixth-century Athens his adventures were deliberately retold and extended both to emphasize their parallels with the popular Heracles and to give them a political dimension, making him responsible for acts that led to the foundation of Athenian democracy.

Theseus was conceived when Aegeus, king of Attica, who had no children, was visiting Troezen and made love to Aethra, the daughter of his host. It is said that the god Poseidon also made love to her on the same night. Before Aegeus returned to Athens, he left a sword and a pair of sandals under

(Argos Museum) Theseus fights the Minotaur, a man with a bull's head, in the labyrinth at Knossos in Crete. Vase painting by Hermonax, 5th century BC.

a heavy stone. He told Aethra that when her coming child was strong enough to lift the stone and claim these things, he should go to Athens and reveal himself to his father – until that time Aegeus feared that his ambitious nephews might harm the child.

In due course Theseus lifted the stone and claimed his birthright. He chose to take the hazardous inland route to Athens because he wanted to test his courage against the dangerous men and creatures who had begun to infest the land once again while Heracles was away serving Omphale.

First he dispatched the club-carrying brigand Periphetes, and took the club for his own weapon. Next he used the method of a murderer called Sinis on the murderer himself: he tied him between two pine trees that he had bent to the ground then released the trees; as they sprang up they tore Sinis apart. He then hunted and killed the notorious grey sow of Crommyon. On a narrow coastal path he met Skiron, who compelled those who wanted to pass to wash his feet, then kicked them over the rocks to a giant turtle that waited below. Theseus succeeded in tipping Skiron over the cliff. Nearing Athens he dealt with Procrustes, who offered travellers a large or a small bed, then stretched or shortened the travellers to fit the bed. Theseus killed Procrustes by fitting him to one of his own beds.

When the hero arrived in Athens he found that Aegeus was now married to Medea, the sorceress, who had convinced him she would bear him sons. She secretly divined the identity of Theseus, and wished to be rid of him, so she persuaded Aegeus that this strong newcomer might be dangerous and that he should be sent to Marathon to kill the ferocious bull that Heracles had driven from Crete. Theseus achieved that feat.

On his return a celebratory feast was prepared, at which Medea persuaded Aegeus to set poisoned wine for him. Before drinking, Theseus took out his father's sword to carve his meat. Aegeus saw it and recognized his son. He embraced him with joy, sweeping the poisoned cup aside. Medea was banished from the kingdom and Theseus overcame the nephews of Aegeus who had been a threat to his rule.

Theseus had arrived in Athens at the tragic moment when the city's tribute to Crete was due. Minos, the king of Crete, had never forgiven Athens for the fact that his son, Androgeos, had been murdered there. In compensation, he demanded a savage tribute: every three years, seven young men and seven young women had to be sent from Athens to Crete to enter the labyrinth and serve as food for the Minotaur who lived there.

The labyrinth, whose name possibly has some connection with the *labrys*, or double-axe symbol of Minoan civilization, may represent memories of the great, complex palace of Knossos. The myth says that the labyrinth was a dark maze of confusing passages, at the heart of which lived the Minotaur, a monstrous man with a bull's head. The maze had been designed by Daedalus. He had also designed the hollow bronze cow in which Pasiphaë, the wife of Minos, disguised herself in order to mate with the bull for which she had conceived a passion. The Minotaur was the result of that union.

Theseus pleaded to go to Crete as one of the victims, although they were normally chosen by lot. The ship set off, rigged with black sails, and Theseus promised his father to change the sails to white ones if he and the other victims returned home alive. On his arrival in Crete, Theseus met Ariadne, the king's daughter, who fell in love with him. In return for his promise of marriage, she gave him a ball, or clue, of thread to help him find his way out of the labyrinth.

As the Athenians entered the labyrinth, Theseus secretly fastened one end of the thread to the door, then he paid it out behind him as he moved towards the centre where the monster lurked. Once there, Theseus struggled long and hard with the Minotaur and killed him at last. Then he followed the thread back to the door and made for the boat with Ariadne and his fellow victims.

They sailed to Naxos where, for some reason, Theseus abandoned Ariadne, who was later discovered there by Dionysus. The usual version of the story is that the gods made Theseus forget Ariadne and sail on without her. Either in his joy at returning home, or in grief at the realization that he had lost Ariadne, Theseus forgot to change the black sails of his ship to white ones. Aegeus, waiting on the cliffs for the boat's return, saw the black sails and threw himself to his death.

Theseus succeeded to the kingdom of Attica and took steps to reorganize it. His most notable achievement was the unification of the small rural communities of Attica under the political rule of Athens, which made possible the future development towards democracy there. He continued to have adventures, however, including an expedition against the Amazons that parallels the one Heracles undertook. He also helped his friend Peirithous, King of the Lapiths, to defeat the Centaurs in the famous battle that broke out when the Centaurs invaded the Lapiths' territory during the King's wedding.

On two occasions he and Peirithous rashly

abducted the daughter of a god. They seized Helen when she was only twelve years old, and she was rescued by her brothers. Later, Peirithous conceived a desire for Persephone and Theseus helped him abduct her from Hades. For this, they were both confined to the Underworld, from which Theseus alone was rescued by Heracles.

When he was old, Theseus was displaced from ruling Athens. He took refuge in Skyros, where he died when the king, his host, treacherously threw him from a cliff-top.

JASON

Came from Thessaly. His father, Aison, who was King of Iolchos there, was driven out by his half-brother Pelias. Jason's mother, fearing for his safety, took him to the Centaur, Cheiron, to be brought up. The usurper, Pelias, consulted an oracle about his future and was told to 'beware a man wearing one sandal'. He was very concerned therefore on the day when a young man arrived at Iolchos wearing only one sandal, having lost the other as he helped a traveller across a flooded river. He was even more concerned when he discovered that the young man was his nephew, Jason. In the way of jealous kings, he sent Jason on a mission that he assumed would cause his death – the recovery of the Golden Fleece from Colchis at the far end of the Black Sea in Asia Minor, where it hung on a tree, guarded by serpents, in a grove sacred to the gods.

The fleece has its own story. King Athamas of Orchomenos, who was incidentally Jason's grandfather, had married Nephele, by whom he had a boy called Phrixos and a girl called Helle. He then took a second wife, Ino, who was jealous of her stepchildren. One year she encouraged the women of the kingdom to roast their grain before sowing it. Naturally there was no harvest, and Ino persuaded messengers who had been sent for advice to the Delphic oracle to return with the answer that the land would not be fruitful again until Phrixos and Helle were sacrificed. Preparations were made and, just as the children were about to be sacrificed, their mother, Nephele, came to the altar leading a sacrificial golden ram that had been sent to her by Hermes. The children clambered on to its back and it flew off towards Asia. Sadly, Helle fell from its back into the sea at a place that was named the Hellespont in her memory. The ram carried Phrixos safely to Colchis, however, where it was duly sacrificed to Zeus and its precious fleece hung in the sacred grove.

Jason accepted the challenge to travel to Colchis to bring back the Golden Fleece. Both Athena and Hera helped the craftsman, Argos, to build a good ship in record time. Athena brought oak for its prow from a tree sacred to Zeus at Dodona; this had the power of speech and was able to advise the crew. Fifty heroes eagerly joined the expedition. They were called the Argonauts but their identities vary in different versions of the story because many people later wanted to have an

(National Archaeological Museum, Athens) Ivory relief of a warship, from Sparta, late 7th century BC.

187

ANTIMAXO

(National Archaeological Museum, Florence) Detail of the François Vase painted in Athens by Kleitias, c.570 BC. It shows a ship that has come to pick up Theseus and the other young Athenians he has rescued from the Minotaur. One sailor swims ashore, eager to join in the dance of victory that has already begun.

Argonaut hero among their forbears. In the crew were certainly Argos, the boat-builder, the fathers of two of the heroes of Troy – Achilles and Ajax, Heracles, who seems to have been a late addition to the story, and Jason himself.

The crew made their first landfall at Lemnos, where they were delayed for a year by the women of the island who all needed new husbands, having recently killed their existing ones because of their misdeeds. The Argonauts finally dragged themselves away, but they had many other adventures on their way to Colchis, after one of which they were forced to abandon Heracles. In Thrace, they came upon the blind soothsayer, Phineus, who was starving to death

because every time he began to eat, the terrible winged women called the Harpies swooped down and either carried his food away or excreted foully on what was left. Two of the crew, who were sons of Boreas, the North Wind, flew after the Harpies, driving them on until they promised not to plague Phineus any more.

Phineus told the crew how to deal with their next hazard, the terrible Symplegades Rocks that clashed together. Jason took his advice and sent a dove between the rocks to test them. It emerged with only one tail feather missing, so the sailors made all speed between the rocks themselves, and found that only the stern of the Argo was slightly damaged.

At last they disembarked near Colchis and Jason went to meet the King, Aietes, and to plead for the return of the Golden Fleece. Aietes agreed, but first gave Jason a trial. He told him to yoke up two fire-breathing brazen bulls, the gift of Hephaestus, and use them to plough some land, which he must then sow with the teeth of the serpent that another hero, Cadmus, had killed.

Medea, the daughter of Aietes, was enchanted by Aphrodite into falling in love with Jason. She was a sorceress, like her aunt Circe, and gave Jason a magic ointment that would protect him and his armour against fire and weapons for a day. He smeared this on and managed to yoke the bulls and plough the field. When he had sown the dragon's teeth, hundreds of armed men sprang from the soil. He threw a stone among them so that they turned on each other and fought until they were all dead.

Medea, knowing that her father would never give up the Golden Fleece, guided Jason to the sacred grove and provided him with a drug that tamed the serpent. Jason lifted the Golden Fleece from the tree; then he and his crew, together with Medea and Medea's young brother, Apsyrtos, hurried to the ship and cast off as soon as they could.

Aietes pursued the ship, but the ruthless Medea killed her brother and dismembered his body, scattering it into the sea in pieces so that Aietes was forced to gather up the body slowly for burial. Zeus, in his anger at this impious murder, stirred up a storm. Jason and the crew therefore put into Circe's island for ritual purification.

The Argo took a long and wandering route home, during which the crew had further adventures. When they arrived at Iolchos, they handed the fleece to Pelias and carried the Argo to the sanctuary of Poseidon. Medea decided to remove Pelias, the usurping king. She demonstrated to his daughters a method she had of revitalizing an old, sick ram: she cut it up and boiled it in a cauldron with certain herbs, until it emerged as a healthy young lamb; she suggested that the same treatment would rejuvenate their ageing father. Pelias, of course, died from the treatment.

Medea and Jason went to Corinth where they lived for many years, bringing up their children. Then Jason decided to take a new young bride called Glauke, who was the daughter of Creon, a local king. Medea prepared a robe for her, which she smeared with a terrible poison that seared the flesh of Glauke and also of her father when he tried to rescue her. Medea flew away from Corinth in a chariot pulled by dragons. As her final revenge on Jason, she killed their children. Then she went on to Athens where she married Aegeus, the father of Theseus.

Jason continued to rule in Corinth until the day when, as he sat peacefully near the Argo, in the spot where he had dedicated it to Poseidon, a timber from it fell on him and killed him.

OPPOSITE
(Vatican Museum) Attic relief, 5th century BC. The enchantress Medea instructs the daughters of the usurper, King Pelias, how to prepare a cauldron with boiling water and herbs to 'rejuvenate' their father.

CHAPTER SIX
THE TROJAN WAR AND THE RETURN OF ODYSSEUS

No one knows whether or not the Trojan War actually took place. When the archaeologist Schliemann, guided by Homeric evidence and his own instinct, discovered the remains of an important ancient city at Hissarlik, near the Dardanelles in north-west Turkey, he identified the city with Troy. Most archaeologists now think that the city he uncovered was too early to have been the one besieged in the Trojan War. All we can say is that there probably was an expedition to Troy from the Greek mainland in about 1200 BC, a time when evidence suggests that the weakening of the Hittite kingdom might have tempted invaders to attack some of its towns. Warriors from Greece might have mounted an important expedition to Asia Minor then with the intention of settling on the north-west coast, which had so far resisted them. It seems likely that they besieged and captured a number of towns, among which might have been a later, less magnificent Troy than the one Schliemann found, but that they returned home because they could not overcome the whole area.

Whatever the truth, for the Greeks the war against Troy was an established fact of their heroic past, and for that reason ought perhaps to be treated as legend rather than myth. Between the Mycenaean period and the writing down of Homer's poems in the eighth century, tales of that and other wars and the memorable feats of particular warrior heroes had clearly been repeated, elaborated and linked together as part of the material of the adventure to Troy. The heroes were named, and their names, together with

those of their ancestors and their homes, were repeated by singers or story-tellers in rhythmic lists and catalogues that made them easy to remember. In this way they became historicized.

Their feats may have been inspired by memories of the warrior Mycenaeans of the Bronze Age or from wonder at the imposing structures they had left behind them. Homer, living in the Iron Age, seemed to think of the Trojan heroes as Bronze Age warriors, since he gave them bronze weapons, although he anachronistically described one of them as being iron-hearted. The two poems that are said to be by Homer, the *Iliad* (so-called because Ilium was established on the site of ancient Troy) and the *Odyssey*, are unquestionably the greatest of the epics that remain, but they do not tell the whole story of the war and the warriors' return from it, even though they allude to events outside their narrative framework.

The *Iliad* is centred on the hero Achilles and deals with a period of just over fifty days towards the end of the ten-year war, ending before the sack of Troy. A later collection of epic poems, known as the Epic Cycle, dealt with the events leading up to the opening of the *Iliad* and took up the story where Homer left off, recounting not only the sack of Troy but the return to their homes of Greek heroes other than Odysseus. In some cases these add different or later versions of events. Only fragments of them remain, but a summary has fortunately survived. There is sufficient space here to give merely a brief outline of the events of the war; its importance to

Greek audiences across several centuries may be guessed at by the hundreds of illustrations they made of it that still survive.

As so often in Greek myths, early events in the lives of some of the participants are crucial to what followed and may, in some cases, have been added at a later stage by way of explanation. There are early warnings in the lives of three people central to the story: Achilles, the Greek hero; Paris, the Trojan seducer, and Helen, the most beautiful woman in Greece, who was seduced.

Achilles was the son of a sea divinity, a Nereid called Thetis. Both Zeus and Poseidon desired her, but feared to mate with her because an oracle had said that her son would be more powerful than his father. They jointly encouraged a mortal, Peleus, to marry her, against her will. The gods attended the wedding, during which Strife threw a golden apple to the ground, saying it was 'for the fairest', an act that was to have important consequences. Disappointed of an immortal father for her child, Thetis tried to make the baby immortal: she is said to have held him either in a fire, to burn out his mortality, or in the River Styx, but the heel by which she held him remained untreated and therefore vulnerable. She took him to Cheiron to be brought up with other heroes and he soon excelled in the arts of war.

Paris was the son of the Trojan king, Priam. When Paris was born his mother dreamed that she was giving birth to a flaming torch and Priam was warned that this meant his baby son would cause the destruction of the city. Paris was therefore exposed to death on a mountainside, but he was rescued and brought up by shepherds. He became a shepherd himself, and was admired for his handsome looks and his courageous defence of his animals.

Paris lived a secluded life on Mount Ida, so when Hermes needed someone to judge who was the fairest of the three goddesses disputing their right to the golden apple he chose Paris, who was personable, yet sufficiently remote from events not to feel threatened by disputes among the gods. Hermes escorted Hera, Athena and Aphrodite to Mount Ida. As Paris looked at the goddesses in turn, each tried to influence his choice by offering him a gift: Hera offered power, Athena skill as a warrior, and Aphrodite the love of the most beautiful woman in the world. He judged Aphrodite to be the fairest and Hera and Athena became his undying enemies.

Some time later, Paris went to Troy, where he chanced to enter an athletic contest and win every event he entered. Inquiries were made, his identity revealed and he was accepted back by his father, Priam, into the royal family of Troy.

The most beautiful woman in the world at that time was Helen of Greece. Her beauty was probably inherited from her parents since her birth resulted from the rape of her beautiful mother, Leda, by Zeus who had disguised himself as a swan to trick her into submission. When Helen was old enough, all the kings and princes in Greece sought to marry her and seemed likely to fight each other for her. Some stories say that it was Odysseus who suggested the plan that she should choose her own husband and that all the suitors should then respect her choice and come to the help of her husband if she were ever abducted. Helen chose as her husband Menelaus, the rich king of Sparta. Her sister, Clytemnestra, was already married to Agamemnon, the great king of Mycenae.

The destinies of all these people began to intertwine when Paris visited Sparta, where Helen and Menelaus lived happily together with their children. He abducted Helen and took her back with him to Troy. Menelaus accordingly called upon all Helen's former suitors to mount an expedition against distant Troy to recapture Helen. Most joined him immediately, but some were reluctant. Odysseus had to be tricked into going. Thetis and Peleus knew that their son, Achilles, was fated to die if he went to Troy, and they tried to conceal him in female disguise among the women of Skyros: but when Odysseus and Diomedes came to Skyros and made a call to arms, Achilles betrayed his presence by instantly seizing some weapons.

At last, the huge fleet was ready to set off from Aulis under the leadership of great Agamemnon, but the wind would not blow. Urged by a soothsayer, and much against his will, Agamemnon sent for his daughter, Iphigenia, and sacrificed her on an altar there. The longed-for wind sprang up, but his wife, Clytemnestra, never forgave him.

There are many stories of delays on the way to Troy, and of raiding parties along the coast. Finally, the ships arrived and were drawn up on the beach in view of the city. The Greeks and Trojans could reach no agreement about Helen. Troy had impregnable walls that had been built by Poseidon. For nine years the Greeks attacked neighbouring supporters of the Trojans and cut off supplies to the city. They occasionally skirmished with warriors who ventured out of the city, but the situation remained at stalemate. The gods took sides in the war, with Hera and Athena supporting the Greeks particularly strongly because of their animus against Paris, the Trojan. In the tenth year, as had been foretold, matters came to a head. This is the point at which Homer takes up the story.

(Berlin) An Attic red-figure cup shows Achilles binding the wounded arm of Patroclos, who sits on his shield, baring his teeth in pain.

Agamemnon, the commander of the Greek army, had taken a woman called Chryseis as part of his spoil after a battle in which Achilles had fought particularly bravely. The father of Chryseis, who was a priest, begged for her to be ransomed, and called down a plague on the Greek camp when he was refused. Agamemnon therefore gave her up but, to compensate himself, seized Briseis, a female prisoner who had been given to Achilles, and of whom Achilles had become fond. Achilles was furious at this insult and vowed that neither he nor his Thessalian soldiers would fight again in the war. He withdrew to his camp in spite of a visit from the other Greek leaders, who pleaded with him and promised to return Briseis and compensate him generously.

Without Achilles, their ablest fighter, the Greeks were driven back to their ships by the Trojans, who were led by Priam's eldest son, Hector. Even the hero Ajax (Aias), with his strength and staunch courage, could not stop the Trojans. Achilles' dearest friend, Patroclos, begged that he might borrow both Achilles' soldiers and his armour in order to terrorize the Trojans on the following day. He fought bravely indeed but Hector killed him, with the help of Apollo, and took the armour of Achilles for himself. Achilles was almost mad with grief at the death of Patroclos and vowed to return to the battle at once. His mother, Thetis, persuaded Hephaestus to make him new armour that night, and the next day Achilles swept into battle. He was inspired by rage and displayed an *aristeia*, or individual valour, that destroyed all before him. At the end of a day of carnage, he met and killed Hector in single combat and dragged the body behind his chariot back to the Greek camp.

A great funeral was held for Patroclos, which included funeral games and elaborate ceremonies. In revenge for his death, Achilles continued to defile the body of Hector, dragging it round the walls of the city each day; then he left it to rot in the open air. Hector's grief-stricken father, Priam, was safely escorted by Hermes through the enemy lines to Achilles' tent, where his pleading at last moved

(British Museum) The Greek hero Achilles fights the Trojan Hector on this vase from Athens, c.490 BC.

Achilles to return the body for decent burial. The *Iliad* ends with Hector's funeral in Troy.

After this a number of allies came to the aid of Troy, including the Amazons and the Ethiopians, whose leaders were also killed by Achilles. Achilles had always known, however, that if he went to Troy he was destined to die there. It was an arrow shot from the bow of Paris, and guided by the hand of Apollo, that penetrated the unprotected place in his heel and killed him. He loss was mourned sorrowfully by the Greeks.

Some other method than valour was now needed to defeat the city. Some say Odysseus planned the stratagem of the wooden horse, others that it was the idea of the craftsman, Epeius, who constructed it. Once the horse was built, a picked group of Greek warriors climbed inside it, including the terrified Epeius who, according to some stories, was put near the door to manage the fastening. The Greek fleet then sailed round the coast out of sight, leaving one man, Sinon, behind.

The Trojans captured Sinon, who pretended that he had been intended as a sacrificial victim to obtain a wind from the gods, but had been hastily abandoned when the wind needed by the fleet sprang up spontaneously. He said the Greeks had made the horse as an offering to Athena, whose favour they felt they had lost recently, and they had made it too large to be taken through the city gates into Troy, because its presence there would protect the city. If it was left outside, Troy would fall.

Cassandra, the seer whose prophecies were doomed never to be believed, warned the Trojans that the entry of the horse would mean the destruction of the city. Laocoön, a priest of Poseidon, hurled a spear at the horse and said that he feared the Greeks, even when they brought gifts. He went to make a sacrifice on the shore; at this, two huge serpents surged out of the sea and strangled him and his young sons. The Trojans interpreted this as an omen that Laocoön was wrong, and immediately dragged the horse into the city, pulling down part of the wall in order to do so. Helen guessed that there was something amiss, and walked round the horse, speaking softly to each of the heroes in turn, mimicking the voices of their wives. Odysseus had to prevent them physically from answering her.

At night, Sinon signalled to the fleet, which

(British Museum) Apulian vase with some details of the sack of Troy; Cassandra seeks sanctuary at an altar, 4th century BC.

returned to Troy. The Greek warriors let themselves down from the horse and opened the city gates to their comrades from the ships. The men and children of Troy, and some of the women, were horribly slaughtered; the remaining women were taken as slaves and concubines, although some stories say that Menelaus rescued Helen. Old King Priam was murdered at an altar in the courtyard of his palace. Only Aeneas, the son of Aphrodite, escaped with his father and his son. The city was burned to the ground.

There are many stories of the difficult journeys undertaken by the Greek heroes on their return to their own lands, and few are happy. The return of Agamemnon, which was particularly tragic, will be described in the next chapter. Only Nestor, a good and wise old warrior, had a quick and easy journey home to Pylos to a quiet and contented life.

The return of Odysseus to Ithaca is recounted, largely in flash-back, in the *Odyssey*, which is so different in character from the *Iliad* as to have made many

scholars insist that the two poems are by different authors. Odysseus had the great advantage of being assisted throughout his journey by Athena, but Poseidon, the sea-god, was hostile to him and vented his hostility in savage storms. Odysseus had been told that he would be away from his home for twenty years altogether if he went to Troy, which is why he had been reluctant to go. He had another ten years to endure when he set off for home after the sack of Troy.

He and his crew began by raiding the Cicones, who killed many of them. A violent storm then took them to the land of the Lotus-eaters, who persuaded a number of his men to eat the lotus fruit, which made them forget their homes and friends and want nothing but to stay and eat more. Odysseus removed some men by force, and they sailed next to the fertile island of the Cyclopes, where many sheep and goats grazed. The Cyclopes were monsters, each of whom had one eye in the middle of his forehead.

Odysseus disembarked with a few men and went

200

LEFT
(Delphi Museum) A small bronze statuette of Odysseus, or one of his men, escaping from the cave of the blinded Polyphemus, having tied himself under a sheep.

BELOW
(Argos Museum) Detail from a vase showing Odysseus and one of his companions using the stake they had sharpened to put out the single eye of Polyphemus the Cyclops, c.7th century BC.

to visit the Cyclops, Polyphemus, who was a son of Poseidon. As his cave was empty, the men made free with his food and waited for his return. When Polyphemus returned for the night with his sheep he closed the entrance to the cave with a huge rock, and dined on two of the men he found there. He had another two for breakfast, and went out again, closing the cave behind him with the rock that no human could move. While he was out, Odysseus sharpened a strong stake. Polyphemus ate two more men that night, but also drank deeply of some powerful wine. While he was asleep, the men heated the stake in the fire then drove it into his one eye. Polyphemus cried out for help, but Odysseus had told him that his name was Nobody, so the giant was ignored when, in response to enquiries from outside about his screams, he cried out 'Nobody is hurting me!' When Polyphemus opened the cave and let his sheep out in the morning, he felt their backs blindly, but could not tell that Odysseus and his men had lashed themselves beneath the bellies of the sheep. As Odysseus reached his ship, he shouted out his real name in triumph, and Polyphemus called upon his father Poseidon either to prevent Odysseus from reaching home, or to let him arrive there alone and find great trouble awaiting him.

The ship next reached the island of Aiolia whose king, Aiolos, was ruler of the winds. When Odysseus left, the king gave him a good wind that would drive his ship straight home to Ithaca, then enclosed some other winds in a tightly-tied bag, which he also gave him. After several days' sailing in the right direction, Odysseus fell asleep and his men opened the bag, thinking it might contain treasure. Contrary winds rushed out and blew the ship back to Aiolia. The king was angry, so they made for another island, which proved to be the home of the Laistrygonians. They were cannibals and they destroyed all the ships except Odysseus' own, and ate all the crews but his.

Odysseus sailed the remaining ship to the island of Aiaia where the enchantress Circe, the aunt of Medea, lived. The crew explored the island in two parties; one group came upon the home of Circe. She gave them food and drink and by doing so turned them into pigs, who nevertheless retained their human sensibilities. When Odysseus heard of this, from one of the group who had refused her hospitality and escaped, he went to their aid. Hermes met him and gave him a herb called Moly, an antidote to Circe's drugs, and told him how to master the enchantress by making love to her. Odysseus was able to persuade her to turn the pigs back into men and promise not to harm them again. Odysseus then stayed happily with Circe for a year.

When his crew urged him to depart, Circe told him that he must visit the dead in the Underworld and

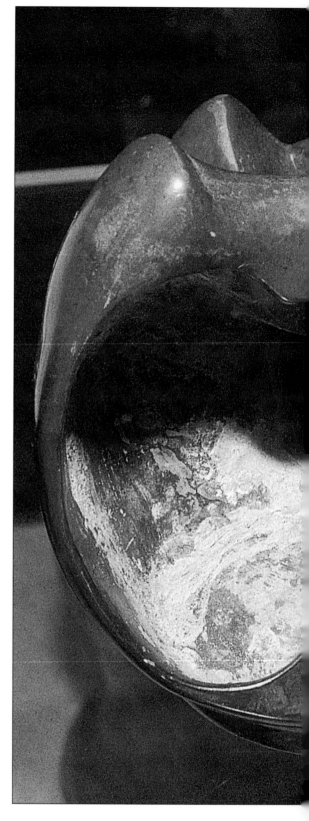

consult the ghost of the blind prophet Teireisias in order to find how to get home. Although appalled at the prospect, Odysseus set sail across the river Ocean and found his way to the Underworld. He made libations and a sacrifice. The souls of the dead came in a throng to drink the sacrificial blood, but he managed to consult Teireisias about his journey. Odysseus was told that his wife, Penelope, was being besieged in Ithaca by many suitors who wanted her to choose one of them as a husband to reign in his place now that they

presumed him to be dead. He talked with, but could not embrace, the souls of some of his family, and of Achilles who had died at Troy and Agamemnon who had been killed on his return to Mycenae.

He saw men who were being punished in Hades for their impiety to the gods: Sisyphus who was condemned endlessly to push up a hill a great stone that endlessly fell back again, and Tantalus who stood in a pool that receded when he wanted to drink, and above whose head were bunches of fruit that withdrew as he

tried to grasp them. He even saw the ghost of the hero Heracles, but then he fled as hordes of spirits surrounded him. He was now free to return to Circe's island, and she gave him some useful advice about the next stage of his journey.

The first hazard Odysseus and his crew had to pass was the island of the Sirens, bird-like women who sang so enchantingly from the rocks that sailors rowed towards them and smashed their boats. Having been advised by Circe, Odysseus stopped the ears of his

men with wax so that they could not hear the song and caused himself to be tied to the mast so that he could not steer towards the ravishing song, although he ached to do so.

Then they had to pass between Scylla and Charybdis. In order to avoid the deadly whirlpool, Charybdis, Odysseus chose to go closer to Scylla. She was a six-headed monster who waited concealed in a cave high on a rock; in spite of Odysseus's preparedness, she snatched six men from his ship as it passed beneath her rock.

The remaining men were utterly weary and depressed and insisted on anchoring at the next island. This was Thrinakie, where Apollo kept his sacred herds of cattle, and both Circe and Teireisias had insisted that Odysseus should avoid it. He made his men promise not to eat the cattle, but they were delayed there by a storm that raged for a month so that their provisions ran out, and when Odysseus was away one day the men slaughtered some of the cattle, made sacrifices to the gods, and ate the meat. The gods were angry. They sent a lull in the storm, which tempted the crew to cast off; once the ship was at sea, they sent a mighty storm that destroyed the ship and all its crew except for Odysseus himself. He clung to some wreckage and drifted for ten days until he found himself cast ashore on the island of Calypso.

He became Calypso's lover and, lacking a ship, stayed with her for seven years, although his desire to return home grew stronger all the time. He daily mourned his inability to depart from the island. Sympathetic Athena finally sent Hermes to persuade Calypso to give him the materials with which to construct a raft, and also food and drink for his journey. Some time after Odysseus had set sail, however, Poseidon sent a storm that destroyed the raft. The sea-nymph, Ino, came to his rescue by giving him a veil to wrap round himself while he swam for the nearest shore. After swimming for two days and nights he arrived naked and exhausted at the mouth of a river, and threw Ino's veil back into the sea for her. He was on the shore of Phaicia.

He was discovered the next morning by Nausicaa, daughter of the king, who had come down to the shore with her women to wash clothes. While she found him some clothes, he covered his nakedness with a leafy branch. She led him back gently to the palace, where he was received hospitably and given generous gifts. The king sent him home in one of the special ships of the Phaicians that could travel very swiftly, but which Poseidon turned into stone on its arrival in Ithaca.

Odysseus did not at first recognize Ithaca, but Athena met him and showed him where he was. Then she disguised him as an old beggar so that he could observe events in his kingdom without being recognized. He met some of his former servants and found that they were still loyal to his memory, especially his swineherd, Eumaeus. Athena removed his disguise for long enough for him to be recognized by his son Telemachus, who welcomed him with joy and relief.

His old dog, Argos, recognized him even in his beggarly disguise, and died happily, having seen him once again.

Then Odysseus approached his wife, Penelope, who treated him kindly as she would have done any beggar. He discovered that she was being driven to distraction by the suitors who had taken up residence in the palace and were eating and drinking as though they were at home. She had delayed making a decision by telling them that she must finish weaving a shroud for the father of Odysseus before she married again. She wove this all day, then unpicked the work at night, but her trick had been discovered. The disguised Odysseus won her confidence sufficiently to persuade her to tell the suitors that she would marry the one who could string her husband's great bow and send an arrow from it through twelve axe-heads set up in a line.

The competition was held the next day. None of the suitors could find the strength or expertise necessary to bend the bow and string it. Odysseus, still disguised as a beggar, asked to try. He was mocked, but finally allowed to do so. He handled the bow easily, as one accustomed to it, strung it, and shot his first arrow straight through the line of axe-heads.

The suitors were amazed, but then they were dismayed because Odysseus turned his arrows on them. He was joined in his attack by Telemachus and Eumaeus and assisted by Athena. The suitors were killed and order was restored.

Penelope tested his identity by asking her woman servant to move the bed from the room she had once shared with Odysseus. Only Odysseus could have known that the bed was immoveable, since he had himself constructed it round a living olive tree. Once Penelope saw that he knew this, she recognized that he was indeed Odysseus and welcomed him home with joy.

CHAPTER SEVEN
THE ROYAL HOUSES OF ARGOLIS AND THEBES

The cycles of myths about two ruling dynasties have special significance for us because of their treatment by the dramatists of the fifth century BC. In early historical times, Argos supplanted Mycenae and Tiryns as the chief centre of Argolis, and it may have been then that the myths of the Argolid rulers, descended from Pelops, were developed. Myths about the Theban ruling family, descended from Cadmus, were similarly brought together and embellished. Much later, the playwrights Aeschylus, Sophocles and Euripides refined the stories and gave them not only dramatic power but lasting value. Their plays show how the lives of individual men and women are influenced by the actions of their forbears, how they react emotionally and morally to situations that are forced upon them, and how they try to square their actions with their perception of their duty to the gods. Thus, the dramatists took primitive and barbaric material and made sense of it for their more enlightened world.

The myths of the Argolid family, the Pelopidai, begin with Tantalus, a king of Lydia, who lived happily and was at one with the gods, even receiving them as guests. One day, however, as an ill-judged test of their discernment, he served them the flesh of his son, Pelops. The gods drove him to eternal punishment in Hades for this hideous act, but they restored Pelops to life.

Pelops moved into Greece, where the Peloponnese still bears his name. He won his wife Hippodamia from her father, the King of Pisa, by taking up his challenge to a chariot race; in order to win, Pelops secretly arranged that the wheels should fall from the king's chariot. He thus won the race and a wife, but the king was killed and Pelops' guilt was inherited by the next generation.

Pelops and Hippodamia had many sons, among them Atreus and Thyestes, who were notorious from youth for their mutual discord. When Pelops sent them into exile, they went to their sister's husband, Eurystheus, King of Mycenae. When he died an oracle said that one of Pelops' sons should have his throne. So began a long and devious struggle between them, which ended when Atreus discovered that his wife, Aerope, was secretly the mistress of Thyestes. He killed her; then he killed Thyestes' sons and invited Thyestes to a feast, at which he served him their roasted flesh.

Thyestes asked the oracle how he might take revenge on his brother, and was told that only a son of his begotten on his own daughter, Pelopia, could do it. He took the oracle literally, disguised himself and raped her. Pelopia, finding herself pregnant, married her widowed uncle Atreus, and Thyestes' new son, Aegisthus, grew up thinking he was the son of Atreus. When Aegisthus discovered the truth, he killed Atreus after cursing him and all his descendants.

The true sons of Atreus were Agamemnon and Menelaus. Agamemnon became ruler of Mycenae and married Clytemnestra; Menelaus ruled Sparta and married Helen, Clytemnestra's sister. As we have seen, both kings were away in Troy for more than ten years. Clytemnestra hated her husband who

(Capitoline Museum, Rome) Portrait bust of Aeschylus. Aeschylus (c.525-456 BC) was the first of the three great dramatists of the Classical period, the others being Sophocles and Euripides, and he is the only one from whom a complete trilogy of tragedies survives, telling a continuous story. He said of the writers of his period that 'We are all eating crumbs from the great table of Homer.'

had sacrificed their daughter, Iphigenia, in order to obtain a propitious wind for the Trojan fleet. She and Agamemnon had other children: a son called Orestes and daughters called Electra and Chrysothemis.

While Agamemnon was away in Troy Clytemnestra took Aegisthus, the son of Thyestes, as her lover. Perceiving the danger of this situation to Agamemnon's heirs, Electra, the eldest daughter, smuggled her young brother Orestes away to safety in Phocis. Some stories say that she herself was forced into marriage with a peasant so that Agamemnon's royal line should not continue. When, after ten years, watch-fires flared across the landscape to announce the return of Agamemnon from Troy, the lovers agreed to murder him. Clytemnestra met her husband with sweet ceremony and prepared a bath for him. While he was helpless in his bath, she trapped him in a net and killed him brutally with an axe.

Guilt for this murder passed to the next generation, for when Orestes grew up it was his duty to avenge his father. Summoned by Electra, he returned secretly seven years later, with a friend called Pylades, and left clues of his presence for his sister at an altar where she worshipped. Electra persuaded him that he must kill Clytemnestra and Aegisthus, in spite of his reluctance. He did the deed but then, as a punishment for his matricide, the Furies pursued him wherever he went. In some stories he travelled the world in a desperate attempt to escape them. In his play the *Eumenides* (The Furies), Aeschylus chooses, rather, to show that Athena brought Orestes to Athens to appear before Apollo at a court of law, the Areopagus, where Orestes was 'cleared of the charge of blood' and allowed to go home. Athena persuaded the vengeful Furies to become instead the Eumenides, 'Kindly Ones', who brought benefits to

ABOVE
(National Archaeological Museum of Athens) A relief showing actors making offerings to Dionysus, the god of wine, at whose festival plays were performed as part of a religious rite. The actors hold their dramatic masks in their hands.

LEFT
The Theatre of Dionysus in Athens. A theatre was built here in stone in 342-341 BC to replace the earlier one in which the masterpieces of Aeschylus, Sophocles, Euripides and Aristophanes were first performed. It has been greatly modified since then. It is likely that there was an Orchestra, or dancing ground, and an altar here in the 6th century BC, and that by the 5th century BC the audience sat in wooden seats. The theatre was sacred to Dionysus, during whose annual spring festival, the Great Dionysia, the plays were performed competitively in groups of three tragedies and a satyr play. Performances were subsidized by the city of Athens.

NEXT PAGES,
LEFT
(Sparta Museum) Clytemnestra murders her husband, Agamemnon, on his return from Troy.

RIGHT
A spring landscape in Phocis, a small territory in central Greece which contains Delphi. Electra sent her young brother, Orestes, there to grow up out of danger from their mother's lover, Aegisthus. It was in Phocis also that Cadmus found the cow that led him to the fertile plain of Boeotia, where he founded Thebes.

(British Museum) A bronze
representation of one of the Erinyes,
or Furies, minor goddesses who were
born from the drops of blood spilt on
the earth at the castration of
Ouranus. These winged creatures
tortured to madness those who had
committed serious offences, especially
against the family, such as Orestes'
murder of his mother.

Athens. The cycle of bloody and revengeful acts was
thus brought to a close by a merciful decision.

The city of Thebes in Boeotia also had its cycle
of myths. These began with Agenor, a king of
Phoenicia. His daughter, Europa, was abducted by
Zeus in the shape of a bull, who carried her on his
back to Crete. Agenor sent his sons to search for her.
After much travelling, his son Cadmus went to the

Delphic oracle to ask for help and was told to stop
searching for Europa but instead to follow a cow that
he would see in Phocis; at the place where the cow
sat down to rest he should build a city. He obeyed,
and built the city that became Thebes. He killed a
serpent, a son of Ares, that he found guarding a nearby spring and, needing men to people his town, he
sowed the serpent's teeth in the ground. Armed war-

riors sprang up, but they were too many and too fierce, so he threw a stone into their midst and, each suspecting the other, they fought until only five men remained. These became the ancestors of the leading Theban families, whose descendants continued to call themselves spartoi, or 'sown men' into historical times.

Cadmus married Harmonia, the daughter of

Aphrodite's affair with Ares, at a wedding attended by the gods. We have already encountered some of the couple's daughters in other myths: Semele bore Dionysus to Zeus; Autonoë was the mother of Actaeon, and Agaue became the unfortunate queen who tore her son Pentheus to pieces when he tried to stop the spread of the cult of Dionysus.

Cadmus's male descendants became kings of

(National Archaeological Museum, Palermo) Metope from a Temple at Selinunte, 6th century BC, showing Europa sitting on the back of Zeus, who has disguised himself as a bull. She holds on to his horn as he rushes her away from Phoenicia to Crete.

Thebes in their turn. His great-grandson, Laius, married Jocasta, who is known by the name Epikaste in earlier versions of the story. Laius was warned by an oracle that any son of his would be destined to kill his father and marry his mother. Therefore when Jocasta had a son Laius pinned the baby's feet together and had him abandoned on Mount Cithaeron.

The baby was found by a shepherd who took it to his master, Polybus, the King of Corinth who, being childless, adopted it as his son, calling him

Oedipus, or 'Swollen Foot'. As a young man, Oedipus visited the oracle at Delphi, where he was told that he was destined one day to kill his father and marry his mother. He determined never to return to Corinth, to the couple he thought were his parents, but set off to find some other home where he might escape his destiny.

One day, as he arrived at a crossroads, he was almost crushed by a chariot. In the tussle that followed, he overturned the chariot and killed its passenger. He went on, however, and came to Thebes.

The city was plagued at that time by a monstrous winged creature, part-woman and part-lion, who sat on a precipice and cast to their death all those who could not answer the riddle she set them. This was: 'What is it that walks upon four legs, upon two legs and upon three legs?' Oedipus courageously went to encounter her and found the answer to the question – it was Man, who crawls on all fours as a baby, goes upright in his prime, and uses a stick as a third leg when he is old and lame. Defeated at last, the Sphinx threw herself from her rock.

Laius, the king of Thebes, had failed to return from a journey, and was presumed dead. Oedipus was considered the saviour of Thebes because he had defeated the Sphinx so Jocasta gave him the kingdom by marrying him. They lived contentedly together and had two sons, Eteocles and Polyneices, and two daughters, Antigone and Ismene.

In time, however, a terrible plague laid low the citizens of Thebes, and the crops failed. Jocasta's brother, Creon, went to the oracle at Delphi and returned with the message that the plague would be lifted only when the murderer of Jocasta's first husband, Laius, had been found; the unknown man was in Thebes and was the source of pollution.

In his play *Oedipus Tyrannus*, Sophocles shows in almost unbearable sequence how Oedipus gradually unravels the true story of his own birth and his killing of his real father, Laius, at the crossroads. When he found that he had not escaped the oracle, but had indeed killed his father and married his mother, he blinded himself with Jocasta's brooches because he was no longer fit to see the light of day. Jocasta hanged herself. In Sophocles' version of later events, in *Oedipus at Colonus*, Oedipus left Thebes and went to Colonus, guided by his daughter Antigone, and ended his days by vanishing from a sacred grove in a miraculous yet peaceful fashion.

The story of Thebes was not yet played out, however. His incestuous union left its mark on his children. The two sons of Oedipus, Eteocles and Polyneices, both wanted to rule in Thebes, and agreed that each should rule for one year at a time. Eteocles would not give up the rule at the end of his year, however, and Polyneices collected support from Argos and, with his companions, mounted a failed expedition against the city, known as 'The Seven Against Thebes'. When the two brothers finally met in single combat, they killed each other. Creon, their uncle, took charge of the kingdom, and refused to allow Antigone to bury Polyneices. Greek custom demanded that bodies should be buried in order that the spirits of their owners should find rest. Antigone therefore defied Creon and buried her brother. Creon condemned her to death for this, and Creon's son Haimon, who was to have married her, chose to end his life too.

The words of the Chorus at the end of Sophocles' play, *Antigone*, show clearly the relation between men and the just gods, the impossibility of escaping what they have decreed, and the foolishness of opposing them with pride: 'Of happiness the crown and chiefest part is wisdom, and to hold the gods in awe. That is the law that, seeing the stricken heart of pride brought down, we learn when we are old.' That lesson can be learned from most of the myths. No one is forced into any particular belief and minor irregularities of behaviour may be overlooked; the gods, in any case, do not behave very differently from imperfect humans, but are gods and must be respected and not challenged. That was the wise way to live.

The Romans

INTRODUCTION

It is often said that the Romans had no myths. In the sense that myths are significant traditional stories concerning supernatural beings or historical or natural phenomena, this appears at first sight to be true. Yet it seems unbelievable that such stories should not have grown up among the early Latins in the same way that they did among other people. Roman literature and art, however, show mere traces of native myths that are almost impossible to identify and dislodge from the Greek literary tradition that absorbed and changed them.

Myths usually originate from an oral tradition, in which they are handed down from one generation to another. Sometimes such myths come to the surface and are frozen for posterity when they are gathered up and written down while they are still current, as they seem to have been in Greece by Homer, for example, who in the eighth century set down myths that had probably been told there since the Bronze Age.

Rome arrived on the scene too late for this to happen. When the works of Homer were being written, Rome was nothing more than a collection of huts on a hill near the Tiber. Once the city had become powerful it took its place in a world whose culture had been overwhelmingly Hellenistic since the conquests of Alexander in the fourth century BC. There were Greek kings and Greek cities in the east from Asia Minor to Afghanistan, in Egypt, and of course in Greece itself. From as early as the eighth century BC, Greek colonists had settled round the southern coast of Italy, and in coastal areas of Sicily.

All these cities shared a language, the *koine*, or common language, of Greece that had superseded its earlier dialects. The culture of their rich and educated classes was Greek. A particular feature of that culture was its taste for explaining the foreign cultures it dominated in terms of its own myths, for superimposing its own kind of stories on the stories of other people. Later Greek writers even suppressed local myths completely and invented new ones of their own to explain some local incident or phenomenon. For example, elements from the Greek myths about the god Dionysus were imposed on stories about the Egyptian god, Osiris, and even on stories about the Buddha. Sometimes, in their urge to make a good story, they turned local deities into people, as we shall see.

It seems likely that traditional oral myths and legends once existed among the Latin tribes who were the first inhabitants of Rome. If so, they were lost before the Romans developed the art of writing. Instead, their remnants were written down and re-interpreted later by Greek writers in their own tradition. Once Rome became an important city, its own educated classes were also Hellenized. They might have thought little of the Greek ability for practical affairs, but they aspired to the Greek culture of the Mediterranean and Near Eastern world.

The gods of the Romans were, in fact, probably never surrounded by the same kind of myths as the gods of the Greeks because the Romans seem to have perceived their gods in a way that was unusual in Europe at that period. The early Romans were still essentially animists, that is they responded to the sacred power within natural and man-made objects. It was the *numen*, or powerful spirit, of each deity that was important to the Romans, and the function that it was able to perform or withhold according to its disposition. Consequently the Romans were concerned with man's ability to hold himself in a mutually stable and profitable relationship with all the gods. They did not, at first, perceive their gods in human form, as the Greeks did, and therefore did not supply them with families and histories. What mattered to the Romans was not stories about the gods, but their powers and the dutiful and proper manner by which man might propitiate them and so maintain the all-important *pax deorum* or peace of the gods. Briefly, Romans seem to have been more interested in the function of a god than in his personality. It was inevitable, therefore, that when poets and artists wished to express their religion in mythical, anthropomorphic terms, they turned to Greek models.

The myths that have become essentially Roman are not to do with gods but with the history of Rome. These have been called, quite justly, 'pseudo-myths' because they were, for the most part, deliberately created by writers, usually Greek ones, rather than evolving gradually from a native folk tradition. They are foundation-legends, stories about the origin and early development of the city itself and it is almost possible to watch the myth of the foundation and early history of Rome developing over the centuries to suit the people for whom it was told.

The first historians of Rome of whom we are aware wrote in the third century BC in Greek. Since traditional Greek myths and legends represented history for educated Romans, it was natural that they were not averse to having their city placed in that tradition. In spite of the fact that a native foundation myth of Romulus and Remus, which will be considered later, was already current, Greek writers pushed the story of the origin of Rome further back into their own cultural past by developing the tale of Aeneas, the Trojan who, with his young son, had escaped from the sack of Troy, bearing his father on his shoulders.

Various stories of the later travels of Aeneas had been current in the Greek world for a long time, and at some stage it became clear that his destiny had been to travel to Italy, where he founded a Latin town, Lavinium, from which his son would found Alba Longa, near Rome, thirty years later. A long line of Alban kings then had to be invented to account for the many years that elapsed between the Greek story of Aeneas, which followed on from the Trojan war, and the Roman story of the founding of Rome by Romulus, which was traditionally thought to have happened in 753 BC.

The stories of Aeneas and Romulus and the early kings and heroes of Rome form what became essentially the myth of Rome. They are not myths in the strict sense of the word, but they became myths for the Roman people in the sense that they embodied the high ideals and values to which they referred over the centuries when they wanted to explain to themselves what it was to be Roman. It is a legitimate function of myth to create patterns that help people understand why things are as they are. In this way, the stories of Aeneas and Romulus may have been deliberate creations, but they could be said to have assumed mythical status over years of repetition and reference.

For mythical stories about the gods, the reader should turn to books about the myths of Greece and simply relate a Roman god to the stories told about his or her Greek equivalent. The equivalents are set out and explained later in this book, but there has seemed no point here in repeating the stories, which were not in any sense Roman, and which are readily available elsewhere.

The Capitol, seen from the Forum, at Ostia Antica, the port of Ancient Rome.

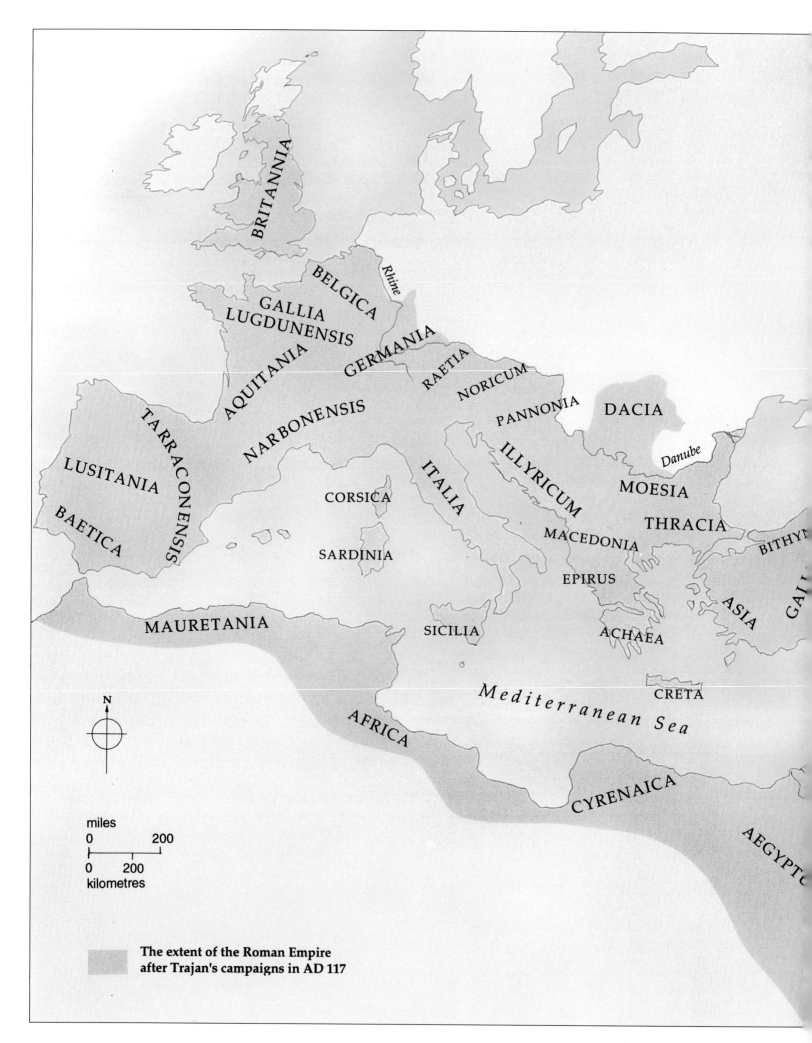

The extent of the Roman Empire
after Trajan's campaigns in AD 117

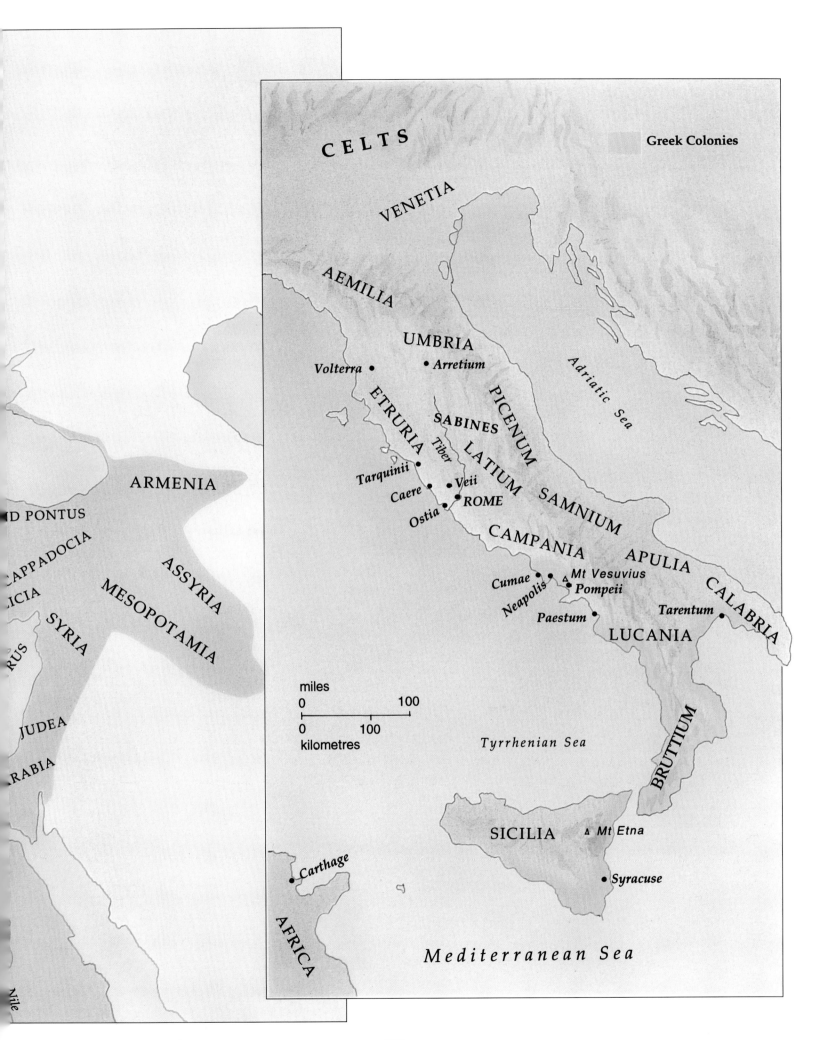

CELTS

Greek Colonies

VENETIA

AEMILIA

UMBRIA

Volterra •   • Arretium

Adriatic Sea

ETRURIA

SABINES

PICENUM

Tiber

LATIUM

Tarquinii •

Caere •   • Veii

ROME

Ostia •

SAMNIUM

CAMPANIA

APULIA

CALABRIA

Cumae •   △ *Mt Vesuvius*

Neapolis   • *Pompeii*

Paestum •   • *Tarentum*

LUCANIA

miles

0   100

0   100

kilometres

Tyrrhenian Sea

BRUTTIUM

SICILIA   △ *Mt Etna*

Carthage •

• *Syracuse*

AFRICA

Mediterranean Sea

ARMENIA

D PONTUS

APPADOCIA

ASSYRIA

ICIA

MESOPOTAMIA

RUS

SYRIA

JUDEA

RABIA

Nile

221

CHAPTER ONE
ROME: FROM VILLAGE TO EMPIRE

The gods and myths of Ancient Rome developed with and helped to define and sustain the Roman Empire. A settlement of farmers near the river Tiber in Italy grew into a city that gradually united and led all the peoples of Italy, then spread its rule across Europe and the Mediterranean world north-west as far as the border with the Scots, south-west through the Iberian peninsula, across the Mediterranean and along the North African coast to Egypt, as far east as Syria and Asia Minor, and north to the Elbe. The period from the origin of Rome until the end of its western empire was about eleven hundred years, while its eastern empire survived, though latterly in a weakened state, for about two thousand years.

During this long period the Romans maintained some of their own early cults, sometimes without remembering their origins; but they also absorbed cults from their neighbours and from the people they traded with or ruled over and, in many cases, they assimilated their own gods to foreign ones who seemed to have similar functions or powers. The extraordinarily flexible and tolerant polytheism of the Romans survived as an established state religion until 313 BC when the Emperor Constantine put in motion changes that allowed Christianity to take its place.

They were particularly influenced by the religious and cultural traditions of Greece that were already well established and had been shaped into a coherent literary and artistic form by the time Rome became a city of any consequence. But because there were so many influences on the gods and myths of Rome, it is necessary to begin with a brief account of what is now known about the origin and development of the city, and to summarize the expansion of its empire before looking at the myths that grew up to explain the phenomenon of Rome and the gods the Romans worshipped.

The geographical position of Rome was of prime importance to its history. The Alps divide Italy from Europe in the north then, beyond the Po Valley, the peninsular has a mountainous spine, formed by the Apennines, that leaves a relatively narrow, dry coastal plain on the eastern, Adriatic side of the country, and a relatively wide, fertile plain on the western, Tyrrhenian side, where the mountains slope down into the plains of Latium and Campania and into hilly, but fertile, Etruria. As the Apennines run almost due south into Lucania and Calabria, the 'toe' of the peninsula, they leave another plain, Apulia, in the 'heel' on the eastern side.

Only the rivers Po, Arno and Tiber have ever been seriously navigable, and there are very few bays or potential harbours along the shallow Tyrrhenian coast. Land routes have to find their way through the hills and mountains, usually following river valleys.

Rome lies about half way down the western coast, about 15 miles (24 km) inland, at the lowest point at which the Tiber can be crossed, where there is also an island in the river. It happens that this position was, and is still, a junction of the major land routes through the hills and along the coast, routes that once included the salt route to the eastern moun-

LEFT
Sixth-century BC tombs in the Etruscan city of Caere, not far from Rome. The tombs were set out in street formation in the necropolis, or cemetery, that therefore looks literally like a 'city of the dead'. The interiors of the tombs were often fashioned like houses, with frescoes on the walls, and lavishly furnished.

BELOW
Foothills of the Apennines in the Upper Tiber valley above Sansepulcro, Umbria.

tains. Grouped near the flood plain of the Tiber are certain low, volcanic hills, some of which have sheer, defensive sides. These would have provided dry settlements above the flood plain. Clearly this was a very desirable position, but one for which there would have been competition.

Archaeologists have found evidence of Neolithic and Bronze Age cultures in Etruria and Latium, the central areas of Italy with which we are concerned. It was not until the early Iron Age, however, that Italy began to show signs of developing in any way that could be compared to the civilizations further east in Greece and Asia Minor. In the early Iron Age a culture known as Villanovan, from the town of Villanova near Bologna, on which it was centred, appeared in the Po Valley, then in Etruria and Latium, whence it spread further south. This was succeeded by the more highly developed urban culture of the Etruscans, whose origin is still debated; some scholars think they came from Asia Minor, others from northern Europe. Whatever their origin, their language was not Indo-European and some of their texts have proved resistant to translation. They began to move into the central area of the peninsula by about 700 BC, and exercised a great deal of influence on surrounding cultures until about the fourth century BC.

From the middle of the eighth century BC Greek colonists began to settle in what came to be known as 'Magna Graecia', an area round the southern coast of Italy and the coast of Sicily, where they founded cities such as Cumae, Tarentum, Catania and

Syracuse, which in their turn founded other important cities: Selinus (Selinunte), Neapolis (Naples), Paestum and Agrigento, for example. The cultural influence of Greece on the rest of Italy was very important, particularly on the Etruscans, with whom they had early contacts.

In the centre of Italy, between the two powerful groups of Etruscans in the north and Greeks in the south, lived a divided population made up of groups having an extraordinarily diverse mixture of ethnic, linguistic, social, economic and religious identities. These included the Latins in Latium, on the coast, and the Sabines and Umbrians in the interior.

It seems likely that Rome itself began as a Latin settlement in about the middle of the eighth century BC. Archaeologists have discovered traces of Iron Age hut dwellings of this date on the Palatine, one of the hills overlooking the Tiber, and evidence of graves in the plain below the hill, which later became the Forum, of a slightly earlier date. There is also evidence for slightly later dwellings on the Esquiline and Quirinal hills. This evidence all suggests that Rome began in the eighth century as a hill settlement of farmers, probably shepherds, who had their cemetery in the plain below. Thus it was comparable with other Iron Age settlements scattered through the

Remains of the Greek city of Selinunte in Sicily, showing the remains of Temple C on the Acropolis.

plain of Latium, but very different from Etruscan cities to the north, Greek cities to the south, and the mountainous homes of surrounding tribes.

Other villages came into being on the hills around the plain and gradually linked themselves together, as many Latin communities did, until by about 650 BC Rome was probably a small Latin town. It continued to grow slowly for the next hundred years, during which time the meeting place, or Forum, was drained and no longer used as a cemetery. Archaeological evidence suggests that between about 550-475 BC there was a great spurt of development, which probably coincided with a period of Etruscan rule in the town. Evidence of walls, drains and monuments and fragments of Greek pottery and Etruscan painted terracotta ware date from this period. Remains have been found of temples, most importantly the great Capitoline temple that was dedicated in 509 BC to the triad of gods, Jupiter, Juno and Minerva. It seems likely that by the time the Etruscan rulers left Rome and retreated to their own territory further north in about 475 BC, Rome was a large city spread over several hills, surrounded by a wall, and ornamented with a number of sanctuaries to the gods of Latium and Etruria.

Roman tradition is probably correct in saying that the city was ruled by kings in the early period since kingship was the normal system of rule among the local tribes then. Throughout central Italy there was, however, a decline in rule by kings at the end of the sixth century BC, and administrative and religious power began instead to reside in the hands of colleges of magistrates, elected from aristocratic families. The histories of Rome written in the first century BC give 509 BC as the date of the end of its monarchy and the beginning of republican rule. Modern scholars suggest that it was probably as much as twenty five years later than this; but in any case a Republic can be said to have settled in by 450 BC, in a more painstaking and less dramatic fashion than the myths about Rome suggest. It took the form of government by two consuls, elected annually by the aristocratic ruling group.

Once the Republic was established, it was forced to take notice of the fact that, although the geographical position of the city was favoured, it was also tempting to invaders both from the interior and from the Mediterranean basin – from Sicily, Carthage and Sardinia. Roman literature suggests that the city's rulers never lost the sense of being vulnerable and beleaguered. They had to be strong to discourage threats to their security. It seems likely, therefore, that subsequent expansion began chiefly as an active response to a perceived threat.

Rome was by this time already a mixture of Latins and Sabines who had been strongly influenced by Etruscan civilization. One period of rule by Etruria was, however, felt to be enough, and the city saw the nearby Etruscan city of Veii as a constant threat. Rome gradually worked towards removing such threats by a well-judged mixture of war and diplomacy. Etruscan power was already waning by about 400 BC, and in 396 BC Rome succeeded in destroying Veii and annexing its territory. After that it used diplomacy in its relations with other Etruscan cities and managed to contain the power of Etruria while leaving its cities free to continue their normal industrial and commercial life.

Celtic tribes had been pressing down the eastern side of Italy since the fifth century BC, and in 390 there was a Gallic raid on Rome, which weakened the city's influence on its Latin allies by suggesting that it was vulnerable. Yet it was a raid for plunder rather than possession and in the long term served to stimulate Rome to greater efficiency. The Servian Wall was built round the city, and the army learned better defensive strategies. New officials were created to handle the affairs of the expanding state, and by 348 BC Rome was strong enough to enter into a treaty with Carthage, the great trading city on the coast of what is now Tunisia.

After fighting a war against her former allies, Rome was in a sufficiently strong position to organize Latium under her leadership, using a system that she later employed successfully much further afield. Rome became the political centre of the area without actually centralizing her rule. She allowed

autonomy to the cities she was responsible for, but asked in return that they should follow her foreign policy and provide troops for her army in emergencies. She thus ensured that other cities would combine with her in mutual defence against an aggressor.

Rome gradually extended this system to the cities of Campania, where the Greek cities also accepted a flexible system that allowed them to live their own life except in time of war. In order to secure strategic positions in neighbouring regions, Rome set up a system of colonization by which land was given to retired soldiers in return for their past service. The colonies were adapted to local circumstances, but clearly brought Roman influence to distant areas without terrorizing or even dominating them. The city could fight brutally at times, however, and after such occasions took the remaining population as slaves. By this combination of procedures Rome gradually united Italy, building roads and sometimes aqueducts in the process. The city thus built up a confederacy in Italy, which gave special privileges to the Latins.

This confederacy was clearly a power to be reckoned with, and one that was perceived as a threat by Carthage, which at that time controlled western Sicily as well as Sardinia and part of Spain. In 264 BC a minor incident caused the first of three major wars between Rome and Carthage; these are known as the Punic Wars from the Latin word for Phoenician since the Carthaginians were Phoenician in origin. Rome entered the First Punic War (264-241 BC) almost by accident, but then had to address the problem seriously, which she did by establishing a fleet and learning how to fight at sea in order to defeat Carthage. Having driven the Carthaginians from Sicily, Corsica and Sardinia, and after intensely destructive campaigns by both sides, Rome won the war and found herself in possession of her first overseas provinces.

The Second Punic War (218-201 BC) affected the population of Italy more directly since the great Carthaginian general Hannibal invaded their country expecting local Italian tribes to support him against Rome; he was disappointed in this, however, which suggests that the Roman system of confederation was working successfully. Hannibal had a great victory at Cannae in Apulia, where probably more than 30,000 people were killed, and at this the Romans despaired. Nevertheless they continued to pour men and resources into the war, which extended into Spain, Sicily and North Africa, until Hannibal was finally defeated at Zama and negotiated a settlement between Carthage and Rome.

Throughout the wars, Rome was able to rely on the support of the Italians, while Carthage on the contrary had very little manpower on which it could rely. This foreshadowed the future strength of the Romans, which always lay in its armies. As a result of the war, Rome had gained two more provinces in Spain. Later, after the Third Punic War, which ended in 146 BC, Rome destroyed the city of Carthage utterly and took her territory, which she ruled as the Province of Africa. Rome then dominated the western Mediterranean.

Response to a threat followed by prolonged, determined, destructive but ultimately professional and successful warfare, became a pattern in the development of Roman power. To the east, she was drawn successfully into the Macedonian Wars in 197 BC, but did not expand her direct rule there until she claimed Macedonia as a province in 146 BC. When King Attalus of Pergamum died in 133 BC he bequeathed his kingdom to Rome, and it became the province of Asia. Rome went to the help of the friendly city of Massilia (Marseilles), defeated the Gaulish tribes who were threatening it, and consequently absorbed southern Gaul in the process. When Mithridates of Pontus threatened Rome, the brilliant general Pompey took Pontus, Syria and Cyprus as provinces. In the 50s Julius Caesar fought the constantly threatening Gauls in the north of Italy and at last incorporated Cisalpine Gaul into the rest of Italy.

Thus, during the period of the Republic, Rome can be said to have become controller of the whole Mediterranean region either directly or through the exercise of influence over native rulers. This expansion was not without problems, however. The Roman army was drawn from the free peasant class, and it has been estimated that such men spent about seven years of their lives in the army, during which time their care and labour was withdrawn from the land they normally farmed. Meanwhile, Roman victories abroad resulted in thousands of conquered slaves being sent back to the city. As the ruling families in Rome grew rich through such offices as arranging contracts for supplies to the army, they invested in large, landed estates, which they then ran with the free labour of slaves. Thus the returning peasant soldier found he had lost his land to the upper classes and his work to the slaves he had helped to create. This lead to unrest and political struggles in Rome itself. By this time the city was overcrowded, unhealthy, full of poor people who had flocked there from the countryside, and ruled by men drawn from a limited group of families, many of whom had succumbed to the temptations of profitable office.

Military campaigns were lead by men from the ruling group who were elected by their fellow senators. Increasingly, the power of men who led successful campaigns abroad became a threat to the stability of the Republic at home. There was a strong tradition of annual elections to high office, but military campaigns sometimes lasted for several years, during which a successful leader could accumulate reputation, honour and popularity. The success of men like Sulla, Pompey and Julius Caesar led eventually to civil wars.

After his brilliant campaigns in Gaul, where he was Governor for two long terms, the great military leader, Julius Caesar, crossed the river Rubicon in the north and made it clear that he was invading his own country, but he then interspersed war with rival leaders at home with successful campaigns in Asia Minor, Africa and Spain. Once in power in Rome, he instituted many reforms – political, social and administrative – in Rome itself and in the Roman army. Instead of being consul for a year in the accepted fashion, however, he acted like a king. He refused the title *rex*, or king, but showed little regard for the political institutions of the republic. His murder in 44 BC was probably inevitable for these reasons. It led to a renewed struggle for power and yet more civil wars. These ended when Octavian, or Gaius Julius Caesar Octavianus, great-nephew and adopted heir of Julius Caesar, defeated the combined forces of Mark Antony and Cleopatra at Actium in 31 BC, thus conquering his Roman rival and bringing Egypt under Roman control.

Octavian was now in control of the Roman Empire, and in 27 BC he accepted the title of Augustus, under which he ruled as a constitutional *princeps*, or first citizen, until his death in AD 14. His rule, which with hindsight we notice coincided with the birth of Christ, was also a turning point in Roman history, as it marked the beginning of the period of Empire in the sense that he arranged that one of his family should succeed him as emperor after his death and so brought to an end the republican period and introduced a new régime that lasted for several hundred years. He himself was a reforming and popular ruler with great administrative powers, who tactfully chose to live a relatively austere life.

The rule of Augustus is particularly significant to the study of the gods and myths of Rome because, following a long and chaotic period of civil unrest, he deliberately instituted a return to what he perceived as the true Roman tradition in religion, morality and government. Festivals and cult rites that had long been neglected were revived, and temples and sanctuaries renewed. His ideals were propagated successfully by a brilliant group of poets and prose writers who lived in Rome at that time. Above all, it is from the poetry of Virgil and Horace and the prose of Livy that we derive our sense of what it was to be Roman. Ovid, who retold the Greek myths so vividly and gracefully did not, however, meet with approval and, possibly for reasons of morality, was banished from Rome.

Under Augustus, the frontiers of the Empire were settled at a point he felt was far enough, and for many years after his death the *Pax Romana*, or Roman Peace, prevailed in the Empire, with the western part dominated by Latin culture and the

(Museum of Pagan Art, Arles) A Roman portrait bust of a young Octavian, who later became the Emperor Augustus.

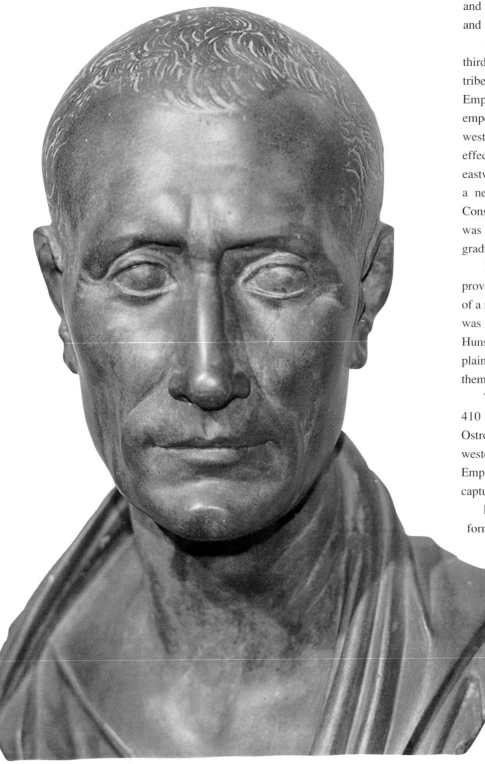

(Vatican Museums) A vivid Roman portrait bust of Julius Caesar.

and included the provinces of Armenia, Assyria and Mesopotamia.

More had to be done in the second half of the third century to stem incursions by Goths and other tribes across the northern and eastern frontiers of the Empire. By AD 284, when Diocletian became emperor, he split the empire into two parts, east and west, in order that it should be supervised more effectively. Gradually the centre of gravity shifted eastwards, until the Emperor Constantine established a new, Christian, capital at Byzantium, renamed Constantinople, in AD 330. After this, although it was in theory governed by joint rulers, the Empire gradually split into two halves.

In their weakened state, the Empire's outlying provinces were attacked by invaders, who were part of a relentless surge of tribes, whose tidal movement was initially set in motion by a nomadic people, the Huns, when they migrated from their home on the plains of central Russia, pushing other tribes before them as they went purposefully forward.

The city of Rome was sacked by Visigoths in 410 and by Vandals in 455, and in 493 the Ostrogoths established a kingdom in Italy. Thus the western empire fell to the invaders. The Byzantine Empire survived, however, until Constantinople was captured by the Turks in 1453.

Roman influence survived in the West in the form of the 'romance', or Roman, languages of France, Spain and Italy, in law and in engineering feats such as roads and bridges. Of all its religions, the last arrival, Christianity, survived into the 'Holy Roman Empire' whose Pope was called *Pontifex Maximus* just as the chief priest of pagan Rome had been.

This very simplified survey of an extremely complex period is intended to suggest the mass of influences that must have worked on Roman perceptions of their place in the world, and on the kind of gods they needed to placate. How did religious ceremony help them? What myth of Roman greatness sustained its soldiers and its citizens? These are some of the questions we shall try to answer in the following pages.

eastern part by Greek culture in the form of the Hellenism that followed the earlier conquests of Alexander the Great.

The period from about AD 70-235 is generally agreed to have been the high point of the Empire. The province of Britain had been added after Claudius's invasion in AD 43, but nothing more until in AD 101-02 and 106, Trajan's wars in Dacia, that had begun as a defence of the northern frontier, were so successful that he added the kingdom of Dacia to the Empire. At the end of Trajan's reign, in AD 117, the Empire had reached its greatest extent,

CHAPTER TWO
MYTHS OF ROME (1): THE STORY OF AENEAS

(Bardo Museum, Tunis) Mosaic of the poet Virgil. The muse of epic poetry stands on his right and the muse of tragedy on his left. The manuscript roll on his knees lies open at lines eight and nine of the first book of the Aeneid.

The aristocracy of Rome set great store by tradition and by the genealogies of their own families. They are likely to have recorded the genealogies by telling them over from one generation to the next. The leading *gentes*, or families, of Rome were important because they virtually governed the state between them. They looked for their traditions, as people often do, in a past that never actually existed. Unusually, they recreated this past in a form that had the appearance of comparatively sober history rather than myth or folklore.

Their heroic men and women were perhaps unusual too in that they displayed, first and foremost, certain moral qualities that created a set of values against which their descendants could measure themselves for all time. Roman heroes were not simply brave but acted as patterns or examples of endurance and loyalty and dutiful and proper Roman behaviour in relation to the gods and the state.

Yet the first histories of Rome were written not by Romans but by Greeks, and they attempted to fit Rome into their own cultural tradition. One means of doing this was to use the story of Aeneas's wanderings after the Trojan War to provide an early precursor of the founding of Rome. The hero was then made thoroughly Roman when the story was retold by Virgil in the time of Augustus.

As we have seen, Rome probably actually emerged as a real city late in the sixth century BC. In Greece, Homer's *Iliad*, which told the story of the Trojan War, had probably been in existence for two hundred years by then. It was an inspired and pow-

229

erfully written version of already existing oral myths, legends and genealogies, dealing with events that probably happened in the Bronze Age.

Homer says that the god Poseidon intervened to save one of the Trojan heroes for a greater future. This was Aeneas, the son of Anchises and the goddess Aphrodite – Venus to the Romans – who escaped from the sack of Troy, holding his son by the hand and bearing his father on his shoulders. Some scholars actually think this episode might have been added to the poem at a later date to account for the gradual development of the story of Aeneas.

Illustrations on Athenian vases found in Etruria tell us that the story of Aeneas was already known there in the sixth century BC, and various versions of Aeneas's search for a new home after the Trojan War appear in both Greek and Latin literature, as do stories of Greek veterans of the Trojan War who, finding no welcome at home after a ten-year absence, settled in Sicily and on the southern Italian coast. These stories, of course, were typical foundation myths, designed to give historical significance to the leading families of Magna Graecia, the areas of Italy and Sicily colonized by the Greeks. The end of the Trojan War was clearly seen as a time of the dispersal and wandering of the great Bronze Age heroes and therefore as an opportunity to claim them as founders of new cities and respectable new genealogies in the west.

The story of Aeneas was told most memorably and completely in the age of Augustus in an epic poem by Virgil (Publius Virgilius Maro). It deliberately set out to create a myth about the origins of Rome, and it worked. Virgil was born in the north of Italy near Mantua in Cisalpine Gaul, a city that still had a strong Etruscan tradition. He first lived in Rome at the age of 16. Augustus urged him to write the poem to celebrate Rome under his rule, and it developed into a national epic, in twelve books, which sets out the Roman virtues through the portrait of its hero. It does not glorify Rome in a brazenly triumphalist manner but with discretion, stressing the need for duty as well as victory. Because it is set in the distant past it suggests, through its hero, the difficulties that had to be overcome before Rome was able to achieve the glory that culminated in the rule of Augustus.

It is humane, moving and beautifully written. It creates a mythical past, partly by following the Homeric style of allowing certain gods to speak throughout as participants in the drama. By Virgil's time the Romans had assimilated their own deities to the Greek gods and they were thus able to appear as characters in the drama in a way the early Roman divinities, who were simply spirits, would not have been. It also follows Homer's pattern by having set pieces in which warrior heroes fight to the death. It departs from Homer in portraying its hero throughout as a man whose significance lies in the future. He is seen as the ancestor of Augustus through the Julian family. Virgil also uses a device by which various characters from the past within the poem make important prophetic speeches that prompt the reader to look forward to the greatness of the Augustan age. He praises Augustus discreetly by this method and at the same time places him in the context of a heroic past.

Because the Trojan War happened long before the creation of Rome, Virgil shows that Aeneas founded an earlier city, and that it was his son's heirs who would found Rome itself. What he could not have known is that his poem created a new myth through its own power. This was ironic since it had not been perfected when he died, and he is said to have asked for it to be destroyed.

The hero of the Aeneid is often described as *pius* Aeneas; the word pious in Latin has the sense of 'dutiful to the gods', a quality highly valued in Rome. Throughout his adventures Aeneas subjects himself to the will of the gods, although sometimes reluctantly. In this, he acts as a pattern of behaviour, displaying the pre-eminent Roman virtues.

We first meet him and his emigrant Trojans at sea, wearily searching for a new land in which to settle, 'so hard and huge a task it was to found the Roman people.' Early in the poem we learn that the goddess Juno (Hera in Greek mythology) is the implacable enemy of all Trojans, partly because the Trojan prince Paris did not choose her as the most beautiful goddess, and she will do all she can to prevent the Trojans founding a new city that will one day come into conflict with the city she favours, Carthage. In her jealous fury, she causes the Trojan fleet to be shipwrecked on a Libyan shore.

After the storm, Venus (the Greek Aphrodite), who Greek myths tell us is the mother of Aeneas, questions the great god Jupiter (Greek Zeus) about her son's fate. Jupiter explains to her, and us, that Aeneas will fight a massive war in Italy, then rule for three years in a new city in Latium. His son Ascanius, who was also called Ilus while he lived in Ilium – another name for Troy – will now have Iulus instead as his second name. In this way Virgil links the descendants of Aeneas with the Julian family, from which came Julius Caesar and his nephew Octavian, later Augustus.

Ascanius/Iulus, will have power for thirty years, but will transfer his capital to Alba Longa. That city

will be ruled for three hundred years by descendants of Trojans until its priestess, Ilia, bears twins to the god Mars. They will be brought up by a she-wolf and one of them, Romulus, will found the city of Rome itself. For the Romans, says Jupiter, 'I set no limits, world or time, but make the gift of Empire without end,' and from them will come the 'Trojan Caesar'. The words of Jupiter therefore set Aeneas into the context of the traditional history of Rome's foundation and show that he is the pre-ordained precursor of that city, not its actual founder, and that he was the forefather of Augustus.

Venus appears to Aeneas on the Libyan shore as a beautiful young huntress. He recognizes her as a goddess but sadly not, until just before she disappears, as his mother. When he complains to her of his fate, she tells him the story of the local queen Dido who, like Aeneas, has been forced from her home. Dido and her followers left Phoenicia after her brother, the Prince of Tyre, killed her husband, and they are building a new city of Carthage in Africa.

Virgil thus draws a comparison between the origins of Carthage and Rome, although he makes the foundation of Carthage mythically contemporary with the end of the Trojan War, instead of more accurately with the actual foundation of Rome. Juno's partiality for Carthage enables Virgil to suggest that divine intervention was responsible for the enmity between the two cities that exploded in the Punic Wars whose horrors were still remembered in Rome in his day.

When Aeneas meets the beautiful Dido, he tells her his story, rather in the manner in which Odysseus recounts the tale of his wanderings in Homer's *Odyssey*. Aeneas begins with the sack of Troy and the death of his wife, Creusa, who later came to him as a spirit and forbade him to mourn, foretelling his long exile and his future settlement 'on Hesperia where Lydian Tiber flows', where he would marry and found a kingdom.

He describes how he set off from burning Troy with his father, his son Ascanius, his people and his 'hearth gods and the greater gods'. The carrying of his gods to Italy was a crucial part of the story in many of its versions, and may have been an important reason for its first having been told, as an explanation of a cult-transfer from one region to another. Like many Greek heroes before him, Aeneas made for the island of Delos to consult the oracle of Apollo about where he should take his people. The oracle told him to 'look for your mother of old.' Old Anchises, the father of Aeneas, immediately interpreted the motherland as meaning Crete because Teucris, the forefather of the Trojans, had set off

(British Museum, London) On this marble relief Aeneas and his son Ascanius discover the white sow that was to mark the end of their journey. Helenus and the god of the river Tiber had both prophesied this moment.

from there to found Troy in the far distant past.

After a short stay on Crete, the Trojan exiles fell sick with a plague. On this occasion Aeneas's household gods appeared to him at night and explained that Hesperia, the land he must make for, was actually Italy; it was the Trojans' true home from which their forefathers, Dardanus and Iasdius, had originated.

The Trojans set off again, and landed on one of the Strophades islands, where they slaughtered some unattended cattle to sacrifice and eat. They were prevented from eating by an instant attack by Harpies, monstrous bird-women from Greek myth, who swooped on the food and fouled what they did not carry off. When Aeneas's men attacked them, the leading Harpy prophesied that, as punishment, the Trojans would find Italy but would not create their city until hunger had made them eat their very plates.

Their next landfall was Epirus where, to their pleasure, they found that Helenus, a surviving son of King Priam of Troy, was now ruler. He told Aeneas that when he reached Italy he must look out for a giant white sow suckling thirty snow-white piglets. This detail suggests that the story is of quite a late date since it seems to be intended to symbolize the fact that thirty was the number of cities in the Latin League. Aeneas would find the sow on the further coast of Italy. On his way there, he must stop at Cumae to visit the Sibyl, a prophetess who would tell him more.

Aeneas landed first in Sicily, at Drepanum near Eryx, where there was a shrine to his mother, Venus.

Virgil is here making both a mythological and a tactfully political point, since the shrine had originally been made to the Phoenician goddess, Astarte, who was assimilated to their goddess Aphrodite by the Greek colonists in Sicily, and who was then identified with Venus in Roman times. Since Homer claimed in the *Iliad* that Aeneas was the son of Aphrodite (Venus), Virgil can be seen here to be emphasizing his hero's cultural and genealogical links with much of the Mediterranean world.

To the sorrow of all, old Anchises died in Sicily. When the Trojans continued their journey, they were shipwrecked on the Libyan shore after passing many dangers, such as Scylla and Charybdis and Polyphemus the one-eyed giant, that Homer had described Odysseus encountering earlier.

Dido listened to these stories with wonder and was consumed with a fierce love for Aeneas. Venus and Juno together had fanned the flame of her love, Venus because she wanted to protect her son from further harm and give him a beautiful wife, and Juno because she wanted to ensure that Aeneas would stay in Carthage so that Rome would never come into being. The next part of the poem, Book VI, tells Dido's tragic story, and has in itself become a powerful myth of betrayed love.

One bright day Dido and Aeneas went hunting together, but Juno raised a storm from which the couple took shelter in a cave. Goddess and nymphs were on hand to witness the 'marriage' of Dido and Aeneas in the cave, and from that time Dido 'thought no longer of a secret love but called it marriage.'

Aeneas responded to her love and seemed to forget his mission, dressing in Phoenician clothes, taking pleasure in his life with Dido, and even supervising work on the building of Carthage.

Jupiter himself sent Mercury to remind Aeneas forcibly of his duty to his son and his descendants. From that moment Aeneas allowed himself to be ruled only by his destiny. He determined to leave Carthage, keeping the news from Dido until the last moment. When she discovered the truth, Dido pleaded passionately with him to stay, but he was resolute. In a fury of rejection, she called upon her people to ensure that they would in future make no pact with Aeneas's people, but 'contend in war, themselves and all the children of their children', thus foretelling the wars between Rome and Carthage. She had a pyre made of everything Aeneas had abandoned.

Then she mounted it and plunged a knife into her breast. Aeneas's ships left Carthage in the tragic glow from Dido's funeral pyre.

The Trojans sailed once again to Sicily, where they commemorated the anniversary of the death of Anchises with funeral games. While the games were in progress, Juno incited the women to set fire to four of the ships in an attempt to bring an end to their weary journeying. Aeneas therefore left some of the older, weaker travellers with a leader to stay and settle in Sicily. Venus pleaded with Neptune to allow the travellers to continue unmolested by Juno, and he agreed, save that one of the crew must die as a token sacrifice. Somnus, Sleep, therefore overcame the helmsman Palinurus, who fell from the ship and drowned.

At last, Aeneas landed in Italy and found the

(Bardo Museum, Tunis) The journey of Aeneas from Troy to the western coast of Italy as described in the Aeneid *deliberately evokes echoes of the journey of the Greek hero Odysseus (Latin Ulysses) from Troy to his home in Ithaca as described by Homer in the* Odyssey. *This Roman mosaic shows Ulysses tied to the mast as he passes the Sirens in order not to be lured by them on the rocks. Mosaic from Dougga.*

The view from the site of ancient Carthage today: the Bay of Tunis in the evening.

Sibyl at Cumae, as he had been advised. Once again, Virgil is being tactful in setting one of Aeneas's most important experiences in a Greek colony, at a place sacred to Apollo, the god whose cult Augustus had exalted in Rome as a sign of reconciliation between Greece and Rome. The Sibyl told Aeneas that he might enter the Underworld only by carrying with him a golden bough from a certain tree sacred to Juno. His mother, Venus, then sent two doves to direct him to the tree.

Aeneas crossed the river to the Underworld, almost sinking Charon's ferry with his living weight. Once there, he encountered Dido and pleaded for her forgiveness, but she turned from him to the shade of her first husband, to whose love she was restored. Aeneas's most important meeting, however, was with the spirit of his father, Anchises, who explained the Underworld to him in an interesting mixture of philosophies popular in Virgil's day. He then showed him his future wife, Lavinia, and his descendants, who would be future kings of the Latin city of Alba Longa (now Castel Gandolfo). He foretold the founding of Rome by Romulus and then showed Aeneas future Roman rulers, culminating in Augustus, its second founder, 'who shall bring once again an Age of Gold to Latium' and who would extend his power throughout the earth. After this,

Anchises listed the kings of Rome who would rule between its foundation and the Republic, showing the important things each would do. He mentioned a number of great Roman families, and after describing the heroic actions of future Roman generals, said:

'Roman, remember by your strength to rule
Earth's people – for your arts are to be these:
To pacify, to impose the rule of law,
To spare the conquered, battle down the proud.'

Anchises then spoke to Aeneas of wars he would have to fight in the future and of what he must do, then escorted him and the Sibyl to the Ivory Gate, through which they re-entered the world.

Aeneas rejoined his small fleet and they rowed safely past the island of the sorceress, Circe, disturbed by the howls and roars of the chained beasts who had been men before they drank her magic potions. In the calm dawn, they came at last to the mouth of the river Tiber. After pulling the ships onto a tree-lined shore, the company made a feast, piling wild fruit on to the hard wheaten crusts they used as plates. Hunger drove them to eat the crusts as well, at which young Ascanius observed that they had even eaten their plates. Aeneas recognized this as the prophecy he had been given and blessed the land, which he realized was meant as their new home and fatherland.

Aeneas then made an embassy to the local king, Latinus, to ask for a strip of coastal land. Latinus, the old and peace-loving king of Laurentum, welcomed him warmly. He was, says Virgil, the son of Faunus and a Laurentine nymph, and therefore descended from Saturn (Greek Kronos), whose rule in those parts had been a golden age. Here Virgil can be seen using an artificially created genealogy that has turned early Italian deities into the king and queen of a Latin tribe. Latinus had no sons to follow him, but he had a daughter. Portents and oracles had clustered about her that suggested she would bring renown to her people, but also war; it was said that she should marry a man from abroad, a stranger. From that marriage rulers of a great empire would spring.

When Latinus met Aeneas, he recognized him as the stranger his daughter should marry. A local prince, Turnus of the Rutulian tribe, had already claimed Lavinia, however, and Lavinia's mother was sympathetic to his claim. Herein lay the seeds of discord. Juno sent Allecto, a Fury, to poison the minds of the Queen and Turnus and to inflame their anger against Aeneas. Turnus incited his supporters to join him, and Latinus was no longer able to keep the peace when Ascanius, the son of Aeneas, unknowingly influenced by Juno, killed a pet stag that was cherished by the daughter of Turnus's herdsman.

Her brothers, together with other herdsmen and farmers all armed themselves for war. Thirteen Italian chieftains joined Turnus against Aeneas, including Mezentius, former king of Caere in Etruria, who had been exiled for his outrageous acts of cruelty. Tarchon, the reigning king of Etruria, joined Aeneas because he had learned it was the only way to rid himself of Mezentius; other Etruscans also joined Aeneas.

While these events were taking shape, Aeneas,

(Paestum Museum) The upper section of this Lucanian funerary stele from Paestum in southern Italy shows the spirit of the deceased entering the ferryboat of Charon in order to cross the River Styx and enter the Underworld.

235

(Louvre Museum, Paris) Statue of the River Tiber as a god; he can be identified by the wolf that nurses Romulus and Remus, the founders of Rome. It shows the extent to which the spirits of place were anthropomorphized in the later period. Virgil makes this god appear physically to Aeneas, although in early Rome he would have been perceived simply as the spirit of the river.

stantly at war with the Latins. These genealogies are again transparently Greek, invented on the basis of a mistaken link between the words Pallas and Palatine.

On the next day Aeneas prayed to the river god for confirmation, and saw the white sow and her litter lying on a grassy bank. After dedicating the animals to Juno, the Trojans rowed upstream to Pallanteum, which was built on the Palatine Hill that later became the earliest part of the city of Rome. It was, as yet, 'a meagre town'.

Evander's conversation with Aeneas is a most significant part of the poem. He explains that, although he is Greek and Aeneas Trojan, they share a common ancestor in the Giant Atlas, who holds the heavens on his shoulders. In this way, Aeneas can be seen to share in the Greek heritage, in spite of having been a Trojan enemy.

Evander and his people were celebrating their annual festival dedicated to Hercules, and he tells Aeneas how Hercules had come to that spot in earlier days and killed the monster Cacus, who lived in a cave there. The cult of Hercules, who was the Roman version of the Greek hero Heracles, was widespread in the western Mediterranean, where he was seen as a god rather than as a hero who had been assumed into the Olympian pantheon at the end of his life, which is how he appears in Greek myths. Virgil here draws a parallel between heroic qualities of Hercules in driving evil forces from the land and Aeneas's own potential for doing so.

Evander explains that the golden age of Saturn once reigned in that land and that he himself had come there in exile, urged by his mother, the nymph Carmentis, and through her by Apollo. From the Palatine Hill, he shows Aeneas some of the places that were to become significant in later Rome. In this way Virgil uses invented myths to account for and give importance to names that were used but not fully understood in his own day. Among these are: the Carmental gate, named after Evander's mother; the wood where Romulus would seek refuge; the Lupercal grotto; the Tarpeian Hill; the rock on which the Capitol would be built, and the Janiculum, founded by the god Janus. The reader suspects a contemporary joke when Virgil makes Aeneas hear cattle lowing 'in what is now Rome's Forum and her fashionable quarter, Carinae'. With great generosity, Evander then gave his son Pallas to Aeneas as a companion in war.

Aeneas left Pallanteum at the head of his army. When they paused, Venus presented him with some powerfully protective armour that she had persuaded her husband, Vulcan (Greek Hephaestus), the smith and fire-god to make. The shield was particularly

'heartsick at the woe of war' rested by the river Tiber. The god of the river raised his head from the water and urged Aeneas to stay in that land, promising him that the next day he should see the white sow and her piglets, as had been prophesied. Roman readers would have recognized in the white sow an ancient portent signifying the foundation of Alba Longa, since the word for white in Latin is *alba*. The river god also urged Aeneas to search out an Arcadian tribe, that is a tribe of colonists from Arcadia in Greece, who were descended from a forebear called Pallas, and had founded a town called Pallanteum, under King Evander. They were con-

remarkable because on it the god, with his fore-knowledge, had wrought the future story of Italy. By describing the details of the shield, the poet is able to summarize the traditional history of Rome – its foundation by Romulus; the threats of Porsenna and others and the heroic response of people like Horatius and Manlius; and, closer to his own age, Cato's law-giving and the sea-battle of Actium, led by Augustus Caesar, from whose 'blessed brow twin flames gush upward'. The shield also shows Augustus's triumph following Actium, in which many conquered races from Africa to the Rhine, speaking varied languages, passed 'in long procession'.

War now breaks out and much of the rest of the poem recounts the epic contests between the warriors fighting on the sides of either Aeneas or Turnus. Young Ascanius has his moment of heroism, after which he is addressed by Apollo, who calls him, significantly, by his other name of Iulus. Apollo also calls him 'son of gods and sire of gods to come', a reference to the deification of Julius Caesar and successive emperors, which will be discussed later.

On one occasion Turnus describes himself as a 'new Achilles', a reference to the great Greek hero

who fought the Trojans, and this is typical of the heroism Virgil allows to the enemy of Aeneas. Turnus was, after all, Italian and thus, in a historic sense, engaged in a civil war with Aeneas. He was not an enemy from outside, and Virgil must give credit to the bravery of the warring tribes of Italy and suggest how they became united under Rome. Yet he sees the pity of it.

Jupiter is distressed by the conflict. 'The time for war will come,' he says, and predicts the future savagery of Carthage in its attack on Roman towns. In the struggle between Juno and Venus, Jupiter refuses to take sides, and leaves the outcome to Fate.

Aeneas is overcome with guilt when Turnus kills Pallas, the young son of his ally Evander, but he himself kills the hated Etruscan, Mezentius. Interestingly, Aeneas has an ally in another Etruscan, Tarchon, who is clearly a good man. Thus Virgil shows two sides to the Etruscan story in Italy.

Aeneas tries in vain to make peace and challenges Turnus to single combat as a way of settling their differences and putting an end to the killing of so many innocent people, but Turnus refuses. Seeing the carnage, Jupiter finally forbids Juno to go any

Detail from the Ara Pacis Augustae, *or Altar of Augustan Peace, in Rome. Aeneas, with his cloak drawn over his head in the manner of a priest, offers a sacrifice, probably the one made at Lanuvium on his arrival in Italy. It echoes a figure of Augustus similarly offering sacrifice on another panel of the altar.*

further in stirring up men to war. In return, she pleads that once Aeneas and Lavinia are married Latin people will not have to become Trojans in any way. She pleads:

'Let Latium be
Let there be Alban kings for generations,
And let Italian valour be the strength
Of Rome in after times.'

In other worlds Italian toughness and vigour will help to make Rome great in the future. Jupiter agrees, saying that no nation on earth will honour her so faithfully, and Juno withdraws from the scene.

The final act of the poem is the single combat between Aeneas and Turnus, reminding us of that between Achilles and Hector in the *Iliad*. At the last, when Turnus is at Aeneas's mercy and pleads for his life, Aeneas pauses, but then sees that Turnus is wearing the sword belt he had taken from young Pallas after he killed him. At this, anger blazes in Aeneas, and he kills Turnus on behalf of Pallas. The poem ends as the soul of Turnus passes to the shades.

The *Aeneid* demonstrates the human cost of achieving power, as well as its glory. Details throughout the poem reveal Virgil's sensitivity to the effect of power on humble, individual lives. Yet the poem clearly declares that Roman domination of the world was foretold by the gods, and that Roman power will impose peace and civilization upon those who come within its orbit. It takes up a number of strands in Rome's history – Etruscan, Italian, Greek, Sicilian – and tries to give value to each and to reconcile them. The poem became extremely popular and extremely influential, and ultimately the Roman people accepted their Trojan origin as part of their own myth.

ABOVE
(Florence Archaeological Museum)
Aeneas fought one Etruscan warrior but was supported by another. This warrior is painted on a Etruscan sarcophagus of the 4th century BC.

LEFT
The view from the Palatine Hill today. In the foreground are the remains of the Roman Forum, the great central meeting place of Rome, where Virgil's Aeneas saw cattle grazing long before the city existed.

The story of Romulus and Remus, to which Virgil refers, had been told in various versions for several centuries by his period, and illustrates the complex growth of a foundation myth. It is another of the national legends that formed part of the myth of Rome and, like the story of Aeneas, probably owed its importance to the concentration on the family and the state in Roman religion and to a veneration of ancestors that verged on ancestor-worship.

By the fifth century BC, Greek writers were using the name Rhomos for the founder of the city who also gave his name to it; the Italians, however, used the term Romulus, meaning 'of Rome'; hence possibly the distinction into two separate men, Latin Romulus and Greek Rhomos, corrupted to Remus in Latin. In fact the origin of the names is probably much more complicated than that, as one or both of the twins occur in a number of written stories from the fourth century BC, stories that had probably been told orally before that.

It will be seen that their story has many characteristics of early myths and folk-tales from other traditions: jealousy between brothers leading to fratricide, the fathering of children on a mortal woman by a god – a frequent feat of the Greek gods, but not of early Italian deities – children abandoned in a floating cradle, the suckling of infants by an animal and the restoration of sons to their family. The story was written down in the third century by Fabius Pictor, apparently from a Greek original, and then frequently repeated in various versions in the first century

BC. It was probably largely a Greek invention overlaying what may have been a traditional story.

The version that became accepted by the Romans of the Empire was the one written by Livy in the period of Augustus. Livy, or Titus Livius, who was born at Padua in about 60 BC, devoted his life to writing his *History of Rome* in 142 books, of which 35 survive. It soon became regarded as authoritative by his contemporaries, although what strikes us now is the way in which he dramatizes events, and views them through the eyes of a moralist, rather as a novelist might do today.

He places the brothers Romulus and Remus in the line of Alban kings descended from the son of Aeneas that was invented in order to fill in the time gap between Aeneas's departure from Troy, which was thought to have been in about 1100 BC, and the founding of Rome, thought to have been in 753 BC. In the tradition of Roman historians, he uses the ancient events he describes to account for and dignify the contemporary topography of his own Rome. It was possibly this that helped to give his version authenticity for his first readers who saw daily the places he described.

Livy lists a selection of the kings of Alba until he arrives at the brothers Numitor and Amulius. The younger of these, Amulius, drove Numitor from the throne, murdered his male children and made Numitor's daughter, Rhea Silvia, a Vestal Virgin so that she would have no children to threaten his reign. His plans promised to come to nothing when Rhea Silvia was raped by the god Mars, as she claimed, and gave birth to twin sons. Amulius imprisoned her and condemned the children, Romulus and Remus, to drowning in the river.

The river had flooded and the men entrusted with the drowning carelessly left the children in a basket in shallow flood water near the Ruminal fig-tree, a tree that grew in Rome in Livy's day and that he suggests once took its name from Romulus. Other versions of the story suggest that *ruma* or *rumis* was an early Latin word for breast, and as Rumina was the goddess of nursing mothers and the fig tree oozes a milky juice that was thought of as a fertility charm, this was an appropriate place for the twins to be nourished.

The surrounding country was still quite wild, and a she-wolf, coming to the river to drink, heard the children cry and offered them her teats to suck. Faustulus, the king's herdsman, happened to pass and saw her gently licking the children with her tongue. He took them home to his wife, Larentia, who nursed the children and brought them up. Livy adds that some people think the origin of this story was that Larentia was a common prostitute, who was called 'Lupa', or Wolf, by the other shepherds. He also links the site with the ancient Roman festival, the Lupercalia, that was still celebrated with unusual rites in Livy's life-time, but whose origins had become obscure.

(Capitoline Museums, Rome) This famous she-wolf of Rome is thought to be an Etruscan bronze of the late 6th or early 5th century BC, which originally stood on the Capitol. The twins, Romulus and Remus, are not part of the original composition, however, but were added in the early 16th century.

RIGHT
In this Etruscan bronze a seated
augur closely observes a flight of
birds to see what they portend.

TOP RIGHT
This relief in the Roman Forum
illustrates the seizing of
marriageable Sabine women by
young Romans in need of wives.

RIGHT
In this relief the boundaries, or
sacred furrows, of a new city are
ceremonially ploughed. This custom
originated with the Etruscans whose
Books of Ritual insisted that each
city had to be surrounded by a
pomerium, or sacred boundary, to
safeguard the population.

He does not refer the Lupercalia to the wolf that nourished Romulus and Remus, however, but to an annual festival in honour of Pan Lyceas, or 'wolfish Pan', a Greek minor deity, whose worship, said Greek story-tellers, had been instituted on the Palatine Hill by Evander, the Arcadian ruler who had welcomed Aeneas there many years earlier. Scholars now suggest that the names of the herdsman and his wife, Faustulus and Larentia, were actually those of local rural deities, and that Greek writers before Livy had turned them into people in a way that was fashionable among writers at the time.

One day, when the Festival of the Lupercalia was in progress, some brigands arrived on the scene, angry because Romulus and Remus, who were now shepherds, had been seizing from them goods they had stolen and sharing them out with the other shepherds. They attacked the twins and succeeded in capturing Remus and handing him over to king Amulius. Remus was charged with stealing from Numitor's land and was therefore passed to

him for punishment.

The truth about the twins' identity was then revealed and, once Remus had been released by his newly-discovered grandfather, the two young men attacked and killed the usurper, Amulius. Numitor summoned his subjects, confessed the whole story and assumed responsibility for the murder of his brother. Romulus and Remus supported him, and he was established once more as King.

Romulus and Remus then determined to found a new settlement on the spot by the Tiber where they had been both abandoned and nourished, and they were encouraged to do so by the fact that Alba was by now over-populated. Sadly, they succumbed to jealousy and ambition, just as their uncle had done before them. As twins, neither could assume authority, so they asked the gods of the countryside to send omens to determine which of them should govern and give his name to the new town. Romulus went to the Palatine Hill and Remus to the Aventine to observe the omens or auguries.

Remus was the first to see a sign – six vultures, but double that number of birds then appeared to Romulus. Supporters of both men claimed that the evidence of the omens favoured their side and in the affray that followed Remus was killed. A more common explanation of that death is, however, says Livy, that Remus taunted his brother by jumping over the half-built walls of his new settlement, at which the enraged Romulus killed him, threatening to do the same to anyone who leapt over his battlements.

It was in this fratricide that some Romans saw the seeds of the civil wars of the first century. The threat about the battlements, in fact, encapsulated the seriousness with which the Romans treated the sanctity of their *pomerium*, or boundary. This had originally been a sacred area, a clear, ploughed strip on both sides of the boundary of any town, on which nothing might be built and which no unauthorized person might cross.

Romulus fortified the Palatine Hill and sacrificed to the gods. Following Evander's example, he worshipped Hercules in the Greek fashion, that is, presumably, bare-headed. He gave laws to his subjects and created a hundred senators, or fathers of the city, *patres*, whose descendants became the patricians, the aristocrats of Rome, as opposed to the plebeians or common people.

He then created a sanctuary for fugitives in order to help increase the population of his new city. This has been seen as a traditional explanation for the later mixture of people who lived in the city. There were, however, not enough women to ensure the future of the city and requests to other cities for female immigrants were scornfully refused.

The problem was solved by a desperate measure. Romulus invited the surrounding tribes, including the Sabines, to the great annual festival of the Consualia, held in honour of Neptune. First, his people courteously showed their visitors, who had brought their sons and daughters with them, round the new city. Immediately the festival began, however, the marriageable men of Rome ran through the crowds and seized all the marriageable daughters who had come with their parents. Certain senators ensured that particularly desirable young women were seized on their behalf. The festival broke up in panic, and the girls' angry parents escaped, lamenting the deception.

Romulus reassured the terrified young women in turn, telling them that they would be honoured as married women and, eventually, mothers, sharing the privileges of the community. The men assured their chosen wives that their action had been

244

prompted by love, and the women gradually accepted their husbands and settled down happily enough to motherhood.

The neighbouring communities began a series of attacks on Rome and were beaten back until the Sabines, under their king Titus Tatius, entered Rome through the treachery of a young Roman woman, Tarpeia, the daughter of the commander of the Roman citadel. She was bribed by Tatius to admit some of his soldiers into the citadel. Once inside, the soldiers crushed her to death under their shields; some say this was her punishment because she had asked, as her price, 'what they had on their shield arms'. By this she had meant their rings and gold bracelets, but they chose to interpret it as their shields. Tarpeia's name was probably once that of an ancient local goddess, or it might have been the Sabine form of the Etruscan name Tarquinia, but Livy's story about her gives sinister significance to the Tarpeian Rock on the Capitoline Hill, from which criminals were once thrown to their death.

The Romans and Sabines fought together on the marshy ground between the Palatine and Capitoline Hills, and it seemed that the Sabine hero, Mettus Curtius, might sink into the swamp. The situation was saved when the Sabine women, fearless of danger, threw themselves between the armies. They begged their fathers and brothers to stop fighting their husbands, who were now also the fathers of their children. They cried that they would rather be killed themselves than be widowed or orphaned. Silence fell and not a man moved. Peace was concluded and the two states were united under a single government, with Rome as the seat of power. The Romans, as a gesture to the Sabines says Livy, began to call themselves Quirites, after the Sabine town of Cures. The marsh in which Curtius had almost drowned was renamed Lacus Curtius.

In telling this story, Livy has accounted for a fact of history, which was that the Romans were descended not simply from a Latin community but also from Sabine communities on surrounding hills that were later incorporated into the city. It seems likely that the story of the rape of the Sabine women may have developed to account for a noticeable Sabine element in the population of Rome, and also in an attempt to explain an obscure but lasting feature of the Roman marriage ceremony, which is still familiar to anthropologists as 'marriage by capture'. When, after the wedding feast, the bride was led to the bridegroom's house she was dragged away from her mother's arms in a show of force by the bridegroom.

Romulus continued a successful reign, and was particularly loved by the commons and the army. One day, while he was reviewing his troops on the Campus Martius, a violent storm broke. A thick cloud enveloped him, and from that moment he was never seen again. When the soldiers saw the empty throne and realized Romulus had been carried up to the heavens by a whirlwind they proclaimed him a divinity, hailing him as a god and son of the god Mars. Livy nods to a story that the senate had torn him to pieces, but dismisses it.

The matter was settled later by a wise man, Julius Proculus, who addressed the Assembly one day, telling them that Romulus had descended to him from heaven at dawn and told him to tell the Romans that 'by heaven's will my Rome shall be capital of the world', that they should learn to be soldiers and teach their children that no power on earth could stand against Roman arms. Romulus had then been taken up again into the sky.

This incident is significant. It reflects the experience of the great hero Hercules, who was lifted up to heaven from his funeral pyre and deified. It places Romulus and therefore other Roman rulers in that tradition, and it foreshadows events in Livy's own day: the first moves towards the deification of the Emperors of Rome, about which more will be said later. The story of deification also helps to explain how Romulus became assimilated to the very early Roman god, Quirinus, who was the third of the

Roman triad of great gods, with Jupiter and Mars. Quirinus was probably originally a Sabine god of war, and possibly of agriculture, and his name may be associated with the Sabine town, Cures, or with the Sabine word for lance, *curis*.

In common with other historians of his age, Livy accounts for the period from the traditional foundation of Rome in 753 BC to the beginning of the Republic in 509 BC with rule by seven kings. He shows how the population of the city increased by means of gradual victories over surrounding cities and the absorption of their population into Rome. It is thought that there may be some historical truth in his detail, but the pattern of kingship he presents is sufficiently schematic to cast doubt on much of what he says.

A warlike king is usually succeeded by one dedicated to social administration or the construction of buildings and temples, and a good Etruscan king is followed by an equally bad one. It seems likely that elements of folk-lore, legend, fact, cult and oral tradition had been converted into a myth intended to stress the Latin origins, valour and great virtues of the Roman people.

NUMA POMPILIUS was the successor to Romulus; he was a Sabine from Cures and thus neatly accounts for the amalgamation of the two peoples. Unlike Romulus, he was not a man of war, but was deeply learned in the laws of god and man. Characters like him are often found in legend or folklore as inventors of customs and ceremonies that seem to later generations ancient but inexplicable. He gave the city a 'second beginning', on a solid basis of law and religious observance. He instituted the Temple of Janus, an important Roman monument, whose doors were left open in time of war so that the god could come to the help of the Romans, but kept closed in time of peace.

It is easy to see in Numa the deliberate creation of a figure who inspired the essentially Roman virtues admired by men like Augustus, and who could be credited with the introduction of a number of Rome's major religious and administrative practices that must have actually grown up over the centuries. Numa was troubled by the behaviour of the Romans in his day, so he decided to inspire them with 'fear of the gods'. To this end, he invented the fiction that he met each night with the goddess Egeria who gave him the authority to establish certain religious rites and priesthoods.

His story includes one piece of possibly genuine folklore. When Numa summoned the god Jupiter in order to discover the expiatory ritual to adopt when something was struck by lightening, Jupiter listed the materials to be used in the sacrifice. He demanded a head, 'of garlic', said Numa; 'human...' 'hair', interrupted Numa, and 'the life...' 'of a sprat', said Numa. Because he was amused, Jupiter agreed to the garlic, hair and small fish, which were, in fact, the puzzling materials used in the rite.

Numa established a Calendar of twelve lunar months with intercalary months to provide adjustment to the full cycle. Then he fixed the 'lawful' and 'unlawful' days on which men might or might not transact business, an important feature of Roman life that we shall look at later.

He established virgin priestesses for the cult of Vesta, which he imported from Alba. Among the priesthoods he established were the twelve Salii, or dancing priests, whose annual ritual, in which they danced through Rome chanting words no one could any longer understand, survived in Livy's day. He ensured that no natural religious rite should be neglected and that foreign rites should be properly adopted, a feature of religious life that was to be rather more important in later years when Rome had contact with many other countries. He reigned for forty-three peaceful years, and his reign acted as a balance to the warlike reign of Romulus.

TULLUS HOSTILIUS, the next king, was a soldier and conducted a bitter civil war with Alba, whose citizens were of the same descent as the Romans. During the war two families made a typically Roman sacrificial gesture in which they put loyalty to the state before their own interest, and thus they serve as one of a number of mythological examples to later Romans. A set of triplets from each side, the Horatii from Rome and the Curatii from Alba, fought each other to decide the outcome of the war. The three Curatii killed two of the Horatii fairly quickly, then the third of the Horatii ran off so that the Curatii were forced to follow him. As they reached him, separately and exhausted, he succeeded in killing each in turn. Horatius returned in triumph to Rome, carrying the armour of the Curatii. When the sister of Horatius, who had been married to one of the Curatii brothers, saw her husband's cloak across her brother's shoulders, she wept for her dead husband. Horatius instantly stabbed his sister for showing her love, saying 'so perish all Roman women who mourn for an enemy.'

Although Horatius was tried for his horrifying deed, his father defended him, saying his daughter had deserved her death. The young man was acquitted, but his father had to perform certain expiatory ceremonies, which then became traditional in the Horatian family. Horatius had to pass under a beam in the roadway, as though under a yoke of submis-

Pavement mosaic at Ostia Antica, the port of ancient Rome, showing a lighthouse and two ships. 2nd-3rd century AD.

sion; the timber, says Livy, is still to be seen, having been replaced from time to time, and is known as the Sister's Beam. In this story, the family pride of the Horatii is celebrated and a respectably antiquarian explanation given for the beam across the road.

Tullus Hostilius destroyed Alba completely, and took its people into Rome, thus doubling the size of the city and increasing the number of families of senatorial rank by the admission of some of the Alban nobility. He built the Senate House for their deliberations, and Livy points out, accurately, that the building had been known until recently as the Curia Hostilia. Tullus Hostilius also fought the Sabines and defeated them. A number of omens, such as a shower of stones on the Alban Mount, warned that the Alban gods should not remain neglected in their deserted temples. When plague broke out in Rome, the king became subject to superstition and, while he was engaged one day in performing secret, and apparently incorrect, expiatory rites to Jupiter, his palace was struck by lightning and he burned to death.

ANCUS MARCIUS, the next king, oversaw a return to religion. He was both soldier and administrator. Under him, ceremonials were established for the formal declaration of 'just wars' after consulta-

tion with the gods and the elders of the city. He also extended the city, built a prison, made better defences and founded the port of Ostia at the mouth of the Tiber, so that Rome could more easily conduct its maritime trade.

LUCIUS TARQUINIUS PRISCUS (Tarquin the First) was a particularly interesting successor to the kingship. He was not a Roman but was born in Tarquinii in Etruria, and was actually an alien, being the son of a Greek immigrant called Demaratus, a noble who had settled in Etruria after leaving Corinth for political reasons. Since Livy places the first Tarquin's reign at the end of the seventh century, there may be some truth in the story of his father's origin. Corinth was ruled by autocrats at that period, and archaeological evidence shows that unusually large amounts of Corinthian pottery were being used in Etruria then.

Before he became king, Tarquinius Priscus was known as Lucumo, which scholars say is simply an Etruscan word for 'lord'. He was a poor but ambitious young man, and his wife, Tanaquil, who was equally ambitious, urged him to try his fortune in Rome. When they arrived there, an eagle swooped down and snatched off his cap; having taken it high into the sky, the bird swooped down again and replaced the cap on Lucumo's head. Tanaquil, reading the omen in the practised manner of an Etruscan, saw this as a sign of greatness to come.

Lucumo courted popularity and when the time came for the choice to be made of a successor to the throne, he ensured that the sons of the previous king, Ancus, were away from Rome. He then secured the vote by a popular majority. He was a man of good ability, but also a schemer, so he added a hundred new members to the Senate, drawing them from the 'lesser men', and knowing that they would support him.

Archaeology suggests that some civic building began in Rome in this period, and it is interesting that the first Tarquin king is credited with building the Circus Maximus, in which he instituted games on Etruscan lines, and with improving the Forum, along with a number of other civic undertakings. He also

extended Rome's power by taking the city of Collatia from the Sabines and subduing some of the Latin tribes.

SERVIUS TULLIUS, who succeeded Tarquin, seems to be a mythical figure and may for once have some basis in a genuinely traditional story. Servius came to the attention of Tanaquil, the queen, while her husband Tarquin was still alive. One night, as Servius slept, flames were observed to play harmlessly about his head. Tanaquil felt that he was destined to be great and brought him up as a prince. A different tradition identified him with an adventurous Etruscan hero called Mastarna; in either case he was clearly someone exceptional.

Servius Tullius was said to have been a slave, but Livy cannot accept that, guessing that his mother must have been a prisoner of war. There may be something of a folk-lore element in the story, since

The remains of Roman warehouses in the port of Ostia Antica.

the fourth century BC was a period during which the plebeians, or commons, were agitating for more power in the essentially undemocratic, aristocratic system of government in Rome and his name is a Latin one that would have been used only by plebeian families.

When king Tarquin was murdered by the sons of the former king, Ancus, who had never reconciled themselves to his kingship, Servius substituted for him, at first pretending that the king had merely been wounded. By that time he had become sufficiently popular to be elected king when Tarquin's death was officially announced.

Servius re-organized society, and introduced the census, an invaluable instrument of rule that survived in Rome. He extended the city boundary, taking in two more hills, the Quirinal and the Viminal. One of his most significant acts was to encourage the building of a temple of Diana in Rome as a joint enterprise by the united Latin people; it was a direct attempt to emulate the way in which a combination of Asian people had come together to build a temple of Diana at Ephesus. The mutual venture by the Latin people signified that they had ceased to fight each other, and that Rome was their capital city.

One man from the Sabine people wanted to dispute this notion, however, and saw a chance to do so. On a Sabine farm there was a heifer of such astonishing size and beauty that it seemed to have an almost sacred quality; indeed prophecies had been made that imperial power would belong to the nation whose citizens sacrificed it to Diana. The Roman priest of the new temple of Diana had heard of this prophecy and recognized the heifer when the Sabine brought it to the temple to sacrifice it. The priest asked the man what he could be thinking of to sacrifice the beast without first purifying himself in the living water of the Tiber. While the Sabine went off to suitably cleanse himself, the priest sacrificed the heifer himself, thus confirming Rome's powerful position.

Servius was the last good king; he actually intended to abdicate in favour of a republic but was prevented from doing so by being cruelly murdered by assassins hired by his son-in-law, another Tarquin.

TARQUINIUS SUPERBUS, Tarquin the Proud, who ruled for twenty-five years was a violent usurper who took power without being elected by the people or sanctioned by the Senate. He was an autocrat, ruling without consultation and treating the Latin leaders with contempt. He was, however, a successful soldier and strategist. He conquered the town of Gabii by a ruse. His son, Sextus, went to Gabii, pretending to have fled from the harshness of his father, but in fact he spent his time there gathering friends, reputation and information. When Sextus felt he had the town in his pocket he sent a messenger to his father to ask him what to do next. Tarquinius Superbus walked with the messenger in his garden and, when pressed for an answer, said nothing but knocked the heads off tall-growing poppies with his stick. The puzzled messenger reported this action to Sextus, who understood the silent message and responded by getting rid of all the prominent men in Gabii so that the town fell into Tarquin's hands.

In Rome, Tarquin began to build the temple of Jupiter on the Capitoline. He also set men to work on the Cloaca Maxima, the Great Sewer of Rome. A number of portents began to disturb his reign. When a snake slid out from a crack in a wooden pillar in the palace, Tarquin sent two of his sons, Titus and Arruns, to the oracle at Delphi in Greece. They took with them Lucius Junius Brutus, the king's nephew.

Brutus had learned to feign stupidity when he was with the brothers in order not to appear as a threat to their succession to the throne, and so be killed. Both brothers were intensely ambitious and, after they had put Tarquin's questions to the oracle, they asked one of their own: which of them would be the next king of Rome? The answer came: 'He who shall first kiss his mother shall hold supreme authority in Rome.'

While Titus and Arruns were drawing lots for the privilege of being the first to get back to their mother Brutus pretended to trip. He fell on his face and kissed the earth – the mother of all living things.

Once back in Rome the brothers were sent on a long campaign against the town of Ardea. One day while they were drinking with friends in Sextus's quarters, they began to boast about their wives. One of the young men, Collatinus, suggested they should all ride to Rome and see what their wives were doing that evening. The wives of the two young princes were found at a lavish dinner party with friends. In Collatia, however, Lucretia, the beautiful wife of Collatinus, was sitting with her servants spinning, despite the late hour. Collatinus invited his friends to take supper with him and his wife. Sextus, watching Lucretia, determined that she should be his.

A few days later, he returned to Collatia, where he was treated like an honoured guest in Lucretia's house and escorted to a guest chamber. During the night he found his way to Lucretia's room, where he raped her. She struggled and he succeeded only by threatening that if she refused him he would kill her and leave a dead slave beside her to suggest that she

had died as a result of her adultery with a slave.

When he had gone, Lucretia wrote to her father and her husband asking each to come at once with a trusted friend. When her husband arrived with Brutus she confessed to her adultery with Sextus Tarquinius and asked that he should be punished. They swore he should and tried to comfort her, but she could not forgive herself. She plunged a knife into her breast and killed herself for shame. By doing this she became a pattern of the pure and steadfast wife, and her example has been quoted in literature and shown in painting and sculpture from that day to this.

Brutus took the knife and called upon the men to swear vengeance. He revealed his true nature at last and led a rebellion against Tarquinius Superbus and his family. The monarchy came to an end and a republic took its place. Two consuls were elected by popular vote; they were Lucius Junius Brutus and Lucius Tarquinius Collatinus.

The story of king Tarquin and his son was clearly invented to explain the sudden and violent end of the monarchy, and the end of Etruscan power in Rome. There are features of Tarquin's reign, such as the building of the Capitoline temple, that seem to have a basis in fact, but the rape of Lucretia is probably a fable devised to explain what was in fact a fairly common decline in monarchic rule throughout the Latin tribes.

The deposed king went for help to some local kings, in particular to Lars Porsenna of Clusium. Porsenna mounted an attack on Rome, making for the wooden bridge over the Tiber. A heroic Roman, Horatius Cocles, stayed alone on the bridge, fending off the attack, to allow his fellow soldiers to destroy the bridge behind him. Just as the bridge was severed, he leapt into the Tiber and swam to safety. 'Cocles' means one-eyed, and this feat was later associated with the statue of a one-eyed man near the bridge, which was probably, in fact, a statue of the god Vulcan. Nevertheless, the myth provided another source of pride for the Horatian family. The truth was probably that Porsenna actually captured Rome although he stayed there only briefly. Roman history in its more mythical version does not, however, feel the need to acknowledge that uncomfortable fact.

Whatever the truth of the stories of the kings, the violent ending of their rule reflected the horror of kingship felt by republican Romans, and their determination that no king would reign in Rome again. That determination helps to explain the assassination of Julius Caesar at the moment when it seemed he might accept an offer of kingship.

It is now thought that the stories about the Etruscan kings also contain a grain of truth in that the Etruscans were in power in Rome during a period when the city actually expanded in size and importance. Most importantly, these are myths and legends that were told to and repeated by people who were amazed at the speed at which their city had grown in size and power, who valued their traditions and who wanted to find explanations for them and give them respectability and significance by placing them in a recognized historical tradition.

CHAPTER FOUR
DOMESTIC RELIGION AND THE EARLY GODS OF ROME

It is, of course, impossible now to recover accurately the earliest gods of the Roman people. Our information about them comes chiefly from educated men looking back at the past from a distance of several centuries in an attempt to find the origin of ancient cult traditions. Such information as we have suggests very strongly that the instinctive religion of the early Romans was a kind of animism, in which many things, both natural and man-made, were felt to be operated and informed by the divine spirit that inhabited them. These spirits were known as *numina*, and were probably not originally differentiated as individual gods. Perhaps we can most easily envisage them now in our own reaction to some tree, rock, forest or river-meadow that seems to have a special, almost sacred quality, and in our reaction to objects that we want to be able to use in as trouble-free a manner as possible.

Surviving literature and inscriptions carved in stone suggest that the Romans felt that the gods set in motion all the important activities of their world, and that different activities were the responsibility of specific gods who existed simply to perform them and nothing else. Once people had named the gods, they added adjectives to the names to indicate precise functions. Thus Janus, the god who had power over doors, was known as Janus Patulcius when he opened them and Janus Clusivius when he closed them.

These gods had names but they did not, like the Greek gods, have personalities, personal histories or myths. They simply had functions. On one often-

(National Museum, Naples) A mythological landscape from the walls of the Villa of Agrippa near Pompeii that is typical of fashionable painting there of the mid-1st century AD. While it is derived from Hellenistic art, it shows the continuing Roman feeling for the spirit of landscape.

(British Museum, London) A bronze lar, a spirit who watched over the household, the family and its lands. These early spirits continued to be honoured in the home for many centuries, as is shown by this one dating from the 1st-2nd century AD.

quoted occasion, as late as the second century AD, when priests removed a fig-tree from a shrine, it is recorded that they invoked three gods to help them: Adolenda, or 'Burner', Commolenda, or 'Smasher', and Deferunda, or 'Carrier Away', thus calling upon divine backing for each part of the process.

Such customs were likely to survive among a conservative priesthood, of course, but it seems likely that the same kind of consciousness of the divine forces behind everyday activities remained with the average Roman for a very long time. Educated men later turned for spiritual satisfaction to the Greek gods, to philosophy or to the idea of one divine spirit, but even the sophisticated poet Ovid could still say of a cluster of oak trees that anyone seeing it would say 'a deity lives there'.

Man's relationship with the gods was functional, almost contractual; it was his duty to recognize their help and acknowledge it when things went well, or to find out what the gods wanted and put it right when things went badly. Religion was not a question of belief but of behaviour, and that is why it now looks to us like superstition.

The familiar, domestic gods were recognized particularly in three areas of life: the household, the agricultural year, and those important moments in life we now know as rites of passage, such as birth, the onset of puberty, marriage and death. The Romans, like most people who are primarily agriculturalists or small traders, centred their lives on the family and household. Wealthier households would include servants and slaves. The head of the household, the father or *pater familias*, was responsible for its continuity and, in the early period, also had the power of life and death over its members. He had his own Genius, or guardian spirit, sometimes represented visually as a snake, and was responsible for maintaining the household's relationship with the divinities that surrounded them. These included such precise functionaries as Cardea, the goddess of door hinges, Forculus, the god of doors, Janus, the god of doorways, and Limentinus, the god of the threshold.

Chief among the household gods were the Penates and the Lares. The Penates were the divinities of the penus or store-cupboard. They were not personalized and no one even knew how many of them there were, except that they were plural. They were the gods of the home in a very intimate way, the ones who ensured a supply of food and to whom the family made small offerings at the main meal every day. They would have been among the gods Aeneas carried with him from Troy because they would have represented home. They were worshipped at the hearth, which was the home of the goddess Vesta

254

who, like her Greek equivalent, Hestia, was so ancient that she never acquired a personality.

The other household gods were the Lares, who were often spoken of in the plural, although there was a singular spirit called a Lar. The Lares cared for the household in general, including its land. They were often identified with the spirits of the ancestors of the family, who were extremely important to the Romans, and they guarded the family as a whole from one generation to the next, patrolling the fields to keep away harmful spirits. Each household would have its lararium, or shrine, a cupboard containing small statuettes representing their Lares, which might also be used as a depository for valuables. The family would make them a monthly offering of cakes, milk or wine in gratitude for their guardianship.

Unusually, the Lares watched over slaves as well as the other members of the household, so slaves celebrated their particular relationship with

them at an annual rural festival called the Compitalia, or Laralia. This was held at the *compitum* or point where several properties met, and a shrine would be set up there for each set of Lares, together with a ploughshare. Each free person would be represented by a suspended wooden doll, and each slave by a ball of wool. The festival was imported into the city of Rome by rural immigrants and later came to be celebrated at crossroads in the swarming city by large groups of poor people who actually had by then no rural memories. It frequently gave concern to the authorities.

In the fields, there were even more divine functionaries than there were in the home, with separate, named, gods for the first and second ploughings, the harrowing, sowing, top-dressing and so on. Spiniensis was invoked to help clear a field of thorns and Stercutius to manure it. Robigus, the god of rust, or mildew, was propitiated on 25 April by the sacrifice of a rust-coloured dog. Consus was the god of

Wall-painting from a lararium *or household shrine in the House of the Vetii, Pompeii. The head of the household, the* pater familias, *is shown with his head covered as for a religious ritual, and holds an incense box in one hand. Two* lares *accompany him. The* genius, *or guardian spirit, of the* pater familias *is represented by the snake below. 1st century AD.*

A typical agricultural task of ploughing with an ox is shown in this Roman relief from Nîmes in France.

the granary, and Ops of the wealth of the harvest.

Pales, whose origin is particularly obscure, was possibly once a pair of shepherd-deities, male and female, responsible for keeping flocks safe from disease. This deity continued to be celebrated in later Rome in a festival called the Parilia, held on the Palatine Hill, where Rome originated. It seems likely that by that time the name of the god had become associated with the name of the hill. The celebrations concluded with a great meal in the open air, after which everyone leaped three times through the flames of a bonfire. It had clearly become a festival to celebrate the birth and renewal of the city, rather than having anything to do with flocks of sheep.

Terminus was the stone used to mark property boundaries, and a stone called by that name became a divinity in Rome itself. Each activity had its divinity, and at the edge of the farm, in the woodland, might have lurked the divinities of wilder nature, Faunus or Silvanus.

The rites of passage through life also had their divinities. At birth separate goddesses were responsible for the foetus, the pregnancy, and the birth itself, which was overseen by Juno Lucina. After the birth, there was a ceremony in which evil spirits were driven away with an axe, a stake and a broom, overseen by Intercidona, Pilumnus and Deverra. There were even named spirits who guarded the cra-

dle, induced the first cry, helped with breast-feeding and so on.

In early Rome the patricians and plebeians had different marriage ceremonies. No religious rites were legally required of either group, but among the patricians homage was often made to the gods in a number of ways. The marriage was celebrated at the bride's father's household altar, where the bride and groom shared a cake made of spelt, a kind of wheat, following a sacrifice that had been sprinkled with a gruel made of spelt. On the eve of her wedding day the bride would have made an offering of her dolls to the Lares of her father's household. The marriage ceremony was held in the early morning, but only if the omens were favourable. The bride sought the goodwill of the gods of the threshold of her new home by decorating it with flowers and wool and smearing the door posts and lintels with oil.

Ancestors were very important to the Romans throughout their history, and in later days wealthy Romans employed actors to walk in their family funeral processions wearing masks of their ancestors; or sometimes they carried wax masks or terracotta representations of their ancestors themselves. But early ceremonies concerned with the dead did not end with their cremation or burial. It was believed that their spirits lingered near the remains of the body in a state of half-life. These spirits were

(National Museum, Budapest)
A Roman bronze mask of Juno
Lucina, the goddess of childbirth,
who retained her early Roman
nature. Her continuing
importance is indicated by the
fact that this comes from part
of the later Roman Empire, now
Hungary.

257

called Manes, 'the good people', as a way of appeasing them; they could actually do great harm. They had to be sustained with food, and the remains of funeral meals have been found entombed with the dead. The food had to be renewed each year to prevent the Manes either wasting away or alternatively punishing the living for their neglect. On the anniversary of his mother's and father's deaths, therefore, every Roman had to honour them and ensure that they were supplied with food for the next year.

As well as the Manes, there were mischievous spirits of the dead of the whole household, called Lemures, who came back into the world on certain days in May. After midnight on those days, the father of the household walked through the house in his bare feet, throwing beans behind him so that he could feed the spirits without seeing them. He then beat a gong and the spirits vanished.

Early gods were not just concerned with the household. Each town or community probably had its own divinity who oversaw its activities. In Latium, villages seem to have grouped themselves together in cult-associations; for example Venus, originally a goddess of gardens, was worshipped at Lavinium, Diana at Lake Nemi and Jupiter Latiaris on the Alban Mount. Such divinities were not, however, at first conceived as living physically in the towns nor were they given temples in order to do so. They were, in a sense, guardian gods, perhaps a grander, urban version of the *genius loci*, or spirit of the place, who might be sensed presiding over a grove or a lake. Juno, who looked after the Etruscan town of Veii, was so successful that tradition has it that the Romans only succeeded in capturing Veii after they had ceremonially invoked her to leave that town for Rome. Many of these gods are now unknown, but may persist in place names. Cicero, who lived in the first century BC, claimed that he had seen religious diversity disappearing during his lifetime, but many local gods must have vanished earlier during the gradual Romanization of the Italian peninsula.

Not all gods were domestic or merely local, although some may have begun as local gods who, in the state-cult, grew into protectors of the whole community. The Italian tribes were Indo-European people, just as the Greeks were, and some of their gods may have originated many centuries earlier. The most important of these was Jupiter, or Iuppiter, the father of gods and men, the first part of whose name is linguistically similar to Zeus in Greek and Dyauspiter in Sanskrit, words connected with the light of day; the second part of the name is a version of *pater*, meaning father in Latin. He was thus a sky god in Rome, just as he was in Greece, but he existed in Italy quite separately from the Greek god.

In Rome, Jupiter was associated with two other gods – Mars and Quirinus. Mars, a god of war, was particularly important in this military state. He is also associated with agriculture, either because he was connected with fertility or, as some people think, because the activities of the soldiers he inspired allowed agriculture to continue. Mars came to have especial importance in Rome because he fathered Romulus and Remus, the city's founders. The Roman year began in March, his month, which was also the month in which military campaigns were resumed after the winter withdrawal. Quirinus was a very early god, who may have been Sabine in origin. He is also associated with war, but his name has similarities to the word adopted to describe the assembly of Roman citizens, 'Quirites'. His association with the city of Rome was strengthened when Romulus, after his death and apparent ascent to the heavens, was assimilated with him.

Some other great gods seem to have existed in Rome before the advent of Greek influence. Vesta has already been mentioned, and the goddess of the hearth is an early deity in many cultures for obvious reasons: from the hearth comes heat, food, comfort. The temple dedicated to her in Rome, which housed the city's own symbolic hearth, was built in a round shape and given a thatched roof, in imitation of the earliest hut dwellings in the city.

Janus, the god of the doorway, has already been mentioned. Like Vesta, he has no myth, but in his case it was because, although he remained important to the Romans, he had no Greek equivalent.

Vulcan, a fire-god, was probably introduced to Rome in quite early times, and Diana, a goddess of wild nature, was probably Italic. Minerva, who is thought by most people to have been an Italic goddess of handicrafts, but by others to have been an Etruscan war goddess, became part of the triad of Jupiter, Juno and Minerva who later became closely associated and very important both in Rome and her Empire.

The goddess Bona Dea, the 'Good Goddess', was a very ancient Roman divinity, probably a fertility power, who was worshipped only by women. Her real name may once have been Fauna, and later myths were invented for her to explain the fact that no man might be present at her worship, and no myrtle nor wine might be used at it.

The early Roman gods had names, functions and divine power, but they did not have myths, families or personalities. Sometimes people who addressed them were not clear exactly who they were nor of what sex, and inscriptions have been found asking the help of whatever god or goddess might be in a place. Towards the end of the monarchy, when Rome appears to have been ruled by Etruscans, things began to change: first because of the Greek influence on the Etruscans, second because the Etruscans seem likely to have built the first temples in Rome that housed statues of the gods, which ensured that the gods would become identifiable in a new, much more physical way.

(Museo Nazionale Romano, Rome)
The importance of funeral ceremonies is suggested by the funerary carriages shown on this sarcophagus.

259

CHAPTER FIVE
STATE RELIGION IN REPUBLICAN ROME

The traditional date for the foundation of the Roman Republic was 509 BC and even although historians now question that date, it seems certain that rule by kings came to an end somewhere near the turn of the sixth and fifth centuries BC. The Roman historian, Livy, asserts that, before he was deposed, the last Etruscan king of Rome had begun to build a temple on the Capitoline Hill and that it was dedicated in the first year of the Republic. The finds of archaeologists support his assertion in two respects: the date of the temple is about right and it appears to have been Etruscan in style. It was dedicated to the Etruscan triad of gods, Tinia, Uni and Menvra, that is to say Jupiter, Juno and Minerva.

Its significance to the story of the gods of Rome is that it was constructed to provide a home for the three gods, which meant that a cult statue of each god could reside in its own section, or *cella*, with Jupiter, the most important, in the middle.

In early Rome a *numen*, or divine spirit, could be worshipped out of doors where it was felt to reside, or at a turf altar, or at a shrine near a spring. It could be worshipped in the form of a stone – as Jupiter actually continued to be in Rome in the temple of Jupiter Feretrius (Jupiter 'the Striker') probably because the stone was perceived as one of Jupiter's thunderbolts. No statue was needed because the god had no corporal form. The Etruscans, on the other hand, represented the gods in human form and placed them within a temple. When they did this in Rome, the Romans took a step towards anthropo-morphism, the representation of gods in human shape, which was at that time completely typical of Greek gods, but not of Roman ones.

The cult statue of Jupiter in the Capitoline temple was probably made by the great Etruscan sculptor, Vulca of Veii, from terracotta. Jupiter was already worshipped by Latin tribes in Italy and as Jupiter Optimus Maximus, Jupiter the Best and Greatest, he became the state god of the people of Rome. Once his statue was placed in the temple

OPPOSITE
The partially reconstructed Temple of Vesta of the 2nd century BC in the Roman Forum. Here the Vestal Virgins guarded the sacred fire. The temple's circular form is reminiscent of an early Latin hut and the first temple on the site was probably actually made of wood and straw.

BELOW
Model of an Etruscan temple that would have housed three gods.

people could see his image rather than simply perceiving his powerful spirit.

Temples for the Greeks were never places in which a congregation worshipped; they were dignified and beautiful homes for gods, within which could be found their cult statues. Now this fashion had been spread to Rome by the Etruscans.

Before considering the subject of Greek influence on Roman gods in more detail, something should be said briefly about the religious practices of the Roman Republic, which incorporated into its pantheon new gods who seemed to have something useful to offer, or assimilated old gods to new ones when it seemed convenient to do so. The point of religious practices was to maintain equilibrium between the people and the powerful forces that governed their lives; if it were possible to discover additional deities who needed to be addressed on man's behalf, then the state could only benefit from the knowledge.

Just as the father of the household was responsible for keeping his dependents in a dutiful and successful relationship with the gods, so officials of the state interceded with the gods on behalf of their people, entering into what seems to us now like an almost contractual relationship with them. Most people probably continued to honour their household gods, but all their other religious obligations were conducted on their behalf by functionaries of the state at ceremonies they probably did not normally attend.

The basis of Roman religious practice was ritual. Rites were carried out in order to maintain the established order of things, to keep things going well, with a proper balance between the human and divine. The gods were powerful and unknown; they controlled nature and could bring flood or famine unless they were properly conciliated. Ritual was a way of ensuring permanent prosperity through maintaining the *pax deorum*, the peace of the gods, and it had to be conducted precisely.

Under the Republic, there was a precise order of priests, the most important of whom were not professionals but men who performed that duty as one among their other political offices. An office of Rex Sacrorum, king of religious rites, was created to maintain the tradition of the earlier priest-kings, but this gradually became a largely ceremonial office. More important was the Pontifex Maximus, literally the greatest bridge-maker, in other words the chief priest, under whose direction were the Augurs and the Pontiffs, the chief administrators of the state cult.

There were also individual priests, called Flamines, who were attached to particular deities,

the most important of whom was the Flamen Dialis, or priest of Jupiter. Special groups of priests also existed to perform particular functions. Among them were the Vestal Virgins, six women chosen from leading patrician families at the age of twelve, who served for thirty years, after which they were allowed to marry. Although their position was sought after and honoured, they were severely punished for infringements of their duty such as allowing the sacred fire to go out, and if a Vestal was found guilty of not being chaste she was buried alive. They lived in a building near the Forum and tended the holy fire that burnt perpetually in the Temple of Vesta, the symbolic hearth of Rome; they were responsible for making a special mixture of salt and meal from which cakes were made for offerings. The meal was kept, together with objects used in various sacred festivals, in their store house.

The rituals by which the priests attempted to maintain the city's peace with the gods were chiefly centred on sacrifice, prayer, and the divination of the

ABOVE
(Museo Nazionale Romano, Rome)
Head of a statue of the Emperor
Augustus shown as Pontifex
Maximus, or chief priest. He piously
wears his toga over his head as
though about to offer sacrifice.

OPPOSITE
(Villa Giulia, Rome) Life-size
terracotta statue of Apollo from an
Etruscan temple at Veii. This was
probably made by the Etruscan
sculptor, Vulca, who is said to have
been called to Rome by Tarquinius
Superbus to make the statue and
decorations for the Temple of
Jupiter on the Capitoline Hill. Late
6th-early 5th century BC.

will of the gods. Sacrifice meant literally the making of something *sacrum* or sacred, setting it aside to be the exclusive property of a god, which involved killing it if it was living. Sacrifice was designed to honour the god, and sometimes to expiate, or atone for, a wrong done by man. Lustrations, or processions to keep away hostile spirits, also sometimes culminated in sacrifice. Vows made to the gods before an action was undertaken were often completed by a sacrifice when the action had been successfully accomplished.

In the state cult, sacrifices had to be made scrupulously according to strictly observed rules. For example, the priest must have purified his hands and the offering must be acceptable; no contaminating intruder (such as a dog or a woman) must be present; there should be no intrusive noise, for which reason sacrifice was accompanied by music designed to block out any other noise. The priest making the sacrifice had to cover his head; this was an interesting difference from the more joyful Greek practice where the priest kept his head uncovered in order to open himself to the influence of the god. In meticulous Rome, if any mistake was made in the sacrifice, or if the god was wrongly addressed, the whole thing had to be repeated.

Many animals were sacrificed in Rome according to strictly laid-down rules. White beasts were used for gods of the upper world and black ones for those of the underworld. A set combination of animals formed the so-called *suovetaurilia* sacrifice that was often represented on stone carvings. They were a pig (*sus*), a sheep (*ovis*) and a bull (*taurus*). There were times of celebration or despair in the city when many sacrifices were called for; the altars of the Capitol must have run with blood and the air would have been heavy with the smell of butchery.

Prayer was also surrounded by rules. The right god had to be chosen and his or her attention had to be caught. That could only be achieved by addressing the deity by the correct name for the function he or she was requested to perform. Since many gods had a variety of names and might fail to respond if they were wrongly addressed, a number of names were sometimes listed at the beginning of a prayer; occasionally desperate formulae such as 'to the responsible deity' or 'whether you be god or goddess' are found on inscriptions. Prayers display great anxiety on the part of the Romans to keep the gods benevolently on their side.

Divination, or the skill of discovering the will of the gods from natural phenomena, was part of religion from early times in Rome. It became particularly important, however, as a result of Etruscan influ-

ence. The Etruscans held a number of books related to religious ritual that they believed had been revealed to them in early days. Among these rituals were those for interpreting such signs as thunder and lightning, which were thought to foretell events in man's everyday life.

The College of Augurs in Rome were responsible for divining whether or not circumstances were auspicious before undertaking certain events. The word *augur* may be connected with the Latin word for bird, and it was primarily from birds that the augurs derived their information, just as Romulus and Remus did when they sought to discover which of them should be leader in their new city. The sky was quartered according to the plan of the augurs, who watched to see which birds appeared in each quarter; they watched for certain kinds of birds; they even watched to see how chickens fed; all these things had significance. The writer, Cicero, who was appointed to the office of Augur, admitted in a letter that he thought augury was nonsense, yet the office was a prestigious one and he continued to perform it.

Augury gave way to some extent to haruspicy, at which the Etruscans excelled. The *haruspex* was a man who could discover divine intention by careful-

ly examining the entrails of beasts who had been sacrificed. The books of the *Etrusca disciplina*, or Etruscan discipline, include one that instructed professional *haruspices* in this art. A bronze model of a liver, divided up and inscribed with the names of Etruscan deities, has been found, which suggests that this craft, too, was governed by very specific rules.

As it can be seen, these habits were very close to superstition, and superstitious fear was marked too in the Roman attitude to omens, or prodigies of nature, such as large hailstones, particular kinds of lightning, deposits of sand by an unusual wind; anything out of the ordinary could portend disaster.

The state regulated the city's year through its calendar of festivals. This also set out which days were ordinary, *fas*, and which were *nefas*, days on which no business might be transacted. Many of these were days when festivals took place, some of them to do with honouring and placating the dead, or with ritual purification. It seems likely that these non-working days covered about a third of the year, but people would not have been expected to be present at most of the ceremonies, which would have been conducted on their behalf by the appropriate priests.

(Yorkshire Archaeological Society Museum, York) This Roman altar found in York has the following comprehensive dedication: 'To the African, Italian and Gallic mother goddesses, Marcus Minucius Andens, soldier of the Sixth Legion Victrix... willingly, gladly and deservedly fulfilled this vow.'

mary of great deeds of the past.

Some festivals also appear to have been genuinely popular, and in most cases these were ancient survivals from a rural tradition whose origin was no longer within the grasp of memory or understanding. Certain myths were created partly in an attempt to understand them.

The Lupercalia is an obvious example of a festival that dates back to a forgotten rite, yet it continued to be celebrated until it was stopped by a Christian bishop in the fifth century AD. Its name suggests an association with *lupus*, wolf, and it has been thought to have originated in an ancient cult intended to keep the forest wolves away from sheep folds in the clearings. In Republican Rome it was essentially a lustration, a purifying procession round the Palatine Hill, designed to ward off threatening spirits, but it took a strange traditional form, which suggests that it arose from some much earlier rite. On 15 February two teams of young men, chosen from patrician families, and called Luperci for this occasion, came together in a cave called the Lupercal on the Palatine Hill, a cave that some people associated with the twin founders of Rome, Romulus and Remus. Near the cave they sacrificed goats and a dog, in itself a very unusual sacrifice. The blood on the knife was smeared on the foreheads of two of the Luperci and wiped off again with a piece of wool soaked in milk. The men had to laugh at that point, although no one knew why. In the cave the Luperci then had a feast accompanied by a good deal to drink. They emerged into the February air dressed only in pieces of the goat's skin. In their hands they carried strips or thongs of the skin. Great crowds gathered at this point to watch the young men run a race along a marked course at the foot of the Palatine Hill. As they ran, they used their strips of goat skin like whips, flicking them at people. It was thought that these flicks promoted fertility so women who wanted to have children stood in their way as the Luperci passed.

March, the month of Mars, which marked the beginning of the campaign season for the army and of the agricultural year for farmers, was originally the first month of the Roman year. The priests celebrated a number of festivals to Mars, the god of war who was also a god of agriculture, during the early part of the month. The popular ceremonial was supplied by the dancing priests called Salii, who were twelve elected young patrician men. On 1 March they retrieved from the sanctuary of Mars in the *regia*, or old palace in the Forum, twelve bronze figure-of-eight shields, reminiscent of Mycenaean shields from Bronze Age Greece. One of these was

National pride was, however, encouraged in the citizen by the occasional public ceremonies of triumphal processions and the funerals of important men. Triumphal processions came to be granted to victorious generals, who had to have been responsible for at least 5000 deaths, and the processions became great public holidays. Officers of state accompanied the general and his army who paraded their spoils of war in processions that sometimes included singing and dancing. Funeral processions concluded with orations in praise of the dead man and all his ancestors, which provided a public sum-

said to have fallen from the sky on a distant 1 March and to have been copied on divine instructions by a blacksmith at the time. The young men, dressed in a sort of Bronze Age uniform, danced through the streets, following a traditional route, singing a song whose words no one could any longer understand. They stopped for a celebratory dinner at a different house each night. The shields were finally returned on 24 March, when the celebration came to an end.

Distant memories of human sacrifice were perhaps recalled at a festival in May. This was the completion of an earlier event in March, when puppets or dolls made of rushes or straw were put into 27 small shrines called *sacra Argeorum* that were distributed throughout the city. At the May festival the pontiffs, Vestal Virgins and the Priestess of Jupiter, dressed in mourning instead of her usual wedding dress, led a procession round the shrines to collect the puppets. They then took them solemnly to the wooden bridge near the Palatine and threw them into the river Tiber. A number of theories have been put forward to account for this ritual, which was apparently a popular one. Most suggest that it was a purification ceremony, some that old men had been sent to their death from the bridge in an earlier time, and others that the puppets were an offering to the river god to placate it for the indignity of having its river spanned by a bridge.

The Vestialia, or celebration of the cult of Vesta, was held in June, probably over the course of a week. The Vestal Virgins not only kept the sacred flame going throughout the year but also presided over a store-house, their version of the *penus*, or store-cupboard of every Roman family. This was usually kept locked, and opened only by the Vestals and the Pontifex Maximus. On 9 June each year, married women came to it in procession, bringing items of daily food as offerings. Later, the day came to be celebrated as a holiday for bakers, probably because of the special salted flour which the Vestals made for sacred rituals. June 15 was the day when the Vestals cleaned out their storehouse completely, taking any rubbish down to the river. This ceremony ended the ritual part of the day, and the Roman calendar states that the day should become a working day again as soon as the rubbish had been cleared away.

The final popular ceremony of the year, which had begun as a native agricultural feast of thanksgiving, was the Saturnalia, whose name shows that it had once been associated with the divinity Saturn, who in early Roman times was associated with sowing seed and preventing blight. From 217 BC it became more light-heartedly Greek in tone. It was celebrated on 17 December, after the autumn sowing had ended. Its original significance was clearly lost on urban Romans, but it had become and remained popular as an easy-going winter festival, which has provided the foundation for a number of western Christmas customs. The festival began with a sacrifice followed by a public banquet in the Forum. People stopped working, dressed informally and strolled about the streets. Gifts were exchanged and slaves were allowed considerable licence, even being waited on at table by their masters.

These are only a few of the more popular festivals celebrated in Rome during the course of the year. They show how tradition persisted when the early gods behind the original rites had been forgotten. They were festivals derived from the Di Indigetes, the native gods. Now it is time to account for the Hellenization of native gods and the acceptance of completely new gods.

BELOW
An Etruscan bronze plaque shows a haruspex *closely inspecting the* *entrails of an animal.*

The Appian Way was begun in 312 BC from Rome as far as Capua and was later extended to Beneventum and Brundisium, linking Rome with the Greek colonies further south. For the first part of the way it served as a patrician cemetery and was lined on either side by family graves and statues.

CHAPTER SIX
THE INTRODUCTION OF NEW GODS INTO REPUBLICAN ROME

Through the centuries of the Roman Republic, the state gods were subject to strong Greek influence. The anthropomorphic Greek gods were very different from the disembodied divine spirits of the Romans but when Roman gods were assimilated to Greek ones, they acquired their cults, their personalities, their established networks of family relationships, their developed myths and even specific items of their appearance.

It is important to remember, however, that the Roman peasant in the fields probably continued to call upon his rural deities and the freedman in the city to make offerings to his household gods. Most people leave no record of their lives and most people were probably relatively untouched by the changes to be seen in Roman temples and in the literature read by educated people. In fact, it is clear from their writing that certain educated men regarded the changes as mere fashion that did not affect them at any deep level.

Greek influence came not just through the Etruscans but through the tribes of Italy who had trading contact with the cities of Magna Graecia on the coast of southern Italy and Sicily. Hellenization was at its height in Rome from the fourth to the third centuries BC. This was a period when Greek culture itself had been strongly influenced by Alexander the Great and the notion of victory, and new cults centred on gods of war found their way to Rome, even the cult of Victory herself, to whom a temple was dedicated. Rome probably absorbed most Greek influence when it absorbed Campania, the area of

LEFT
(British Museum, London) Roman bronze figure of Hercules.

OPPOSITE
(Roman Forum) A winged Victory is shown on this detail from the Arch of Septimius Severus, erected in AD 203 in honour of the tenth anniversary of his accession, and in memory of his and his sons' victories.

271

Italy closest to the Greek cities. The importance of the link between the two cultures was made explicit in 312 BC by the building of the Via Appia, the great road from Rome to Capua.

The Romans took new gods into their religious system as they felt the need for them. As the city grew from an agricultural centre to a trading, manufacturing and mercantile base new kinds of help were needed from divine sources, and new gods were found to supply those needs. Greek influence can be seen in the institution of new state cults. One of the first of the Greek gods to come to Rome, possibly from Tibur, a nearby Latin city, was Heracles, whom the Romans called Hercules. His cult was centred on an altar in the Forum Boarium, the Cattle Market. He had not originally been worshipped as a god in Greece, but admired as a hero whose father was Zeus himself. His deification was a later addition to his myth, as were his numerous travels in the west where Greek colonists had settled.

Hercules was said to have arrived at the Tiber after his Tenth Labour, which had involved taking a herd of cattle from the monster Geryon, who lived in

the far west, and driving them home to Greece. As he rested by the river Tiber the cattle were stolen from him by a local shepherd called Cacus, whom Hercules killed, characteristically freeing the country from one of its tiresomely anti-social characters.

Once established in Rome he was adopted as a god with particular influence over commerce, possibly because he had actually been introduced there by Phoenician traders who associated him with their god, Melqart, and because merchants identified with his wanderings and liked the tough way he dealt with anyone who threatened to upset his progress.

The cult of the twin brothers Castor and Pollux was traditionally introduced in Rome in 499 BC, when they are said to have appeared in the Forum to announce a Roman victory against the Latins and the Tarquins at Lake Regillus. They had fought on the Roman side in the battle. A temple was dedicated to them in 484 BC. While they were in the Forum they watered their horses in the lake of Juturna, a female water deity.

The twins, the Dioscuri or 'sons of Zeus', were in Greek myth Castor and Polydeuces, the brothers of Helen of Troy and Clytemnestra. All four children were born from a double conception by their mother Leda, who was inseminated by a god and a mortal on the same day. Jupiter, who desired her, had disguised himself as a swan in order to rape her while she was walking near a river. That night she slept as usual with her husband, Tyndareus. The Romans thought of Juturna, rather than Helen, as the sister of the twins, which might have resulted from an Etruscan attempt to make a convenient triad of Juturna, Castor and Pollux.

Worship of the two gods was already established in Latium, as is shown by a bronze plaque to them in Lavinium, dating to the sixth or fifth century BC. Some people identified them with the great gods, the Penates of the state, that had originally been taken from Samothrace to Troy and were then taken to Italy by Aeneas. Whatever the reason for their arrival in Rome, they became very popular gods there.

In 495 BC, during an economic decline, the cult of Mercury was introduced. His Greek equivalent Hermes was, among other things, the god of merchants and dealers of all kinds and he was presumably felt likely to be a useful influence on commerce during a slump.

The Greek god, Apollo, was known throughout the ancient Mediterranean world for his oracles at Delphi, Delos and Cumae, but he was introduced into Rome primarily as a healing god about the middle of the fifth century BC. In 293 BC, during a period when pestilence raged in Rome, Apollo's son, another healing god called Asclepius, was imported from Greece and was worshipped in Rome as Aesculapius .

From the Etruscans the Romans borrowed the notion of the consenting gods, the Dei Consentes, twelve deities who advised Jupiter on important decisions. The Romans identified them with the twelve most important Greek gods, giving them Latin names, except for Apollo, who was already known by his Greek name. Once the Roman gods had been assimilated to their Greek counterparts, they were assimilated also into their myths, and so took on the relationships that existed between the Greek gods. This meant that the original natures and functions of the Roman gods were largely forgotten.

Jupiter, like Zeus, had always been a sky god, and he retained this characteristic. In Greece, migrating people had taken the worship of Zeus to regions whose people worshipped a mother goddess called Hera, and they had both assimilated her cult to the new cult of Zeus and preserved her status by making her his wife. Consequently, when the Roman god-

dess Juno, who represented the fertile power of women, was assimilated to the Greek goddess Hera, she automatically became the wife of the Roman god Jupiter on analogy with Hera and Zeus.

The Roman god Mars became increasingly the god of war rather than of agriculture because of his assimilation to the Greek god Ares, who was only a god of war. Because Minerva had been an Etruscan craft-goddess, she was assimilated to Athena, who was also a goddess of crafts, but thereafter she shared Athena's wisdom and her talent for war as well. Because Athena had been born from the head of Zeus, so Minerva became the daughter of Jupiter.

The Roman goddess Diana actually had a good deal in common with her Greek counterpart, Artemis, since both were goddesses of untamed nature. She was the sister of Apollo, a relationship accorded to Diana too after her assimilation. The Roman goddess Venus underwent a greater change. She had once been an ancient spirit of cultivated growth, whose name was neither masculine nor feminine; she acquired a much wider area of influence and more glamorous persona through her assimilation to the goddess Aphrodite, the most beautiful of the Greek goddesses, who was the wife of Hephaestus and the lover of Ares. Venus thus became the wife of Vulcan, the *numen* of volcanoes, who was assimilated to the god Hephaestus, the smith, whose fiery work had been suggested by his own early association with volcanoes. She also acquired Mars as a lover on analogy with Aphrodite's adultery with Ares.

The twelve important gods and their counterparts are set out here:

274

Gods		Goddesses	
Greek	**Roman**	**Greek**	**Roman**
Zeus	Jupiter	Hera	Juno
Poseidon	Neptune	Athena	Minerva
Ares	Mars	Artemis	Diana
Apollo	Apollo	Aphrodite	Venus
Hephaestus	Vulcan	Hestia	Vesta
Hermes	Mercury	Demeter	Ceres

(Bardo Museum, Tunis) Roman mosaic of Diana, the huntress, that illustrates the characteristics she shared with the Greek goddess Artemis. 2nd century AD.

OPPOSITE
(Palermo Museum, Sicily) Mosaic of Neptune, the Roman water god who was identified with the Greek Poseidon.

In spite of these assimilations, the Romans continued their habit of worshipping spirits by making shrines and temples to such abstractions as Salus – Health, Fides – Faith, Pietas – dutifulness to the gods, and Moneta – the spirit of the Mint, from which came prosperity. The persistence of this habit suggests a surviving desire to worship in a Roman rather than a Greek way.

Following the early assimilations of the Roman to the Greek gods, over a period of about two hundred years during the Republic new gods and rituals were deliberately introduced to Rome by the Senate, almost as part of policy, at times of crisis when there was need to reassure and quieten the people by diverting them. It seems possible that Livy might have had his own experience of this policy in mind when he made Numa, traditionally the second king of Rome, say of his unruly people that he would find a way to 'inspire them with the fear of the gods.'

It was perhaps in this spirit that the *duoviri sacris faciundis*, the two men who were nominated from the ruling class to be in charge of arranging the sacred rites and who became the *decemviri*, or ten men, in 367 BC, were sent at times of unusual portents or great danger to consult the Sibylline Books. These were said to be the works of the Sibyl, a prophetess of Apollo who presided over his oracle at Cumae.

In early histories of Rome the story goes that she offered nine oracular books to Tarquinius Priscus, king of Rome, but he twice foolishly refused them; on each occasion she destroyed three books and raised the price of the remaining ones and he was finally constrained to buy the remaining three at three times the price of the original nine. It was these books that the *decemviri sacris faciundis* consulted at times of crisis in Rome.

The priests may, in early times, actually have visited the oracle at Cumae, but by about 367 BC the books seem to have been preserved in the Temple of Jupiter on the Capitoline. They were burnt in a fire that destroyed the Temple in 82 BC, then reassembled from a number of sources. The new books, containing oracles written in Greek verse, were copied and kept in two gold chests in the temple of Apollo on the Palatine. Only the *decemviri* were allowed to consult the books, and their advice was almost always followed. The cynical commentator is bound to wonder what convenient adjustments might have been made to the books at various times, but there seems no doubt that their instructions to the Senate to innovate popular rituals at a number of difficult times helped to pacify the populace; and a chief requirement of Roman religion was that it should

establish a peaceful relationship between men and the gods.

When there was famine in the city in 496 BC, the Books advised that a cult of Ceres, Liber and Libera should be introduced. These were early Roman gods, who had previously been conceived as individual spirits of fertility, but they were now brought together as cult figures in a way that parallelled the cult of the Greek corn and wine deities – Demeter, the goddess of grain and the harvest, Dionysus, the god of wine, and Kore, or Persephone, the daughter of Demeter. In introducing this cult, the Senate was departing from its normal intention to keep Roman religion as free as possible from alien influences. Through the cult Romans gradually became acquainted with the Greek story of Persephone's seizure by Hades, who ruled over the Underworld, the barren period on earth during Demeter's search to find her, and the renewal of the process of growth when Persephone returned. These were the elements of the Eleusinian Mysteries, a Greek cult concerning the after-life that took hold in Rome in later years, in spite of disapproval from the authorities.

The Roman historian, Varro, says that the temple to Ceres, Liber and Libera dedicated in 493 BC, was the first to have a Greek rather than an Etruscan statue. Its immediate importance to the ordinary people was that it became the centre of the Roman corn trade.

In 433 BC, during a time of pestilence, a temple was dedicated to Apollo, a healing god. In 399 BC there was pestilence again in Rome when a hot summer followed a particularly severe winter. This time the Sibylline Books suggested an innovation called a *lectisternium*, from the word *lectus*, meaning the couch on which people reclined at meals. The idea was that a feast should be offered to the gods in public. It was a development of an annual Greek celebration when the gods were invited to dine in person with humans but it took a more spectacular form in Rome. During a period of eight days, images of six Greek gods, known by their Latin names of Apollo and Latona (the mother of Apollo and Diana), Hercules and Diana, Mercury and Neptune, were presented to the public. They were displayed reclining on couches, with food and drink spread on tables before them. Everyone in the city was free to see the images and to use the eight days as a holiday in which they might offer hospitality at their own doors, even to strangers.

Five such ceremonies were decreed in the fourth century and presumably offered both a diversion and an opportunity for closer acquaintance with the gods,

280

who must have seemed very different, displayed on their couches, from the formerly invisible Roman *numina*, or divine spirits.

The years of the second Punic War (218-201 BC), when Hannibal led the forces of Carthage against Rome, were very difficult ones. Rome was defeated on a number of occasions and the populace feared that Hannibal would attack Rome itself. After the defeat of the Romans at Lake Trasimene in 217 BC, the Senate consulted the Sibylline Books, which ordained the introduction of certain rites to calm the people.

Great Games to Jupiter were to be instituted, and a temple built to the Venus of Eryx; another *lectisternium* should be held, together with a *supplicatio*, and there should be a *ver sacrum*. This was all done. *Supplicatii*, which tended to be held alongside *lectisternia*, were occasions when the population, wearing garlands, went in procession round the shrines of the city, prostrating themselves in a manner that would normally have been considered hysterical and un-Roman, although perhaps typically Greek. The *ver sacrum*, the custom of the Sacred Spring, had been a very early custom in Italy. When a community grew to the extent that there was insufficient land to support it, a whole year's cohort of young adults were dedicated to a god and sent off to find land for a new home somewhere else. In this new Roman version of the custom, all the animals born that spring were sacrificed to the gods.

All this was followed in 216 BC by a new instruction from the Sibylline Books after the Romans' worst defeat at the Battle of Cannae. In order to expiate whatever wrongs the gods were punishing Rome for, it was decreed that a Greek man and woman and a Gaulish man and woman should be buried alive in the Forum Boarium, the cattle market. The historian Livy found this action disgusting and

'hardly Roman'. In fact, it had something in common with an aspect of Etruscan religion that was normally eschewed by the Romans and the Greeks. Etruscan wall-paintings show that in their later period they were much preoccupied with the torments of the dead at the hands of the demons of the underworld. It seems that they offered human sacrifices to appease the demons, commonly setting their victims to fight each other in duels. This custom appears to have become a model for the much later gladiatorial contests in Rome.

Under pressure of war, the Senate had sanctioned another alien rite in 249 BC, which it repeated in 207 BC when it arranged a festival to appease the Greek deities of the Underworld, Hades and Persephone, under their Roman names of Dis and Proserpina; in this also they seem to have been following Etruscan rather than Roman tradition.

The pontiffs continued to record numerous disturbing prodigies and omens of disaster in those years, and it was clearly felt that the gods had not yet been appeased. A new *lectisternium* was held, on a larger scale, at which twelve pairs of gods, both Greek and Roman were displayed. In an important break with tradition, for the first time no distinction was made between the native gods and foreign ones.

This open attitude to the introduction of foreign gods persisted as long as it suited the Senate to distract the people. Interest in oriental gods, which was surfacing among the mixed population of Rome, could be said to have been officially recognized in Rome during this period of crisis. In 205 BC, the Senate unearthed a prophecy that a foreign invader would be driven from Rome if the Great Mother were brought to the city.

The Great Mother was the Asiatic goddess, known in Rome as Cybele. An embassy was sent to Pessinus in Galatia, where she was worshipped, and King Attalus of Pergamum, unwilling to offend Rome, agreed to send her there. She arrived at Ostia in the following year, in the form of a black meteorite with which she was identified. She was greeted by Scipio and escorted to the Temple of Victory on the Palatine Hill by some of the most important aristocratic wives in Rome. The day, 4 April, was thereafter treated as a holiday and new Games, the Megalensia, were inaugurated.

The cult of Cybele was the last important official innovation based on the Sibylline Books, and it might be said to have been successful in that Rome defeated Hannibal. The Roman Senate had, however, introduced a foreign cult without fully understanding it.

Along with Cybele came her myth, which

Fresco showing a group of children sacrificing to Diana. It might suggest that the Greek association of young, unmarried girls with the untamed, virginal Artemis, was transferred to Roman girls and Diana.

is a strange one with very mixed origins that show how Greek myths were interwoven with eastern ones as well. Zeus attempted to rape Cybele while she was sleeping. Although his seed fell to the earth, as an earth mother she received it and bore a child – a bisexual monster called Agdistis. Dionysus, the god of wine, made Agdistis drunk and tied his sexual organs to a tree so that when he awoke from his drunken stupor and tried to get up he castrated himself.

A tree grew from his blood and one day the daughter of a river god picked some fruit from the tree, which she put in her lap to hold. The fruit impregnated her. When she gave birth, her father first tried to kill her and then to expose the baby. Cybele intervened to prevent this. When the child, called Attis, had grown into a handsome young man Cybele fell in love with him and he is often shown as her companion. He was unfaithful to her, however, and she sent him mad. During a fit of madness he castrated himself under a pine-tree, where he bled to death. Like other vegetation gods, he rose again and his rite included ceremonies both of mourning and of the joyful renewal of life.

What the Roman Senate had not realized was that the priests of Cybele were eunuchs and that their initiation to her service included self-castration while they were in an ecstatic trance. In later years the Senate forbade Roman citizens to take part in the orgiastic rites of the goddess.

The aristocracy had brought the situation on themselves; they had exploited their position by encouraging the introduction of new gods, festivals and games when it suited them to distract the people's attention from the disastrous events of the Punic War. After the war, however, the Senate reversed its policy and, in general, tried to prevent foreign influences from invading the state religion. They continued to maintain the *pax deorum* on behalf of the people, but the state religion had by now become ossified and its ceremonies rigid. The Senate kept a careful eye on more exotic forms of worship, such as that of Cybele, and decreed that they should be conducted privately. Their main fear was, as usual, of disorder among the teeming populace.

Therefore in 186 BC measures were taken throughout Italy against the cult of Bacchus that was

284

becoming increasingly popular: no one was to be an officer of the cult and no more than five people were to take part in its ceremonies. Bacchus, who had long been known in Rome as Liber, was the name used for the Greek god Dionysus in his particular aspect as a god associated with wine and uninhibited behaviour. Because he was a vegetation god, his cult was also connected with fertility, death and rebirth. His cult could only be entered through initiation, during which certain mysteries were revealed to the initiates. Celebration of the cult involved drinking and orgiastic dancing. It had spread very quickly from southern Italy and fears that its orgiastic nature might disturb public order and its initiation mysteries encourage the growth of groups of dissidents with secret views made the Senate treat its member-

Cybele and Attis. Cybele, the Great Mother, is often shown in a chariot drawn by lions. Attis wears a Phrygian cap, which denotes his oriental origin, and leans against the pine tree that forms a crucial part of his legend. Roman altar from Asia Minor, end of the 3rd century AD.

ship as a political offence rather than a religious one.

Although the Republican Senate banned the cult it became popular again under the Empire, and the process of initiation is openly illustrated in some wall paintings of the first century AD at Pompeii.

The state religion had probably never been intellectually satisfying to educated men, although they subscribed to the sense of duty to the well-being of the state that it promoted. They seem to have found some comfort in Greek philosophy, which had found its way to Rome by this period. Two schools of philosophy appear to have been most influential, the Epicurean and the Stoic, of which the Stoic school proved the more lasting.

The philosophy of Epicurus, a fourth-century Greek, did not change very much over time. It was based on a current scientific theory that all matter consisted of streams of atoms flowing in parallel channels that occasionally swerved and so produced new combinations. There might be gods, but they had nothing to do with life, which ceased completely with death when the atoms of the soul dissolved. The chief aim of life was pleasure, not necessarily hedonistic pleasure, but freedom from pain, ambition and power, and the cultivation of the joys of friendship and a quiet life. The arrival of his philosophy in Rome unfortunately coincided with a period of material wealth, which meant that Epicurean notions of pleasure were too often interpreted as self-indulgence.

A number of Epicurean philosophers were

expelled from Rome in 173 BC, which suggests that the authorities were disturbed by their views. Nevertheless Epicurus influenced the poets Lucretius and Horace, and Virgil also shows awareness of his ideas.

Stoicism developed from the ideas of Zeno, a Phoenician, who was so poor that he taught in the Porch, or Stoa, of the market in Athens. His ideas were later disseminated in Rome by Panaetius, who developed them in a way that made a specific appeal to Romans. Stoicism saw the universe as governed by law, which the good man must obey. Stoics were pantheists, who saw god in everything, although he might be called by many names, such as Zeus, Jupiter, Nature, Fire, Breath or Logos (the Word). It was a determinist philosophy, seeing man's actions, but not his will, as fixed. It was also a philosophy of acceptance. It saw man as having within himself some of the divine spark; this governed his behaviour, and made him rule his own life with reason. The fact that it could therefore be applied to man's daily actions and decisions seems to have appealed to the practical Romans. It survived to be an influence even on some Christians.

By the end of the Republic, the introduction of foreign gods had led to the recognition of gods in human shape and to the unquestioned assimilation of Roman gods to Greek ones. It had also led to a far more emotional and intense method of worship than Roman rituals had so far supplied. Cybele was the first deity to be introduced from the East, but it was from that direction that new gods would come in future, including of course the God of the Christians. Educated men seem to have turned away from the new emotionalism and towards philosophy, and this, in turn, tended towards the notion of one god and therefore also prepared the way for Christianity.

OPPOSITE
These 1st-century wall-paintings from the Villa of the Mysteries at Pompeii seem to illustrate the initiation of a woman, or women, into the Bacchic mysteries. Various interpretations have been made of the frieze that runs round all four walls of the room. Here a boy reads from a scroll. To the right, a group of women, who appear to be performing a lustral rite, are approached by a woman carrying a tray who is wearing her clothes girded up in the manner of an acolyte. A Silenus plays a lyre and beyond him a satyr seated on a rock plays on the pipes while a female satyr suckles a kid. Beyond them a woman holds out her cloak and points fearfully at the scene confronting her on the adjacent wall.

(Vatican Museums, Rome) This statue of Augustus shows him in his role as leader of the Roman army. The decoration of his breastplate is used to evoke various mythological and historical references. The figure of the Sky spreads his cloak across the top of the breastplate. Beneath him Sol, the Sun, drives his chariot towards Aurora, the Dawn, who rides off on a winged female figure. At the bottom rests the goddess Tellus, Earth. Above her, to the left and right, Apollo rides a griffin and his sister Diana a stag. The two figures in the centre probably represent Augustus's success in persuading the Parthians to return Roman legionary standards they had captured thirty years earlier. The cupid supporting the Emperor's right leg is the son of Venus and may suggest Augustus's own descent from her through the Julian family. The dolphin may refer to the emperor's victory at the sea battle of Actium. The statue is from Livia's villa at Prima Porta, Rome.

CHAPTER SEVEN
THE GODS OF THE ROMAN EMPIRE

When Octavius Caesar, the adopted son of Julius Caesar, returned to Rome in 29 BC he was acclaimed as a Prince of Peace who had not only won a foreign war but also brought to an end a long period of civil strife. A triple triumph celebrated his conquest of Illyricum, his victory at Actium and the consequent annexation of Egypt to Rome. In 27 BC, his choice of the title Augustus under which to rule was a felicitous one, carrying with it suggestions of a revered man who was consecrated to his task. In 23 BC he was recognized as Emperor. In 12 BC, on the death of the current Pontifex Maximus, or Chief Priest, he was elected to that office, and in 2 BC he was given the title Pater Patriae, Father of the Fatherland.

In the spirit of that title, he stressed the importance of the family, and sought to reform the institutions of the state. For some time the state had neglected its regular religious observances and many temples had fallen into disrepair. Some satirists were making mocking references to the gods in their plays; other writers of the period, however, expressed their belief that Rome could not be great unless piety was restored to the state. Augustus shared this view, and set himself to renew the state cults, first by overseeing the necessary repair and rebuilding of eighty-two neglected temples.

Rather than looking to the new gods and religions that were spreading into Italy from the East, Augustus looked back to the more traditional gods of Rome in his attempts to inspire dutiful worship, or *pietas*, in his people. He had long shown a particular enthusiasm for the worship of Apollo, who appeared to him and supported him at the battle of Actium, and he had founded a temple to him on the Palatine Hill in 36 BC. Now he propagated his worship, not just in his aspect as a god of healing, but as the inspiration for a progressive, peaceful civilization that would cast a new light on the world. In the Hellenistic world, Apollo had by this time become associated with the sun, an appropriate image for the dawning of a new age in Rome. There is a famous statue of Augustus made to stand at the Prima Porta; he is wearing armour, and on his breastplate are figures of the sun and the goddess of dawn.

Augustus also stressed the cult of Mars, particularly in two aspects: first as the father of Romulus, the founder of Rome, and second as Mars Ultor, the Avenger. As a young man, in 42 BC, he had vowed a temple to Mars in a spirit of vengeance for the murder of Julius Caesar. In 2 BC he dedicated a temple to Mars Ultor, expressing the hope that every young man would worship there at the beginning of his military career, and every commander before setting out on an expedition.

The prophetic words of the ghost of Anchises, the father of Aeneas, in the *Aeneid* have already been quoted in an earlier chapter, saying that the arts of the Romans should be to pacify, to impose the rule of law and to spare the conquered while at the same time beating down the proud. Through the two gods, Apollo and Mars, Augustus promoted the twin notion of the spread of Roman civilization and its support by just war. The joint themes were spread

Remains of the temple in Rome dedicated to Mars Ultor (the Avenger) by Augustus in 2 BC. It was a centre for great ceremonies and served as the Imperial Sanctuary.

among educated people by writers of his period, particularly by Virgil.

The Ara Pacis, or Altar of Peace, dedicated in 13 BC, which can still be seen in Rome today in a restored form, presents a similar vision of Rome through its scenes of family worship, religious processions and the arrival of Aeneas in Italy.

Augustus took these ideas to a wider public by means of the Secular Games in 17 BC. These Games were, by tradition, thought to be held every hundred years, but had not in fact been held since 263 BC. The holding of the Games was intended to suggest that a new *saeculum*, or age, was about to begin, and that idea was reinforced by the occurrence of a number of contemporary prophecies about the beginning of a new Golden Age. The games, together with bloodless sacrifices to the Fates, the goddess of childbirth, Mother Earth, Jupiter Optimus Maximus, Juno and Apollo, and hymns to the gods sung by choirs of young people, lasted for three days. As intended, they presumably carried Augustus's message of renewed piety, peace and greater prosperity to most of the population of Rome.

It is scarcely surprising that, after his death, Augustus, like his adoptive father, Julius Caesar, was declared a god himself. It had long been a feature of Greek and Roman religion that exceptional men, at the end of their lives, might be taken into the pantheon of gods; it had happened to the Greek Heracles and the Roman Romulus. Both of them, however, had one divine parent. Alexander the Great had asked for, and been given, recognition of his divinity, mainly as an astute way of establishing his power in his Eastern and Egyptian empires, where kingship and divinity went hand in hand. In Egypt the king had for many centuries also been a god. After Alexander's death the Greek dynasty he founded in Egypt, the Ptolemies, established a cult of the reigning monarch to ensure their position there.

Augustus ruled Egypt as part of the Roman Empire, so he was perforce a divine emperor there. His adoptive father, Julius Caesar, had believed he had a personal association with the goddess Venus because, as a member of the Julian family, he was directly descended from Iulus, or Ascanius, the son of Aeneas, who was himself the son of Venus and Anchises. Augustus never claimed divinity directly, but he allowed himself to be called *divi filius*, son of the god, that is of the divine Julius. His birthday became a public holiday and a month was named after him. He also encouraged the development of two cults that led towards the recognition of his divinity: one was the Numen Augusti, the Divine Will of Augustus, to which altars have been found

A statue of the god Apollo stands in front of the temple dedicated to him in Pompeii. Apollo was one of the most popular gods in Imperial Rome. Vesuvius can be seen in the background.

dedicated as far away as Gaul and Africa; the other was a cult to his Genius, which was invoked at the taking of oaths.

After Augustus died, in September, AD 14, the Senate agreed that the Divine Augustus should be accepted among the gods of the state. A senator claimed to have seen him bodily ascending to the sky. At his funeral, Tiberius compared Augustus with Hercules as a great benefactor to the whole world.

The deification of the Emperor after his death set a pattern for the future, although certain Emperors – for example, Tiberius, Caligula, Nero and Domitian – did not achieve the status, while others pressed for divine recognition during their life-time. The story is often quoted of the Emperor Vespasian joking on his death-bed, 'Oh dear, I think I'm becoming a god.' The Emperor Hadrian actually had his young favourite, Antinous, deified after his death by drowning. The emperor-cult became partic-

294

ularly important in the furthest reaches of the Empire where local people often joined it with the cult of the goddess Roma in an attempt to emphasize their attentiveness to the power of Rome. Its practice in such places was presumably encouraged as one element in the Romanization of the diverse cultures of the Empire.

Julius and Augustus Caesar both associated themselves strongly with a god, Julius with Venus and Augustus with Apollo and, through him, with images of the sun. A study of Roman sculpture and coins will show that later Roman Emperors went further than this and actually identified themselves with particular gods; Caligula went through most of the pantheon, and ordered that his head should replace that of Zeus at Olympia. Nero was identified with Zeus the Giver of Freedom and Hadrian with Zeus Olympius. This habit sometimes extended to their families; for example Julia Domna, the wife of Septimius Severus, who came from a royal priestly family in Syria, was identified with Cybele, and depicted on the throne of Juno.

It has already become clear that Roman religion was not exclusive and that it was possible, even desirable, to worship more than one god. As Rome extended its empire, a greater variety of gods became available for worship and more assimilations of one god to another were made. In this confusing situation, certain new forms of worship spread through parts of the empire and to Rome itself.

One group of gods came from Egypt. They were the family of Osiris and Isis, their son Horus and their servant, the jackal-headed Anubis. Ptolemy 1, the Greek ruler of Egypt, knowing the resistance of both Greeks and Romans to the notion of animal gods, added to the group what amounted to an artificially created god – Serapis (or Sarapis in Greek). Serapis was originally to be found at Memphis, at the sanctuary where the dead bulls of Apis were entombed. Ptolemy merged the spirit of Apis, the sacred bull, with Osiris, the god of the dead, to produce a third deity Osorapis, or Serapis, around whom he created a cult that would enhance his own power. It was so successful in the Roman world that Serapis seems to have replaced Osiris there as the husband of Isis.

Early Egyptian stories make it clear that Isis and Osiris were originally fertility deities; Osiris represented the rising of the Nile flood-waters and Isis the land that awaited them. This particular fertility myth was, of course, fairly meaningless in countries whose fertility depended on rain rather than on the

Detail of a panel from the south side of the Ara Pacis Augustae *the Altar of the Augustan Peace, dedicated in 9 BC. It probably shows some of the people present at the inauguration ceremony, and it also illustrates the Roman ideal of pious and dignified family life. On the left of the procession, flamines, or priests, are recognizable from their distinctive caps, and an assistant at the sacrifice carries an axe. The central figure is probably Marcus Agrippa, a general, and later son-in-law to Augustus. To the right is the figure of the Empress Livia, and to the right of that is probably Tiberius, her son, the future emperor. The children are also thought to be members of the imperial family.*

Detail of the south-east panel of the Ara Pacis. The seated goddess is Tellus, Earth, perhaps perceived here as Italia, the personification of Italy. The children and the fruit on her lap suggest abundance. Breezes surround her and at her feet are healthy beasts, lush vegetation and an overturned urn that suggests the proximity of a spring. The elements of earth, air and water thus flourish in the Augustan peace.

power of a single river. The Roman cult of Isis, which was very different from its Egyptian original, became popular with groups of poorer freedmen and women in the city towards the end of the Republic, but the shrines of Isis and Serapis were destroyed on the orders of the Senate in 50 BC and they were kept outside the city limits of Rome after that until the Emperor Caligula admitted them into the official calendar during his reign (37-41 AD).

The Egyptian gods are thought to have been brought to Rome by sailors and merchants, and the mysteries of Isis became particularly popular among women. She was rapidly identified with the goddess Demeter/Ceres, the goddess of corn, and her mysteries had some similarities to the Eleusinian Mysteries of Greece that gave enlightenment about the afterlife and promised victory over the powers of night.

Other goddesses were assimilated with Isis. She can often be distinguished in statues, however, by her headdress; it sometimes shows the sun's disc sur-

rounded by a crescent moon, or a cow's horns, or the palm leaves of victory, or two feathers that represent the soul. She usually holds a *sistrum*, the rattle that was used in her ceremonies. She is sometimes identified with Tyche, that is the Roman goddess Fortuna, who usually holds a rudder to direct affairs and an overflowing cornucopia, or horn of plenty. The cult of Isis had a professional priesthood, and its processions and complex rites seem to have been popular.

The cult of Serapis persisted until the end of the fourth century AD, and appears to have become respectable in Rome. The Emperor Hadrian had a Serapeum constructed at his villa at Tivoli, outside Rome. Serapis was associated with the sun and the sky gods and yet, like Osiris, was also thought of as a god of the dead. He was even a healing god. On some inscriptions, his worshippers have gone the whole way and described him as 'One Zeus Serapis'.

From about the middle of the second century

AD, the Isis cult gave way to some extent, at least among men, to a new cult whose origins were in Persia, but which developed into what was essentially a Roman mystery cult. This was the cult of Mithras. It was strongly associated with astrology, as might be expected in a cult deriving from Persia, where Babylonian astrologers had been very influential. It clearly had links with Persian Zoroastrianism, which stressed dualism in life, the conflict between the forces of light and darkness.

The newly developed cult of Mithras carried a number of myths with it. One is frequently illustrated in the numerous statues of Mithras slaying a bull. It claimed that in the struggle between light and darkness, the Sun was the chief representative of the divinity Ahura-Mazda. Mithras supported Ahura-Mazda in his struggle against darkness and in the end took the supremacy from him, but with his agreement.

The first living thing created by Ahura-Mazda was a wild bull, which Mithras wrestled into submission, holding it by the horns. He then took it to an underground cave from which it escaped. The Sun sent his messenger, the Raven, to watch where it went and Mithras, guided by Ahura-Mazda, found it.

Mithras pulled back the bull's head and, clinging to its nostrils with his left hand, he sank a dagger into its throat with his right hand. From the flow of the bull's blood sprang all plant and animal life. Ahriman, the force of darkness, sent his servants – a scorpion, an ant and a snake – to drink up the life-creating blood, but it spread throughout the earth. The Sun therefore made a covenant with Mithras, before whom he bowed and by whom he was crowned. They parted after sharing a ceremonial feast, which was afterwards commemorated by adherents to the cult in a ritual sacramental meal.

The importance of the sun in Mithraism may well have encouraged the cult's popularity at that period. Mithras, who usually wears a Phrygian cap, is sometimes shown wearing a radiate crown, that is with a circlet on his head from which the sun's rays project. Such a crown was also shown on Serapis and on Alexander the Great. Some Roman emperors liked to present themselves wearing it on their coins. The dualism inherent in the cult might have made both an intellectual and an emotional appeal to Romans whose state religion had never presented good and evil as rival forces.

The cult also offered a complex ceremonial,

(National Museum, Ravenna) Relief showing the deification, or apotheosis, of Augustus, which was accorded to him after his death. He is accompanied by members of the Julio-Claudian family.

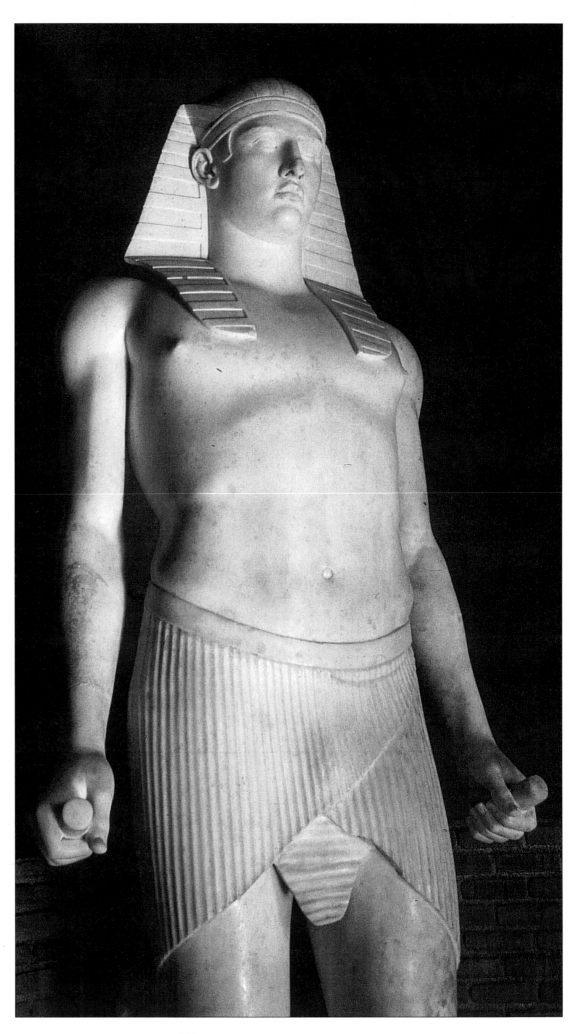

RIGHT
(Vatican Museums) Sculpture of
Antinous, the favourite of the
Emperor Hadrian, shown as an
Egyptian deity. He was drowned in
the River Nile. From Hadrian's Villa
at Tivoli.

OPPOSITE
(British Museum) One panel of an
ivory diptych showing the apotheosis
of the Emperor Antoninus Pius. The
lower part illustrates incidents from
his life and in the upper part he is
lifted up to be among the other gods.
The Antonine family were
particularly enthusiastic about
imperial cult.

trained priests, an ethical code, a strong sense of fraternity among its participants, and secrecy. It advocated that its initiates should actively behave well rather than that they should merely abstain from wrong-doing. It was a religion exclusively for men, and it appealed above all to men from the upper classes of society, to business men, and particularly to military men, especially officers. It seems likely that a number of emperors actually encouraged its spread through Roman military camps, and evidence of its celebration has been found as far apart as England – on Hadrian's Wall and in London – and Africa. Some civilians took to Mithraism as well, but it seems to have been rather exclusive in its appeal.

Its exclusive nature must have been reinforced by its rites. These were celebrated in fairly small vaulted caves, where the ritual feasts were presumably held, but which cannot have held many people. Each cave was decorated with astrological signs, and represented an image of the universe. At one end there was usually a statue representing Mithras slaying the bull, an action which in itself seemed to be taking place in a cave and being watched by a raven.

There were secret initiation rites by which men rose through various grades, from the Raven – an observer, the Nymphus, or bride, and the Soldier up to the Lion, which appears to have been the standard grade. After that there were three further grades, the Persian, the Sun-runner and the Father. Each of these grades was protected by different planets or gods. The lions represented the fire that would burn the body after death, and through which the released soul would ascend to heaven.

One rite – the *taurobolium* – which has often been associated with Mithraism, is actually a rite of the Cybele cult, but may have been used in Mithraism at times. To celebrate this rite, a man went into a pit, above which a bull was sacrificed on a grid of some kind so that the man below was drenched in the blood of the animal. It seems possible that it has become associated with Mithraism after the event because of the bull sacrifice.

Some writers have seen Mithraism, with its dualism, one main god and ethical code as an important rival to Christianity. It seems rather to have been one of a number of religions to which some men turned at a time of intellectual and emotional religious enquiry when a ferment of ideas and cults were moving through Rome's vast Empire.

The Roman Empire gave its people religious freedom, and most people probably continued to worship their local divinities, just as most ordinary Romans probably continued to pay attention to their household gods rather than anything more exotic –

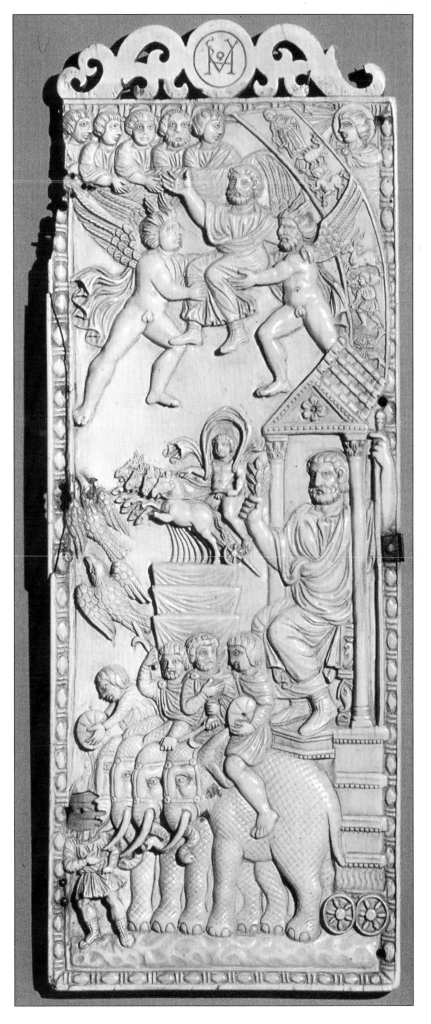

the household altars found below the volcanic ash in first century Pompeii certainly seem to suggest this. Because the religions of the empire were, for the most part, polytheisms that maintained their cults through the common practices of local festivals and sacrifice at local shrines, there was a good deal of possibility for the interchange and assimilation of gods.

As some of the more remote western provinces of the empire became more urbanized, they sometimes chose to give their gods a Roman gloss by introducing some sort of uniformity to them and using Roman names. This was known as the *interpretatio Romana*, where local gods were identified with Roman ones, but it could also work in reverse when Roman settlers abroad chose to use a local name for one of their own gods.

Julius Caesar noted that Mercury was very popular with the Gauls. The Roman god's name was applied to some of their gods where there was a very approximate resemblance between them. He was, for example, associated with the god Lug who gave his name to Lugdunum, modern Lyons. At Trier, there is an example of Mars Lenus, where Lenus, a local healing god has been assimilated to the Roman god. Mars was unsurprisingly one of the Roman gods most often invoked in Britain, since many of the Romans living there would at least at some stage in their lives have been soldiers. There are more than thirty inscriptions, for example, to Mars Coccidius at Bewcastle. Maponus, a British god of youth, was assimilated to Apollo. The Roman town of Bath was known as Aquae Sulis, which shows that the presiding goddess was felt to be the Celtic deity Sul, who was worshipped as a sun-goddess in that area.

Sometimes joint cults were set up, as when some Seine boatmen in Gaul in the reign of Tiberius made a four-sided monument to Esus, Tarvos, Vulcan and Jupiter, honouring two of their own gods together with two Roman ones. Some Celtic gods seem, however, to have kept their own identity, among them Cernunnos, the antler-headed god, and Epona, a goddess associated with the horse.

Roman influence was far less obvious in Greece, which tended to retain its own gods and mythology, already long-established before Rome existed. In Asia Minor, more foreign gods were Greek than Roman because of the influence of Alexander the Great as well as the ancient trading, social and cultural ties between Greece and Asia Minor.

Syria sent some of its gods to Rome; it had an enormous diversity of religions, largely because its mountain ranges created a series of unconnected terrains. The Syrian goddess Atagartis was brought to

Rome fairly early, probably by slaves. Under these circumstances, Syrian deities tended to become naturalized Roman ones, rather as Egyptian ones did. The god Melqart of Tyre, for example, became assimilated with Hercules, and Eshmun of Sidon with Asclepius, the Roman healing god, who was himself assimilated to the Greek Aesculapius. Eshmun was so well assimilated that he cured the sick by incubation, that is by sending them a dream of recovery as they slept, in precisely the same way as Aesculapius cured Greeks who slept near his shrine at Epidauros.

Another Syrian god, Jupiter of Doliche, named after a small town in Commagene near the upper Euphrates, was usually shown as a god of lightning,

standing on a bull, holding a thunderbolt in one hand and a hatchet in the other. He was the patron of ironworkers and therefore popular with soldiers who must have frequently needed his help. Inscriptions have been found to him as far apart as Africa, Germany, Hungary and Britain.

In one of the stranger episodes of Roman history, a fourteen-year-old Syrian called Elagabalus, who had served the god Ba'al at Emesa, became Roman Emperor for fewer than four years, being lynched by his guards in AD 222. He attempted unsuccessfully to introduce his local cult of Sol Invictus, the Unconquered Sun, to Rome. About fifty years later, the Emperor Aurelian had more success when he established the Sun as the supreme deity of

Rome. He came from Illyria, where the sun was worshipped, but some of his army came from Syria, which Aurelian also knew, having visited Palmyra and Emesa. He was thus making an intelligent attempt to unite the eastern and western empire by bringing together the sun-worship of the east with the western Celtic and Germanic gods of healing and light who had become associated with Apollo. December 25, the winter solstice, was the birthday of the sun, a festival that was later appropriated by the Christians.

The Phoenicians who migrated to Carthage took their gods with them and some of these gods later became assimilated with Roman gods. Ba'al, the Lord, became assimilated with Zeus/Jupiter in Palestine and with Saturn in Africa. The latter assimilation to the early Roman fertility god seems appropriate. Tanit, the Carthaginian moon-goddess, was assimilated at first to the Great Mother, who later gave way to Juno, but Tanit also continued as Caelestis, who was herself later assimilated to Aphrodite/Venus. She was also strongly associated with Ceres.

At Corbridge, in England, an altar was dedicated to Jupiter Dolichenus, Caelestis Brigantia, and Salus. In this very interesting triad, the local goddess Brigantia is identified with Caelestis/Juno – the Syrian/Roman goddess – and is thus the wife of Jupiter in his Syrian version; Salus, the personified god of healing, completes the triad which now seems to us exotic, but was clearly quite acceptable to the Roman in Britain who could afford to have the altar made.

When Roman colonists settled abroad they often attempted to recreate the heart of Rome itself by making a citadel on which they built a temple to the triad of gods – Jupiter Optimus Maximus, Juno Regina, and Minerva – who had been the dedicatees of the first temple on the Capitoline Hill in Rome. These capitols are found in the province of Africa, mostly in modern Tunisia, which tried particularly to model itself on Rome. The Capitoline cult was often accompanied by the emperor-cult so that men could not only remind themselves of their national identity as Romans but also associate themselves with the power of Rome and the benefits it brought.

Nevertheless there is, as always, evidence to show that local deities continued to be worshipped in these places. It is interesting to speculate how far the great Greek and Roman gods penetrated through society, and to what extent they ever took the place of local deities for those people who could not afford to leave behind them the evidence of statues, funeral sarcophagi and inscriptions in stone.

Remains of a 3rd-century AD temple of Mithras at Carrowburgh, Northumbria, near Hadrian's Wall. It would have been roofed. Mithraism was popular among the officers of the Roman legions throughout the empire.

CHAPTER EIGHT
ROME AND CHRISTIANITY

One of the eastern religions that made its mark in parts of the Roman empire was, of course, Judaism, which differed from other faiths in its uncompromising and exclusive monotheism. The worship of Jehovah had already spread through the Eastern Mediterranean during the Hellenistic period and there was a Jewish colony in Rome in the last century of the Republic. The fact that Jews, together with astrologers, were expelled from Rome in AD 139 suggests that their presence was at least noticeable and possibly disturbing to the authorities.

The Jews were expecting a Messiah, through whom they would establish a kingdom of peace and their hopes were always pinned on Jerusalem as the centre of their faith. Their hopes for Jerusalem were, however, shattered in AD 70 when the Roman emperor Titus destroyed the sacred city and took the treasures of the temple back with him to Rome. Images of them can still be seen there, displayed in stone carvings on his triumphal arch. Possibly even worse was Hadrian's attempt to assimilate the Jews to Rome by founding a Roman colony called Aelia Capitolina in Jerusalem in AD 132, and erecting a shrine of Jupiter Capitolinus on the very site of the former holy place of the Jews. The consequent Jewish revolt incited the Roman army to destroy many villages, kill thousands of men and women and encourage Gentiles to settle in Judaea. An agreement with Rome eventually allowed the Jews to express their faith, but it left them without a home or a political state of their own.

Before this, in AD 30, during an earlier disturbance of the Roman peace in Judaea, Jesus of Nazareth, claimed to be the son of Jehovah, had been crucified. After his death, the ideas that might otherwise have died with him were taken up and spread by a number of his disciples. The ideas and teaching of the disciples found a reception among certain Jews, who created what must have seemed at first merely a minor sect of Judaism. The teaching then spread further afield both geographically and culturally, greatly helped by men like Paul, formerly Saul of Tarsus. He persuaded the Jewish followers of Christ that their message was universal rather than simply Jewish and that converted Gentiles should be allowed into their sect, which must become less rigid. Paul was a Jewish scholar from Syria, a Greek-speaking Roman citizen and ultimately a Christian apostle. He illustrates in himself the extraordinary range of cultural experience that was sometimes synthesized in the Roman world.

By the second century AD there were Christian communities throughout the Middle East, in Greece, Cyprus, Pompeii and Rome, and possibly in Spain and even India. By the third and fourth centuries, Christianity was the only religion making continuous progress at the expense of other religions. This progress has been explained not only by the quality of the faith itself and by the intelligence of the Greek writers who propagated it, particularly to the people of the eastern empire, but by the fact that it was well organized from the beginning. It provided an interconnecting system of clergy, formal baptism into the

faith, and help for the poor; its members formed themselves into alternative, lateral, dependable social structures that must have been particularly welcome to the poor and needy people who probably formed the majority of its adherents at first if only because they formed the majority of society.

Why then were Christians persecuted? In some cases the reason was political expediency; they were persecuted because failure to do so might have resulted in public disorder. In the early period of their existence, when there were no systematic edicts against them, they were sometimes drawn to the attention of the authorities by people who simply could not accept the fact that they behaved different-ly from other people, a situation not unknown today when some communities still find difficulty in accepting new cultural minorities in their midst.

It is important to remember that in earlier soci-eties, cases to be prosecuted were not brought to trial by a police force, but by other members of society who found certain kinds of behaviour offensive. The Christians were accused of 'hatred of the human race', a vague phrase that perhaps arose from the fact that they did not participate in the ordinary religious festivals of the day. On the contrary, their own ritu-als must have seemed strange; at their Eucharist they symbolically consumed the body and blood of their Saviour; they called each other 'brother' and 'sister'

and kissed on meeting; early rumours of cannibalism and incest were perhaps understandable. Furthermore they treated women with honour and they worshipped a criminal whom the Romans had put to death. Some of this feeling is displayed even by a writer as intelligent as the historian Tacitus, who wrote of their 'detestable superstition', and complained of their presence in Rome 'where every horrible and shameful iniquity, from every quarter of the world, pours in and finds a welcome.'

It is only fair to note that the Christians themselves were extremely intolerant and unyielding. Unusually, they wanted their form of worship to replace other worships, rather than to accept them as equals. When they were accused of crimes, they refused to take the simple step that would have freed them – to offer a sacrifice to the gods or the Emperor. Other religions accepted a variety of gods into their pantheon; the Christians did not. They would not admit that Emperors could be divine, and would certainly not sacrifice to them or pray to them, although they might pray for them. They wanted to change the world, which was always regarded as a dangerously

revolutionary position in Rome, but they went further and talked of establishing a new kingdom on earth. By refusing to behave piously towards the Roman gods, they were abusing the very traditions that had formed the Roman character and the Roman state, as this book has tried to show.

It seems that once people knew them as neighbours, on the whole they came to trust and like them. It was, however, inevitable that the Christians should become an irritant to the authorities. They first appear as a separate group, rather than as a sect of Judaism, at the time of the emperor Nero, when Paul appealed to him on their behalf. Paul himself had provoked a riot in Ephesus, in Asia Minor, when he preached against the city's goddess, Artemis/Diana. Nero did not persecute the Christians systematically but he discovered that they provided him with a convenient scapegoat to blame when things were going wrong for him. For example, he used the opportunity offered by the great fire in Rome in AD 64 to accumulate land, consequently rumours circulated that the fire had been started deliberately. Tacitus claimed that Nero chose to divert attention from himself by blaming the Christians as arsonists and devising exotic punishments for them. This, of course, would have led to their being blamed for almost any disagreeable event in the future.

In the early second century, Pliny indicates the general attitude taken by authority to the Christians by quoting a letter written to him by the Emperor Trajan. Pliny, who was governor of Bithynia from AD 111-113, asked Trajan how to proceed when Christians were brought before him at court hearings. How should he differentiate between them? and what should he do if they had been accused anonymously? Trajan's answer was that Christians should not be sought out, but that if they were reported and the case against them were proved, they should be punished. Any person who denied he was Christian and illustrated this by praying to the Roman gods should be pardoned, however suspect his past. Anonymous written allegations should have no place in any charge.

This policy of not searching out Christians, but of trying them when they had been reported seems to have been the one adopted by most Emperors between Trajan and Decius, that is from about AD 98 until AD 249. It meant that Christians were fairly safe unless they became very unpopular for some reason with the people among whom they lived or found themselves being blamed for some specific circumstances, for which they might not have been responsible. Even then, the authorities were some-

times reluctant to intervene, as they were in the case of the martyrdom of Bishop Polycarp of Smyrna in about AD 157 when a mob brought him to a stadium and insisted that, the games with the wild animals being over, he should instead be burned for refusing to curse Christ. According to the description of his death, the Jews in the crowd were particularly anxious to help with building the fire. The authorities on that occasion tried to persuade him to save himself by simply saying 'Caesar is lord' and performing the sacrifice, but his refusal to do so meant they could not have controlled the crowd without allowing the burning to take place.

Perhaps Tertullian, a Christian writer born in Carthage, was right when he said that 'the blood of Christians is seed', and that the news of such martyrdoms actually helped the spread of Christianity. In the first two centuries the numbers of the Christians who performed the required actions and escaped martyrdom were not recorded so we shall never know how many they were.

Things changed in AD 250 when the Emperor Decius, in view of many troubles in the Empire, decided to secure the *pax deorum* by proving his loyalty to the old gods of Rome. Through doing this, he hoped to restore order.

Among his measures was a determined suppression of Christianity. He commanded all Christians to give up their faith and take part in the normal worship of the Roman gods of the Empire, and he sent

BELOW LEFT
An early Christian baptismal bath, with steps down to it, typical of those found in North Africa. This one was in a Christian church that earlier had been a Roman temple. Sbeitla, Tunisia.

BELOW
The theatre at Ephesus in Asia Minor (modern Turkey) where St. Paul preached against the goddess Diana.

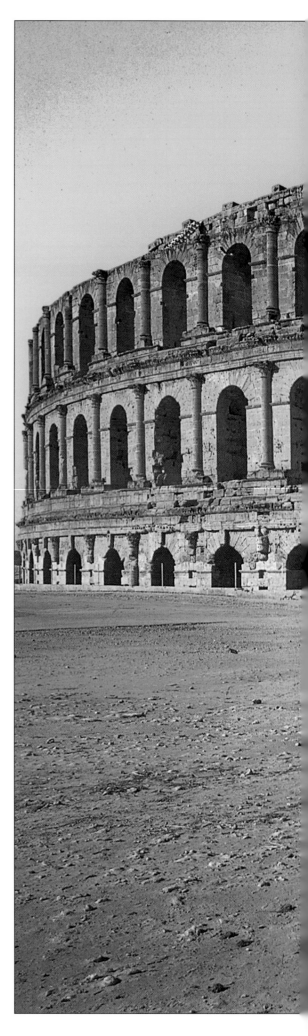

ABOVE
(Hermitage Museum, St. Petersburg)
One panel of an ivory diptych from
Constantinople showing members of
the court seated in an arena watch-
ing men and bears fighting at the
games. Circa AD 500.

RIGHT
Christians were among the victims
forced to fight with men or animals
at the public spectacles held in the
arena of this huge Colosseum at
El Jem in Tunisia. Early 3rd
century AD.

officials to make sure they did. He arrested the most prominent Christian clergy and executed the Pope. All Christians had to make a sacrifice or libation (a pouring out of wine) to the Roman gods, or suffer death or imprisonment. Anyone who performed the sacrifice received a releasing certificate, some of which still survive. Some people might have bought the certificates without performing the actions; others escaped, but many were killed.

Decius died in AD 251, but Valerian renewed the persecution in 257 and Aurelian in 270, so that suppression became official policy for a number of years. After that, things were relaxed and for some years authority turned a blind eye to Christians who refused to worship the emperor, which meant that

they could once more enter the civil service and, in some cases, rise to high office.

The most serious attack on them came under Diocletian and began in AD 303. It was surprising, since Diocletian had seemed tolerant, and had even married a Christian wife. It was Diocletian who instituted the tetrarchy, the system of shared imperial rule by which he hoped the empire would be more efficiently run. The tetrarchy was an agreement between four emperors: two were senior and were known as Augustus; the other two were their lieutenants, or deputies, and were known as Caesar. They co-operated closely, and sometimes linked themselves together by judicious marriages. Diocletian had a particularly anti-Christian deputy, called Galerius, who may have been the inspiration for the worst excesses.

Somewhat in the spirit of Augustus, Diocletian had decided that the time had come to bring back sound moral values to Rome; the gods would be favourable to Rome, he said, if its rulers saw to it that everyone cultivated a pious life. Members of new religions were coming between the Romans and their gods and opposing the older religious practices that had always served Rome well. Perverted and obstinate people like the Christians must be punished.

He did not demand bloodshed, but decreed that churches must be destroyed, the scriptures burnt and higher class Christians deprived of their immunities from punishment; he then went further and decreed that Christians should be captured and forced to sacrifice before being released. While Diocletian was ill, however, Galerius took advantage of his absence and demanded universal sacrifice to the gods on pain of death. This initiated the most serious period of persecution ever known, until Galerius repented on his death bed in AD 311, stopped the persecution and, in an edict, granted Christians what they had always wanted, legal recognition. This edict was also signed by Constantine.

Constantine's father, Constantius, had been Augustus, together with Galerius, when Diocletian retired, but when Constantius died at York during an expedition in AD 306, his troops proclaimed his son Constantine as their leader. Constantine was opposed by two of the other tetrarchs, but he entered Rome in 312, having successfully fought off opposition to his rule at the Battle of the Milvian Bridge outside Rome.

It was said that just before that battle, Constantine dreamed of the sign of Christ, that is of a cross set against the sun. The sun was a particularly important symbol to him because he had been brought up by his father, who came from the Balkans, to the worship of Sol Invictus, the Unconquered Sun. His father had actually been displayed on a victory medallion as *Redditor Lucis Aeternam*, 'Restorer of eternal light'. Constantine

traditional Roman desire.

After his declaration of tolerance, Constantine's greatest help to the progress of Christianity was, perhaps, his supervision of the interminable disputes about dogma and heresy that arose in the Christian Church in the fourth century. It was probably largely through his influence that the Nicene Creed emerged from the meeting at Nicaea in AD 325, for example. Constantine was less tolerant to pagan religions. He forbade any of his staff to offer sacrifice and, while he was building his new city of Constantinople at Byzantium in the eastern empire, he is thought to have despoiled existing pagan temples of precious materials to use there. His son Constantius went further, closing pagan temples in every city and forbidding sacrifice on pain of death.

BELOW
(Louvre Museum, Paris) The Roman
Emperor Julian who was called the
Apostate because once he had
become Emperor he revealed his
life-long adherence to pagan beliefs.

was therefore no stranger to monotheism. He supported Christianity from the time of his vision, but he was not actually baptized a Christian until shortly before his death in AD 337.

Constantine agreed with Licinius, the one tetrarch who had supported him in his claim to power, that the persecution of Christians should be brought to an end. Their policy towards the Christians was stated clearly in AD 313, in the 'Edict of Milan', which said that Christians, and everyone else, should be granted the freedom to follow whatever religious observance they wished, 'so that whatever divinity there is in the seat of heaven may become placated and propitious to us and to all who are under our rule,' This last clause manifestly expresses a very

314

LEFT
(Museum of Christian Art, Arles)
Detail of an early Christian
sarcophagus showing a clean-
shaven Christ healing the blind
man.

OPPOSITE
(Vatican Museum, Rome) A statue
from the Roman catacombs showing
Christ the Good Shepherd in a pose
reminiscent of earlier Greek statues
of Apollo carrying a calf. Christ
was often shown as a young,
beardless man.

The number of edicts on these lines that were pro-
nounced over the years suggests, however, that they
were not very effective.

It is not surprising that Christianity in the period
of Constantine was far more widespread in the eastern than in the western empire. Possibly up to half
the population were Christian in Alexandria and in
other cities in Syria and Asia Minor where Greek
culture and philosophy had in some sense paved the
way for new kinds of thinking. Only a minority of
people in Rome itself and in the west were Christian
by that period. It is interesting to note that the Latin
Bible probably originated from North Africa, and
that an important line of Christian converts writing
in Latin grew up there and influenced the western
empire; they included Tertullian, Cyprian and the
great Augustine.

There was one more pagan Roman Emperor,
Flavius Claudius Julianus, known as Julian the
Apostate, who ruled from AD 361-363. He was born
in Constantinople and, although brought up as
a Christian, he was actually far more attracted
by pagan literature and the philosophers of
Neoplatonism. He kept his ideas to himself during a
very successful military career, but when he became
emperor he shed his Christian upbringing and
decreed that all religions in the Empire were to be
tolerated. He gave his active support to pagan groups
and withdrew it from Christian ones. Nevertheless,
he admitted in writing that the ultimate victory of
Christianity in the Roman world was assured.

Over the centuries, Christians were to show
themselves perhaps more intolerant than the Romans
had been as they set about eliminating paganism.
Compromises had to be made. It has been suggested,
for example, that the suppression of the worship of
local deities by certain campaigning bishops may
well have led to their reincarnation as Christian

The transition from paganism to Christianity is illustrated in this building. The Temple of Antoninus and Faustina, in the Roman Forum, was dedicated by the Senate in AD 141 to the memory of the Empress Faustina and also to the Emperor Antoninus Pius, after his death. Sometime before the 12th century AD it was converted into the Christian church of San Lorenzo in Miranda, and in 1602 it was given a Baroque façade.

saints. The Christians also took existing festivals into their calendar, as they did with the winter solstice and birthday of Sol, 25 December.

In the light of all that has been said here about the merging of cults and images, early Christian images are interesting in the manner in which they demonstrate that their makers have assimilated them to earlier traditions. The crucifix as an image is noticeable by its absence in the early Christian period when Christians were reluctant to associate their religion with the instrument by which the most hardened criminals were put to death. They used instead the chi-ro sign, bringing together the first two Greek letters of Christ's name. This in itself forms a cross against a circle, in the manner of Constantine's vision.

Christ was also visualized as the Good Shepherd, and statues of him are reminiscent of Greek statues of Apollo carrying a calf from centuries earlier. Scholars have seen images of the goddess Isis influencing some statues of the Virgin Mary. In order to represent the delights of heaven, age-old images of the vine and the harvest were used, as they had been in the worship of Dionysus. The first youthful images of Christ gave way to the now familiar bearded figure with a halo. The halo is in itself reminiscent of the radiate crown of those gods and emperors who had been associated with the sun. Themes of the conflict of good and evil are represented by hunting scenes on Christian sarcophagi, and even Bellerophon killing the Chimaera and Perseus slaying the dragon are used to suggest the triumph of good over evil, to the extent that the latter probably produced the notion of St. George.

Discussion of the further development of Christianity lies beyond the scope of this book. It is difficult to see, however, how its propagation would have spread so rapidly without the cultural conditions brought about by the great melting pot of the Roman world. Perhaps even more important for the transmission of Christianity was Rome's administrative ability and the technical prowess that made communication possible from the Thames to the Indus and the Rhine to the Nile.